ALPHEUS THOMAS MASON is one of America's outstanding political scientists and an authority on constitutional history. Among his many publications are *American Constitutional Law* (with W. M. Beaney), *Free Government in the Making, The Supreme Court from Taft to Warren,* and *In Quest of Freedom: American Political Thought and Practice.* Dr. Mason is currently McCormick Professor of Jurisprudence at Princeton University.

THE STATES RIGHTS DEBATE

Antifederalism and the Constitution

THE STATES RIGHTS DEBATE

Antifederalism and the Constitution 🖎

ALPHEUS THOMAS MASON • *with selected documents*

PRENTICE-HALL, INC. ENGLEWOOD CLIFFS, N.J.
A SPECTRUM BOOK

To Julian Boyd

*friend and fellow explorer in the
labyrinth of eighteenth-century
American political thought*

Preface 🌿

It occurred to me in early 1962, as I re-read the wide-ranging debates on the proposed federal Constitution of 1787, that the Antifederalists had not been given due credit. Though Chief Justice Warren had labeled the Bill of Rights —Antifederalist in origin—"the heart" of any constitution, the truth of his evaluation did not quite sink in. Yet the focus in Court and country on the values embodied in the first ten amendments alerts us to the continuing influence of Antifederalist thought. The subject had been much on my mind before I agreed to write a book about it. At the moment, there seemed to be no particular urgency in getting started.

One day in December 1962, Dean Jefferson B. Fordham of the University of Pennsylvania Law School handed me a copy of the so-called "Dis-Union" Amendments, recently proposed by the Council of State Governments. These seemed incredible, fantastic. Yet a few months later two of them, with little or no debate, won approval in a significant number of state legislatures, representing millions of people. A few public-spirited citizens, much alarmed, urged Chief Justice Warren to speak out. His call for a "great national debate" promptly followed. But if the discussion were to be informed, the relevant historical materials had to be made available. Time had become a factor of tremendous importance. Fortunately, I was able to obtain the assistance of Mr. Sanford B. Gabin, without whose help these pages would not yet be in print.

This book has been long in the making; generations of graduate students enrolled in my seminar on American Political Thought have made their contributions, so many in fact that to mention names might seem invidious. My undergraduate friend, Mr. F. C. Johnston, helped in assembling the selected bibliography. Helen Fairbanks, as usual, tracked down hard-to-find sources, and Helen Wright doubled as editor and typist. Last, but not least, the Rockefeller Foundation and Princeton University gave me financial support. To all these people and institutions, I am deeply indebted.

A. T. M.

Contents 🦎

xi

THE STATES RIGHTS DEBATE

Antifederalism and the Constitution

INTRODUCTION

FEDERAL-STATE RELATIONS are again in the headlines. The picture, widely broadcast on June 12, 1963, of Governor George C. Wallace of Alabama standing at the entrance of the State University determined to prevent the admission of two Negroes acting under federal court orders, dramatically highlights the issue. The controversy is, however, more broadly based.

Seared by recent Supreme Court decisions touching areas long considered sacrosanct, the states, speaking through the powerful Council of State Governments, have proposed three far-reaching amendments.[1] One would undo the 1962 Supreme Court decision in *Baker* v. *Carr*[2] in which the Court, striking at the rotten borough scandal, asserted its responsibility for more equitable apportionment of seats in the state legislatures. Another would permit state legislatures to amend the Federal Constitution without consideration or discussion in any national forum.[3] The third would set up a super-Supreme Court—a "Court of the Union" consisting of the chief justices of the fifty states—empowered to overrule Supreme Court decisions in cases involving federal-state relations. Proponents of these amendments moved so stealthily that twelve states approved one or more of them before the most informed citizen knew of the action.[4] Noting this widespread public apathy, Chief Justice Warren, addressing the American Law Institute on May 22, 1963, prodded members of the bar to initiate a "great national debate." [5] Materials for it exist in abundance; indeed, the debate is older than the nation itself.

Antifederalists—men of states rights persuasion in their later orientation—are a hardy breed. Our entire history is studded with their activities. Outraged by the Alien and Sedition Acts, Jefferson formulated the Kentucky Resolutions declaring that when the federal government assumed powers not delegated, state nullification of the act was the constitutional remedy. The union was again imperiled in 1814, when certain New England states adopted the so-called Hartford Convention Resolutions, urging the states to protect their citizens against unconstitutional federal militia and draft legislation. When Congress, in 1828, enacted the "Tariff of Abominations," the protesting South Carolina Exposition declared that a sovereign state has the right to determine whether an act of Congress constitutes such a danger "as to justify the interposition of the state to protect its rights." [6] It was not, however, until 1861 that certain southern states, using states rights to keep a subject race in bondage, committed what Hamilton deplored as gross heresy.[7] Proclaiming state sovereignty in the most extreme form, the South then went on to Harper's Ferry, Shiloh, and Appomattox.

It remained for the present generation, after a united nation had fought and won two world wars, and at a time when our security is gravely tested, to witness the most defiant assertion of state sovereignty since the Civil War. "If proposals of this magnitude [the recent states rights amendments] had been made in the early days of the Republic," Chief Justice Warren observed, "the great debate would be resounding in every legislative hall and in every place where lawyers, scholars, and statesmen gather." [8]

Lა affirming the "sovereignty, freedom and independence" of the states, the Articles of Confederation made inevitable the chaos that worked such havoc in Anglo-American relations prior to 1776. Though the idea of federation had been frequently broached,[9] Britain and the colonies proved unable to convert it into a mutually agreeable plan of government. "There is no possible medium," loyalist Daniel Leonard observed fatalistically, "between absolute independence [of the colonies] and subjection to the authority of parliament." [10] Repudiation of parliamentary sovereignty meant that the provincial legislatures alone would be sovereign. The result would be *imperium in imperio,* the height of political absurdity.

The Revolutionary fathers deplored *imperium in imperio* as a political monster "subversive of all Government." [11] Yet independence had scarcely been won before the new nation found itself plagued by this very monster. Americans were to realize again, as did John Adams in 1774, that it is as impossible for two supreme and independent authorities to exist in the same state as for two supreme beings to rule the universe. Loyalist Samuel Seabury had anticipated the difficulties independence would create:

> If we should succeed in depriving Great Britain of the power of regulating our trade, the colonies will probably be soon at variance with each other. Their commercial interests will interfere; there will be no supreme power to interpose, and discord and animosity must ensue.[12]

Seabury had also suggested the remedy; needed was an over-all common power—perhaps a "medium" between absolute state independence and absolute subjection. Could America find the "middle ground" which the Colonists and Britain alike considered a hopeless search?

By 1786 a consensus had developed in favor of calling a convention to establish a more energetic central authority. The consensus was so overwhelming as to be virtually uncontested.[13] "We all agree in the necessity of new regulations," George Mason told the Philadelphia convention delegates on June 7, 1787, "but we differ widely in our opinions of what are the safest and most effectual." [14] Differences touching basic principles were apparent as soon as Edmund Randolph submitted his plan vesting in the central government authority "to legislate in all cases to which the separate States are incompetent." [15] Also lodged in the central authority was the right of veto over acts of the several states.

James Wilson, promptly disassociating himself from those who would "swallow up" the states, pointed an accusing finger at Alexander Hamilton. The New Yorker disavowed any such intention. "He had not been understood. . . . By an abolition of the States, he meant that no boundary could be drawn between the National & State Legislatures; that the former must therefore have *indefinite* authority. If it were limited at all, the rivalship of the States would gradually subvert it." [16] In short, Hamilton's purpose, the objective generally, was not to eliminate the states but to correct the infirmities inherent in the Articles. "The streams of national power," Hamilton insisted, "ought to flow immediately from that pure, original foundation of all legitimate authority"—the consent of the people.[17] A government designed to meet great national purposes could not tolerate any provision that would make its authority contingent on the existence of a state domain absolutely free from invasion. In *Federalist* essay No. 22, Hamilton refers contemptuously to the "enormous doctrine of a right of [State] legislative repeal," and to the gross heresy "that a party to a contract has a right to revoke that contract." [18]

Luther Martin and William Paterson opposed the Randolph plan vehemently. They argued that national authority of such scope would destroy the states as independent units of government. James Wilson's response went to the core of the issue. If New Jersey, he retorted, would not surrender her sovereignty it was useless to talk about government. To remove this seemingly irreconcilable impasse, William Samuel Johnson with the assistance of Oliver Ellsworth of Connecticut fashioned the Connecticut Compromise, giving the states equal representation in the Senate.

A crucial battle apparently had been won. The high caliber of the delegates opposing the compromise, including Madison, Hamilton, and Wilson, no less than the argument used against it, were calculated to create the impression that a basic Federalist principle had been sacrificed. From the tenor of arguments in opposition, it was easy to infer a purpose to destroy the states. Jonathan Dayton of New Jersey dubbed the Connecticut Compromise "an amphibious monster." [19] In making the Senate "a palladium of residuary sovereignty," seeds of rivalry would be planted. A fundamental principle was involved: the proposition that no government can be solid or lasting unless representation is based on the people. Echoing Leonard's gloomy caveat of 1775, Gunning Bedford observed that "there [is] no middle way between a perfect consolidation and a mere confederacy of States." [20]

Not unnaturally, those wishing to preserve the states as independent units of authority regarded the Connecticut Compromise as a notable victory. A spirit of relaxation set in, enabling the friends of strong union to forge ahead and perhaps regain the ground they had apparently lost.

As a kind of substitute for Randolph's proposal of a national veto over state action, Paterson and Martin introduced what later became the supremacy clause. The Constitution and laws of Congress passed in pursuance thereof were declared to be the supreme law of the land, "anything in the constitution or laws of any state to the contrary notwithstanding." Madison also won approval of the provision calling for the Constitution's ratification by the people rather than by the state legislatures. The advance toward centralized government was alarming to certain delegates, stimulating the not unreasonable fear that the states were doomed.

As the Constitution left the hands of the framers, it contained no provision that smacked of the congenital defect so disabling to effective government under the Articles. The powers of the national government, though enumerated, were "undefined" and "indefinite." No precise line had been drawn delimiting national power in the interest of the states. The "middle ground" long sought in vain had been found. Proposed for ratification was a national government of "indefinite" powers. The states would be retained insofar as they could be "subordinately useful." [21]

Both inside and outside the state ratifying conventions, two complaints against the proposed Constitution became a sonorous refrain. It was contended that the new Constitution would establish a "consolidated system," threatening rights basic to both the states and individuals. The critics, therefore, centered their efforts on winning amendments which would draw protective lines and establish barriers against national power. Their purpose, in a word, was to incorporate limitations which the Convention had failed to provide.

The Antifederalist campaign was both a great success and a disappointment, yielding a gold brick. The battle was waged so effectively that certain commentators, including the late Justice Robert H. Jackson, believe that, without promise of a limiting Bill of Rights, the Constitution's supporters might not have been able to win ratification.[22] Be that as it may, the first Congress elected under the new Constitution proposed, and the states ratified, the amendments known as the Bill of Rights. The provisions which Chief Justice Warren now extols as "the heart of any constitution" [23] were almost forgotten appendages.

In the state ratifying conventions, a storm of protest arose against the provision for national supremacy. Article VI, paragraph 2, the so-called supremacy clause, was portrayed as "clearly designed to make us one consolidated government." [24] Unity, it was feared, had been substituted for union. James Wilson, noting that the word "consolidation" had yet to be defined, proceeded to clarify the issue. If, he explained, opponents of the plan meant by consolidation that the states would be subordinate to the national government, the truth of the charge must be conceded.

But if they meant that the states had been deprived of all independent existence, they were clearly in error. The Constitution itself presumes the continual existence of the states.[25]

The states are integral parts of the amending process. The national government guarantees to each state a republican form of government and pledges assistance, if requested, against invasion or domestic violence. The new system was to be approved only when nine of the thirteen states ratified the document. All these provisions indicated to advocates of ratification that the states would be more than mere administrative districts; they would play an important role in the practical operation of government.

Antifederalists were not convinced. To quiet their fears, the First Congress proposed, and the states quickly ratified, the Tenth Amendment, which proclaims that powers not delegated to the national government are reserved to the states or to the people. Though this amendment manifests sympathy for the concept of union without unity, it was not intended to limit the force and effect of the supremacy clause. When Madison presented the amendment, it read, as now, "powers not delegated . . . are reserved to the states. . . ." Mr. Tucker moved to add "expressly," making the amendment read "[T]he powers not *expressly* delegated." Madison objected, arguing that it was impossible to confine a national government to the exercise of express powers. The upshot was general agreement that "corporate bodies are supposed to possess all powers incident to a corporate capacity, without being absolutely expressed." [26] Despite the Tenth Amendment, the central government was supreme in the exercise of its delegated and implied powers.

Those who feared federal encroachment had to be content with a constitutional tranquilizer, an empty declaration—the Tenth Amendment. Its purpose, Chief Justice Marshall declared, was to quiet "the excessive jealousies which had been excited." [27] In interpreting national power, Marshall never referred to the Tenth Amendment as a limitation. For him its language, for all practical purposes, merely restated the content of the supremacy clause. Within these limits the Tenth Amendment was and is significant. The fears motivating its framers were genuine.

It is one of the ironies of recent Supreme Court history that even the so-called Bill of Rights, Amendments 1 through 8, particularly the First —a notable Antifederalist victory in 1790—is now appraised as a defeat for states rights. In his final address to the Conference of Chief Justices on August 10, 1963, Chairman Edwin Livingston complained that "the Constitution is being remade by judicial fiat without following the lawful processes of amendment and without the consent of the governed." Livingston charged that Supreme Court Justices were using the First Amendment freedoms of speech, press, and religion, and the Fourteenth Amendment prohibiting discriminatory state action, as ammunition for "the systematic destruction of state sovereignty." [28] Thus even the gains of

1790—thanks to the Supreme Court—represent substantial losses for the states in 1964.

Materials for the discussion advocated by Chief Justice Warren span our entire history. The readings collected in this volume may help to set the debate in the context of the time when crucial decisions and action occurred.

Notes ⁂

1. Text in *State Government*, 36, 10-15 (1963). See Chapter IV.
2. 369 U.S. 186 (1962).
3. This proposal was anticipated as early as 1787 in the Virginia Plan submitted to the Federal Convention at Philadelphia by Edmund Randolph. Resolution 13 declared that "the assent of the National Legislature ought not to be required" in the amending process. Max Farrand, *The Records of the Federal Convention*, rev. ed. (New Haven, Conn.: Yale University Press, 1937), I, p. 22. For reasons current states-righters might find ironical, Elbridge Gerry opposed the provision of Article V directing Congress to call a convention upon application of two thirds of the states. Gerry suggested that "two thirds of the States may obtain a Convention, a majority of which can bind the Union to innovations that may subvert the State-Constitutions altogether." Hamilton feared the opposite result. "He did not object to the consequences stated by Mr. Gerry." Pointing to the very situation that today threatens national supremacy, Hamilton warned: "The State Legislatures will not apply for alterations but with a view to increase their own powers." Farrand, II, *id.*, 557-58. George Mason was apparently dissatisfied with Article V, even with the provision allowing the states to initiate amendments. He insisted that "by the Article Congress only have the Power of proposing Amendments at any future time to this Constitution, & shou'd it prove ever so oppressive, the whole people of America can't make, or even propose Alterations to it; a Doctrine utterly subversive of the fundamental Principles of the Rights & Liberties of the people." Farrand, IV, *id.*, 61.
4. See Briggs, "Three-Pronged Movement to Weaken Powers of Supreme Court Quietly Gains Ground," *Louisville Courier-Journal*, 1963; reprinted in *Trenton Evening Times*, May 8, 1963, p. 40, col. 1. See also 21 *Congressional Quarterly Weekly Report*, 662-63 (1963).
5. *The New York Times*, May 23, 1963, p. 1, col. 7.
6. Kelly and Harbison, *The American Constitution, Its Origins and Development*, p. 305 (1948).
7. *The Federalist*, No. 22, p. 199 (Wright, ed., 1961). Hereinafter cited as *The Federalist*. See text accompanying note 18 *infra*.
8. *The New York Times*, May 23, 1963, p. 23, col. 3.
9. See McLaughlin, "The Backbround of American Federalism," in *America and Britain*, pp. 177-221 (1919). See also Boyd, *Anglo-American Union: Joseph Galloway's Plans to Preserve the British Empire 1774-1788* (1949), especially his suggestive Chapter 1, "The Middle Doctrine."
10. Leonard, "Letters Addressed to the Inhabitants of the Province of Massachusetts Bay, Jan. 16, 1775," in *Novanglus and Massachusettensis* (1819), p. 174.
11. Language of Mr. Tucker, *Annals of Cong.*, I, 776 (1789).
12. Seabury, "A View of the Controversy Between Great Britain and Her Colonies, etc., A Letter to the Author of a Full Vindication," in *Letters of a Westchester Farmer* (1774-1775), Vance, ed. (1930), p. 27.

13. See Wright, *Consensus and Continuity, 1776-1787* (1958).
14. Farrand, I, *op. cit., supra,* note 3, p. 161.
15. *Id.,* 21.
16. *Id.,* 323; emphasis added. Yates's report of Hamilton's remarks provides interesting variations: "I did not intend . . . a total extinguishment of state governments; but my meaning was, that a national government ought to be able to support itself without the aid or interference of state governments, and that therefore it was necessary to have full sovereignty." *Id.,* 328.
17. *The Federalist,* No. 22, p. 199.
18. *Ibid.*
19. Farrand, I, *op. cit., supra,* note 3, p. 490.
20. *Ibid.*
21. Hunt, ed., *The Writings of James Madison, 1783-1787,* II (1909), p. 338.
22. *Board of Education* v. *Barnette,* 319 U.S. 624, 636-37 (1943).
23. Christman, ed., *The Public Papers of Chief Justice Warren,* 7 (1959).
24. Lee, "Letters of a Federal Farmer," in *Pamphlets on the Constitution of the United States, 1787-88,* Ford, ed. (1888), p. 282.
25. Elliot, ed., *The Debates in the Several State Conventions on the Adoption of the Federal Constitution,* II (1836), p. 455.
26. *Annals of Cong.,* I (1789), pp. 436, 761.
27. *McCulloch* v. *Maryland,* 4 U.S. (4 Wheat.) 415, 421 (1819).
28. *The New York Times,* August 11, 1963, p. 49, col. 1.

I · SEEDS OF CONTROVERSY · 1774-1786

Essay ✄

Antifederalism antedates the union itself. "Antifederalists" were active even before the "Federalists" fashioned an epithet to discredit them.* The animating spirit is profound distrust of power in general and of centralized rulership in particular. Jefferson, whose life and work are imbued with deep-seated confidence in man and his capacity for self-government, expressed the spirit of free government and of Antifederalism in the Kentucky Resolutions:

> . . . [I]t would be a dangerous delusion were a confidence in the men of our choice to silence our fears for the safety of our rights: . . . confidence is everywhere the parent of despotisms—free government is founded in jealousy, and not in confidence; it is jealousy and not confidence which prescribes limited constitutions, to bind down those whom we are obliged to trust with power: . . . In questions of power, then, let no more be heard of confidence in man, but bind him down from mischief by the chains of the Constitution. . . .[1]

America was steeped in this distrustful philosophy long before it found embodiment in the Articles of Confederation and the Constitution, long before Jefferson denounced the Federalist-inspired Alien and Sedition Acts as evidence of power's corroding influence. *Cato's Letters*[2] was "a favorite textbook of the patriots." [3] James Burgh's *Political Disquisitions,*[4] another major source of Antifederalist thought, was "encouraged" by some seventy-five prominent early Americans.[5]

Each of these works emphasized the baneful effects of power and the consequent need for "political jealousy" to safeguard the rights of man. Cato declared that "Political jealousy . . . in the people, is a necessary and laudable passion." [6] He argued that "Power renders men wanton, insolent to others, and fond of themselves. . . . All history affords but few instances of men trusted with great power without abusing it, when with security they could." [7] "There is a degree of watchfulness over all men possessed of power or influence upon which the liberties of mankind

---

*See Jackson Turner Main's illuminating discussion of the relevant nomenclature in *The Antifederalist: Critics of the Constitution, 1781-1788* (Chapel Hill, N.C.: University of North Carolina Press, 1961), pp. xi-xv.

much depend," Samuel Adams wrote Elbridge Gerry. "It is necessary to guard against the infirmities of the best as well as the wickedness of the worst of men." "Jealousy" was therefore "the best security of public liberty." [8] In later years Adams and Gerry became staunch Antifederalists.

The seeds of Antifederalism, nourished by suspicion, were both strengthened and weakened by the colonial reaction to Britain's attempt to cope with the problems of empire. From our colonial experience stemmed a curious and persisting schizophrenia. Increasing desire for union resulted in part from colonial displeasure with British policy; resistance to union, grounded in our traditional distaste of all centralized authority, was reinforced by Great Britain's arbitrary rule. This tension manifested itself even before independence. In the First Continental Congress of 1774, James Duane, John Dickinson, and Robert Morris, who opposed independence until it became apparent that war could no longer be avoided, urged the creation of a central government. In behalf of his Plan of Union, Galloway commented:

> Is it not necessary that the trade of the empire should be regulated by some power or other? Can the empire hold together without it? No. Who shall regulate it? Shall the Legislature of Nova Scotia or Georgia regulate it? Massachusetts or Virginia? Pennsylvania or New York? It can't be pretended. Our legislative powers extend no further than the limits of our governments. Where then shall it be placed? There is a necessity that an American Legislature should be set up, or else that we should give the power to Parliament or King.[9]

In a similar vein, Samuel Seabury observed: "To talk of being liege subjects to King George, while we disavow the authority of parliament, is another piece of whiggish nonsense." [10] Yet Richard Henry Lee and Patrick Henry, in later years vehement Antifederalists, insisted not only on the independence of the colonies from Britain but also on their continued independence of each other.[11]

The First Continental Congress rejected the Galloway Plan of Union, providing for an American Parliament elected by colonial legislatures and a President-general appointed by the King. Thus the colonies had failed to come to grips with the difficulties inherent in any federal system— the inevitable clash between central and local authority arising from the distribution of power between two authorities. In the mid-eighteenth century Great Britain was in fact a federal empire—a system in which powers were divided between central and local governments. In law and theory, however, the empire was a unified rather than a federal system. Parliament was supreme. After 1768, when British statesmen addressed themselves to the task of reorganizing the empire, they fell back upon the supremacy of Parliament. Given the opportunity to create a viable federalism, British statesmen bungled it by demanding too strong a central government at the expense of colonial autonomy. No serious attempt was made to organize power so as to preserve the advantages of both centralized authority and local autonomy.

America inherited the problem Britain and the colonies proved powerless to solve. Independence and war served only to shift the locus of responsibility for its solution. Independence had been achieved, but not union. In 1783 the war was over, as Dr. Benjamin Rush said, "but this is far from being the case with the American Revolution. On the contrary, nothing but the first act of the great drama is closed. It remains yet to establish and perfect our new forms of government. . . ." [12]

America's first attempt at constitution-making produced a document revealing both "inexperience with federal government and distrust of any centralized power." [13] The Articles of Confederation represented an easy victory for the enemies of a centralized state. Thomas Burke, who led the successful move to write into the Articles the provision that the states retain ultimate sovereignty, was "much pleased to find the opinion of accumulating powers to Congress so little supported." [14]

And yet the drive for unity had made an impact. Burke's revisions were in response to John Dickinson's original draft of the Articles, a plan which would have provided for a truly national government. So effectively did Burke arouse states rights sentiments that the Articles—even with his crippling amendments—evoked lurking suspicion that the power to be exercised by the Congress might be dangerously excessive. The town of West Springfield, Massachusetts, objected that the Articles would grant Congress too much power; "the sovereignty and independence" of the states would be "nearly annihilated." "It is *freedom*, gentlemen," the report affirmed, "it is *freedom*, & not a choice of the *forms of servitude* for which we contend, and we rely on your fidelity, that you will not consent to the present *plan* of Union, til after the most calm & dispassionate examination you are fully convinced it is well calculated to secure so great & desirable an object." West Springfield entertained "no jealousy of the present [Continental] Congress," but it could not be sure that "in some future corrupt times there may be a Congress which will form a design upon the liberties of the people. . . ." [15]

Men like Duane, Morris, and Wilson, all supporters of Dickinson's original draft, faced an uphill struggle. The hardships experienced under British rule could not be erased. "[T]he prejudices which the revolution had engendered against the arbitrary government of Great Britain," William Plumer observed, "made the people jealous of giving to their own officers so much power as was necessary to establish an efficient government." [16] Nevertheless, the Articles were a step—somewhat faltering—in America's long march toward union. They kept alive the *idea* of a "great Federal Republic" at a time when the forces of disunion might easily have prevailed. By recognizing that the war power and foreign relations were national in character, they provided a base on which to build. [17]

Perhaps the greatest service rendered by the Articles of Confederation was the impetus its shortcomings gave the nationalists, particularly James Wilson, John Jay, Alexander Hamilton, James Madison, John Adams, and John Marshall. Despite defects in structure and power, the Articles "prepared the way not for anarchy and chaos but for a more perfect union." [18]

In practice, Antifederalist thought produced a constitutional dilemma. It gave constitutional validity to the supremacy of the states over Congress, reinforcing "the most persistent problem of American constitutional law—the existence of a multiplicity of *local legislatures with indefinite powers*." [19] Inadequate power at the head meant that the central government was too weak to cope with problems of national scope; it was virtually powerless to check the overbearing legislative majorities in the several states. Legitimized state supremacy sanctioned the free play of thirteen state legislatures. The salutary effect was to spur the search for a truly Federalist solution.

Implementation of nationalist doctrine went hand in hand with overt demands for stronger central authority, tending to obscure evolution of the theory itself. Crucial in this development was the emergence of the doctrine of judicial review, a notion which pitted courts against the dominant legislative power of the thirteen states. Jefferson had early lamented legislative invasion of property and contract rights. In his own state of Virginia, he had seen that, "One hundred and seventy-three despots would surely be as oppressive as one." "An elective despotism," he declared,

> was not the government we fought for, but one which should not only be founded on free principles, but in which the powers of government should be so divided and balanced among several bodies of magistracy, as that no one could transcend their legal limits, without being effectively checked and restrained by the others.[20]

While John Adams was arguing for an executive veto to check the excesses of legislative majorities,[21] judicial power was being invoked as a remedy for abuses in the "legislative vortex." In certain states, courts pitted judicial knowledge "against sheer legislative self-assertion," destructive of the rights of property and contracts.[22] Implied was the judicial duty to uphold higher law against legislative usurpations. Meanwhile, along with this development, certain nationalists sought in vain to discover in the Articles of Confederation evidence of legal pre-eminence that might serve as a corrective of "unconstitutional" state legislative enactments. Effective theoretical transformation of the Articles was contingent not only on repudiation of the states' claim to sovereignty, but also on discovering a source of law which could claim higher status than that aspired to by the states. The drastic changes that had to be effected are measured by the lengths to which Wilson and Hamilton went, prior to the Convention of 1787, in their gropings for the foundations of national sovereignty in the Articles of Confederation.

As early as 1780, Hamilton, contending that "the fundamental defect" of the Articles was "want of power" in Congress, had observed: "It may be pleaded that Congress had never any definite powers granted them, and of course, could exercise none, could do nothing more than recommend." Hamilton denied this:

> They have done many of the highest acts of sovereignty, which were always cheerfully submitted to: The Declaration of Independence; the declaration of war; the levying of an army; creating a navy; emitting money; making alliances with foreign powers; appointing a dictator, etc., etc. All these implications of a complete sovereignty were never disputed, and ought to have been a standard for the whole conduct of administration. Undefined powers are discretionary powers, limited only by the object for which they were given; in the present case, the independence and freedom of America. . . .[23]

James Wilson, defending Congress' power to pass the act of 1781 incorporating the Bank of North America, argued in 1786:

> To many purposes the United States are to be considered as one undivided, independent nation; and as possessed of all the rights, and powers, and properties, by the law of nations incident to such. Whenever an object occurs, to the direction of which no state is competent, the management of it must, of necessity, belong to the United States in Congress assembled. There are many objects of this extended nature.[24]

In the same year John Jay, denying state authority to exercise the war power of confiscation, declared that the "rights to make war, to make peace, and to make treaties, appertaining *exclusively* to the national sovereign, that is, to Congress, . . . the thirteen state legislatures have no more authority to exercise the powers, or pass acts of sovereignty on those points, than any thirteen individual citizens." [25]

Challenged was not only the power of the states vis-à-vis the central government, but also the right of the states to withhold from Congress powers commensurate with national objectives. State legislative aggression had been opposed by judicial power; judicial review had been tied to the notion of higher law. It seemed logical to infer, as was later done, that the states were never sovereign. Independence and revolution had been, as Jefferson said, assertions of "the right of the people." The theoretical groundwork had yet to be laid for an effective national government. The arguments of Hamilton, Wilson, and Jay were ingenious rather than persuasive.

In the spring of 1787, James Madison wrote his analytical essay, "Vices of the Political System of the United States." For him the critical period posed a twofold problem: manifold evils in state governments and the alarming decline of national authority, especially "the defect of legal and coercive sanctions," experienced after a period of wartime unity and power. Two sides of the same coin were represented. Solutions for the "multiplicity," "mutability," and "injustice" of state legislation were closely linked with the corrective for that other vice—"want of sanction to the laws and coercion in the Government of the Confederacy." Later on, Madison suggested that the national government "have a negative, in all cases whatsoever, on the Legislative acts of the States." He conceived this check to be "essential and the least possible abridgement of the State sovereignties." [26] That this method was ultimately rejected in favor of judicial review does not lessen the significance of Madison's original remedy.

Nationalist reactions to the defects of the Articles, combined with the aggressive campaign to augment its central authority, only served to intensify opposition. In his letter to Duane, Hamilton had urged the calling of a convention to establish a "solid coercive union." "The Confederation . . . should give Congress complete sovereignty; except as to that part of internal police which relates to the rights of property and life among individuals, and to raising money by internal taxes." Washington's Circular Letter of 1783 also underscored the need for drastic action. "It is indispensable to the happiness of the individual States," he wrote, "that there should be lodged some where a Supreme Power, to regulate and govern the general concerns of the confederated Republic. . . ." [27] Jefferson shared the prevailing sense of urgency. "The want of power in the federal head was early perceived, and foreseen to be the flaw in our constitution which might endanger its destruction," he wrote Richard Price from Paris in 1785.[28] Unless "the band of our confederacy" were strengthened, Jefferson feared that "the States will go to war with each other in defiance of Congress." [29]

To these and other demands for constitutional change, defenders of the Articles of Confederation, most of whom would later become Antifederalists, reiterated the same arguments which had earlier proved so successful in defeating the Galloway Plan of Union and in emasculating John Dickinson's original draft of the Articles. Since amendment of the Articles required unanimity among the thirteen states, even the effort to confer upon Congress a limited power to raise an independent income failed. Dogged resistance to Congress inspired the instructions of Fairfax County, Virginia, to the State legislature: "The proposed duties may be proper, but the separate States only can safely have *the power of levying taxes*. Congress should not have even the appearance of such a power." Congress' plea for power to levy an impost was "found to exhibit strong proofs of lust of power. . . ." [30] These instructions were authored by George Mason, in later years an Antifederalist, one of three who refused to sign the Constitution. Rhode Island delegates submitted a similar message to the Governor of Rhode Island. An impost grant would effect fundamental alterations of the present system; it might "disturb the general harmony, derange the elegant proportions and endanger the welfare of the whole building." The result might very well be fatal to liberty.[31]

During the pre-Convention decade, this basic distrust, a nagging fear that a new aristocracy was in the making, pervaded the states rights literature.[32] Power begat power, the theme went; once granted, it was never surrendered but rather expanded.[33] When the power in question happened to be taxation, the implications were all the more serious. "Taxation is the necessary instrument of tyranny," wrote *The Plain Dealer*. "There is no tyranny without it." [34] Taxation was the most dangerous of all powers; "power, among civilized people as we are, is necessarily connected with the direction of the public money." [35] Abraham Yates, Jr., reminded his readers that it was not accidental that the Articles of Confederation denied Congress the power to raise money by direct taxation. Yates recalled that taxes had been crucial in the dispute with Great Britain; indeed, all history proved that "no important revolutions have taken place in any government, till the power of raising money from the people has been put into different hands. . . ." "This power is the center of gravity," he concluded, "for it will eventually draw into its vortex all other powers." [36]

Just as the forces of union and disunion had produced a dualism in early American political thought, so they also effected a division within the body of early Antifederalist thinking. Most of them recognized the need to bolster central authority, but they were reluctant to operate outside the confining framework of the Articles of Confederation. Skeptical of any radical move, they suspected the motives of those who advocated it. This attitude is reflected in the reaction of Massachusetts delegates in Congress to instructions sent to them in 1785 by the Massachusetts legislature, recommending that the delegates introduce a resolution calling for a constitutional convention. Any commercial power granted Congress, the delegates replied, should be temporary and restricted. A convention might be tempted to alter the basic structure of government. While measures ought to be taken "to guard against the evils arising from the want in one or two particulars of power in Congress, we are in great danger of incurring the other extreme. . . . We are for increasing the power of Congress as far as it will promote the happiness of the people, but at the same time are clearly of opinion that every measure should be avoided which would strengthen the hands of the enemies to a free government. . . ." [37]

It would be a mistake to conclude that all these precursors of Antifederalism were impervious to the evils stemming from defects in the Articles. Some were as narrow in their political outlook as the advocates of reform charged, but the great majority did not oppose all effort to revise the Articles. All agreed that some revision was necessary. Shays' Rebellion did not impress Federalists alone. Included among those who favored stronger government before 1787 were George Mason,[38] Patrick Henry,[39] Elbridge Gerry,[40] George Clinton,[41] James Monroe,[42] William Grayson,[43] John Francis Mercer,[44] and James Warren.[45] All were destined to become staunch Antifederalists.

When the call for a convention was issued at Annapolis in 1786, opponents of major change found themselves in a dilemma. Conceding that the Articles were imperfect and recognizing that amendments were nearly impossible to obtain by the mode prescribed, they could not consistently block the drive for a convention so long as it was authorized only to *recommend* reforms *within* the existing constitutional framework. George Bryan later recalled the circumstances that narrowed the range of Antifederalist action prior to the Philadelphia Convention:

> Previous to the appointment of the Convention there seemed to be in Pennsylvania a general Wish for a more efficient Confederation. The public Debt was unpaid & unfunded. We were deluged with foreign goods, which it was evident might have paid large Sums to the Continental Treasury, if Duties could have been generally laid & collected, & at the same time the levying such Duties would have checked the extravagant Consumption. Whilst Congress could refuse to execute them it was obvious that we were in Danger of falling to pieces.[46]

Antifederalist thought may have been ambivalent, but it was not ambiguous. Most Antifederalists of this period agreed that the central government under the Articles needed invigoration. The basic character of the Articles must, however, remain unaltered. Above all, they did not want the central government removed from control of the state legislatures. Union, not unity, was their goal. Fundamental disagreement with the nationalists lay in the conflict between the desire for some change and their distrust of nationalist objectives.

Experience under the Articles of Confederation, the tangible product of early Antifederalism, eventually culminated in the establishment of a more perfect union, created in spite of, rather than because of, the Articles. Though the Articles cannot be blamed directly for the conditions that made the critical years critical, the central government's lack of coercive power contributed to the crisis. The Articles marked, as John Quincy Adams suggests, a break with the political theory of the Declaration and of the Revolution.[47] Whereas the earlier experience was founded on the notion of *one people,* if not yet one nation, acting in a united sovereign capacity, the Articles were explicitly grounded in the idea of state sovereignty. In this sense, the Articles represented a usurpation by the states of the original sovereignty vested in the people, the authority asserted in both independence and revolution.

The definition of a constitution that Judge William Paterson fashioned in his famous charge to the jury in *Vanhorne's Lessee* v. *Dorrance* had yet to be met:

> What is a constitution? It is the form of government, delineated by the mighty hand of the people, in which certain first principles or fundamental laws are established. The constitution is certain and fixed; it contains the permanent will of the people, and is the supreme law of the land; it is paramount to the power of the legislature, and can be revoked or altered only by the authority that made it. What are legislatures? Creatures of the constitution, they owe their existence to the constitution—they derive their powers from the constitution. It is their commission, and therefore all their acts must be conformable to it, or else void. The *constitution* is the work or will of the *people* themselves, in their original, sovereign, and unlimited capacity. Law is the work or will of the legislature in their derivative capacity.[48]

The Articles fell far short of the goal. The architects of this system had "wasted their time, their talent," as John Quincy Adams said, "in erecting and roofing and buttressing a frail and temporary shed to shelter the nation from the storm." The experience was not, however, without its advantages. These early fruits of Antifederalism should perhaps be tested not so much by the bitter taste they left as by the ultimate result they inspired. Afforded was "an experiment of inestimable value, even in its failure." "It taught our fathers the lesson," Adams observed, "that they had more, infinitely more to do than merely to achieve their Independence by War. That they must form their Social compact upon principles never before attempted on earth." [49]

In his Circular Letter of 1783, Washington had urged that "our Federal government be given such tone . . . as will enable it to answer the ends of its institution." "Binding ligaments" were needed and these could properly be imposed by "no earthly power other than the People themselves."[50] Americans had still to demonstrate whether they could meet the challenge Jefferson underscored many years later: "A generation that commences a revolution rarely completes it."[51]

Notes ᗜᔕᵂ

1. Paul L. Ford, ed., *The Writings of Thomas Jefferson* (New York: Putnam, 1896), VII, pp. 288-309.
2. Thomas Gordon and John Trenchard, *Cato's Letters: or, Essays on Liberty, Civil, and Religious, and other important subjects,* 4 vols., 5th ed. (London, 1748).
3. Arthur M. Schlesinger, *Prelude to Independence* (New York, 1958), pp. 96, 137.
4. James Burgh, *Political Disquisitions; or, an Enquiry into public Errors, Defects, and Abuses. Illustrated by, and established upon Facts and Remarks, extracted from a Variety of Authors, Ancient and Modern,* 3 vols. (Philadelphia, 1775).
5. J. T. Main, *The Antifederalists; Critics of the Constitution, 1781-1788* (Chapel Hill, N.C.: University of North Carolina Press, 1961), p. 9.

6. Burgh, *op. cit.*, I, p. 260.   7. *Ibid.*, II, 36.

8. Samuel Adams to Elbridge Gerry, April 23, 1784, in Harry Alonzo Cushing, ed., *The Writings of Samuel Adams*, 4 vols. (New York, 1904-1908), IV, p. 302; Adams to John Winthrop, December 21, 1778, in Edmund Cody Burnett, ed., *Letters of Members of the Continental Congress*, 8 vols. (Washington, D.C.: 1921-1936), III, p. 545.

9. Debates on the Galloway Plan of Union, 1774, in Charles Francis Adams, ed., *The Works of John Adams*, 10 vols. (Boston, 1850-1856), II, 387-391. The original debates were destroyed. Notes taken by Adams on Sept. 28, 1774.

10. Samuel Seabury, "A View of the Controversy between Great Britain and Her Colonies," Dec. 24, 1774, in Charles H. Vance, ed., *Letters of a Westchester Farmer* (1774-1775). Publications of the Westchester County Historical Society, 1930, Vol. VIII, p. 105.

11. Debate on the Galloway Plan of Union, 1774, in Adams, *op. cit.*, II, pp. 387-91.

12. H. Niles, *Principles and Acts of the Revolution* (Baltimore, Md., 1822), p. 234.

13. Benjamin F. Wright, *Consensus and Continuity, 1776-1787* (Boston, 1958), p. 21.

14. Thomas Burke to the Governor of North Carolina, April 29, 1777, in Burnett, ed., *Letters of Members of the Continental Congress*, II, pp. 345-346.

15. Feb. 16, 1778, Massachusetts towns, Force transcripts; cited in Main, *op. cit.*, p. 16 (n. 43).

16. Richard F. Upton, *Revolutionary New Hampshire* (Hanover, N.H.: Dartmouth College Publications, 1936), p. 184. Cited in Main, *op. cit.*, p. 16 (n. 44).

17. Edward S. Corwin, "The Progress of Constitutional Theory Between the Declaration of Independence and the Meeting of the Philadelphia Convention," *The American Historical Review*, Vol. 30 (April 1925), 527.

18. Julian P. Boyd, ed., "The Articles of Confederation and Perpetual Union," 11, Old South Leaflets, Nos. 228-229 (Boston: The Old South Association, 1960).

19. Corwin, *op. cit.*, p. 513; emphasis added.

20. Jefferson, *Notes on the State of Virginia* (Chapel Hill, N.C.: University of North Carolina Press, 1955), pp. 110-29.

21. John Adams, *A Defence of the Constitutions of Government of the United States of America*, published 1787-88; reprinted in Charles F. Adams, *op. cit.*, IV, pp. 271-588.

22. Corwin, *op. cit.*, p. 523.

23. Hamilton to Duane, Sept, 3, 1780, in John C. Hamilton, ed., *The Works of Alexander Hamilton*, 7 vols. (New York, 1850-51), I, pp. 150-67.

24. James DeWitt Andrews, ed., *The Works of James Wilson* (Chicago, 1896), I, pp. 558, 565.

25. Secret Journals of the Acts and Proceedings of Congress, IV, Foreign Affairs, p. 209.

26. Madison to Randolph, April 8, 1787, in Hunt, ed., *The Writings of James Madison*, II, pp. 336-40. See also his *Vices of the Political System of the United States* in Hunt, II, pp. 361-69.

27. Washington to Governor William Livingston, July 12, 1783. Quoted in A. T. Mason, *Free Government in the Making* (New York: Oxford University Press, 1956), p. 162.

28. Jefferson to Richard Price from Paris, Feb. 1, 1785, in Boyd, VII, p. 630.

29. Jefferson to Randolph, Feb. 15, 1783, in Boyd, VI, pp. 248-49.

30. Instructions of Fairfax County, Va., to its representatives in the State legislature, May 30, 1783, in Kate Mason Rowland, *The Life of George Mason* (New York, 1892), II, pp. 50-51.

31. The Rhode Island delegates to the Governor of Rhode Island, Oct. 15, 1782, in Burnett, ed., *Letters*, VI, p. 506.

32. "The Examiner," in the *Massachusetts Gazette* (Springfield), Sept. 10, 1782. Quoted in Main, *op. cit.*, p. 78.

33. Richard Henry Lee to Samuel Adams, March 14, 1785, in Burnett, ed., *Letters*, VIII, p. 66 (note).

34. "The Plain Dealer," in the *Freeman's Journal* (Philadelphia), May 10, 1783. Quoted in Main, *op. cit.*, p. 79.
35. "Democritus," in *ibid.*, March 26, 1783. Quoted in Main, *op. cit.*, p. 79.
36. "Rough Hewer, Jr.," in the *New York Packet*, April 21, 1785. Quoted in Main, *op. cit.*, p. 79.
37. Massachusetts Congressmen to the State legislature, September 3, 1785, in Burnett, *op. cit.*, VIII, pp. 208-9.
38. Madison to Jefferson, Dec. 10, 1783, in Hunt, II, pp. 27-28.
39. Henry, in William Short to Jefferson, May 14, 1784, in Boyd, VII, p. 257.
40. Gerry to Samuel Adams, Sept. 30, 1785. Cited in Main, *op. cit.*, p. 113.
41. Clinton to Washington, Oct. 14, 1783. Cited in Main, *op. cit.*, p. 113.
42. Monroe to Jefferson, June 16, 1785, in Burnett, ed., *Letters*, VII, pp. 143-45.
43. Grayson to Madison, May 28, 1786; to Wm. Short, April 16, 1787; in *ibid.*, VIII, pp. 374, 581.
44. Mercer to Madison, Nov. 12, and Nov. 26, 1784, in *ibid.*, VII, pp. 609-10, 616.
45. Warren to Washington, Sept. 2, 1785. Quoted in Main, *op. cit.*, p. 113.
46. Manuscript (n.d.), Bryan Papers, Hist. Soc. Pa. Cited in Main, *op. cit.*, p. 114, n. 40.
47. J. Q. Adams, *The Jubilee of the Constitution* (New York, 1839), pp. 17-18, 30.
48. Cited in Ford, *Pamphlets*, by John Dickinson, p. 182 (note).
49. J. Q. Adams, *op. cit.*
50. *Ibid.*
51. Jefferson to John Adams, Sept. 4, 1823, in Ford, XII, p. 310.

Documents 🎋

1 · Samuel Seabury · *A View of the Controversy* · 1774

The Reverend Samuel Seabury, an Anglican minister in New York and a prominent American Tory, addressed himself to the smoldering problem of Federalism in a pamphlet published in 1774.

. . . In every government there must be a supreme, absolute authority lodged somewhere. In arbitrary governments this power is in the monarch; in aristocratical governments, in the nobles; in democratical in the people; or the deputies of their electing. . . .

Upon supposition that every English colony enjoyed a legislative power independent of the parliament; and that the parliament has no just authority to make laws to bind them, this absurdity will follow—that there is no power in the British empire, which has authority to make laws for the whole empire; i.e., we have an empire, without government; or which amounts to the same thing, we have a government which has no supreme power. All our colonies are independent of each other: Suppose them independent of the British parliament,—what power do you leave to govern the whole? None at all. You split and divide the empire into a number of petty insignificant states. This is the direct, the necessary

"A View of the Controversy Between Great Britain and Her Colonies," in *Letters of a Westchester Farmer* (1774-1775), Charles H. Vance, ed. Publications of the Westchester County Historical Society, 1930, Vol. VIII, pp. 103-27, *passim*.

tendency of refusing submission to acts of parliament. Every man who can see one inch beyond his nose, must see this consequence. And every man who endeavours to accelerate the independency of the colonies on the British parliament, endeavours to accelerate the ruin of the British empire.

To talk of being liege subjects to King George, while we disavow the authority of parliament is another piece of whiggish nonsense. I love my King as well as any whig in America or England either, and am as ready to yield him all lawful submission: But while I submit to the King, I submit to the authority of the laws of the state, whose guardian the King is. The difference between a good and a bad subject, is only this, that the one obeys, the other transgresses the law. The difference between a loyal subject and a rebel, is, that the one yields obedience to, and faithfully supports the supreme authority of the state, and the other endeavours to overthrow it. If we obey the laws of the King, we obey the laws of the parliament. If we disown the authority of the parliament, we disown the authority of the King. There is no medium without ascribing powers to the King which the constitution knows nothing of:—without making him superior to the laws, and setting him above all restraint. These are some of the ridiculous absurdities of American whiggism. . . .

I will here, Sir, venture to deliver my sentiments upon the line that ought to be drawn between the supremacy of Great-Britain, and the dependency of the colonies. And I shall do it with the more boldness, because, I know it to be agreeable to the opinions of many of the warmest advocates for America, both in England and in the colonies, in the time of the stamp-act.—I imagine that if all internal taxation be vested in our own legislatures, and the right of regulating trade by duties, bounties, &c. be left in the power of the Parliament; and also the right of enacting all general laws for the good of all the colonies, that we shall have all the security for our rights, liberties and property, which human policy can give us: The dependence of the colonies on the mother country will be fixed on a firm foundation; the sovereign authority of Parliament, over all the dominions of the empire will be established, and the mother-country and all her colonies will be knit together, in ONE GRAND, FIRM, AND COMPACT BODY.

2 • Thomas Burke • *Defense of State Sovereignty* • 1777

Thomas Burke, who ardently and successfully opposed John Dickinson's initial nationalistic version of the Articles of Confederation, embodied the spirit of early Antifederalism in his letters to the Governor of North Carolina.

Letters of Thomas Burke to the Governor of North Carolina, March 11 and April 29, 1777, in *Letters of Members of the Continental Congress,* Edmund Cody Burnett, ed. (Washington, D.C.: 1921-1936), II, pp. 294-96, 345-46.

MARCH 11, 1777

The more experience I acquire, the stronger is my conviction that *unlimited power can not be safely trusted* to any man or set of men on earth. No men have undertaken to exercise authority with intentions more generous and disinterested than the Congress and none seem to have fewer or more feeble motives for increasing the power of their body politic. What could induce individuals blest with peaceable domestic affluence to forego all the enjoyment of a pleasing home, to neglect their private affairs, and at the expense of all their time and some part of their private fortunes, to attend public business under many insurmountable difficulties and inconveniences? What but a generous zeal for the public? And what can induce such men to endeavor at increasing the power with which they are invested, when their tenure of it must be exceedingly dangerous and precarious and can bring them individually neither pleasure or profit? This is a question I believe cannot be answered but by a plain declaration that power of all kinds has an irresistible propensity to increase a desire for itself. It gives the passion of ambition a velocity which increases in its progress, and this is a passion which grows in proportion as it is gratified. . . . Great part of our time is consumed in debates, whose object on one side is to increase the power of Congress, and on the other to restrain it. The advocates do not always keep the same side of the contest. The same persons who on one day endeavor to carry through some resolutions, whose tendency is to increase the power of Congress, are often on another day very strenuous advocates to restrain it. From this I infer that no one has entertained a concerted design to increase the power; and the attempts to do it proceed from ignorance of what such a being ought to be, and from the delusive intoxication which power naturally imposes on the human mind. . . .

These and many other considerations make me earnestly wish that the power of Congress was accurately defined and that there were adequate check provided to prevent any excess. . . .

I enclose you an abstract of the debates in Congress on every question of any consequence that has been determined in Congress since my last. . . . The last matter in the abstract will show you that even thus early, men so eminent as members of Congress are willing to explain away any power that stands in the way of their particular purposes. What may we not expect some time hence when the seat of power shall become firm by habit and men will be accustomed to obedience, and perhaps forgetful of the original principles which gave rise thereto. I believe Sir the root of the evil is deep in human nature. Its growth may be kept down but it cannot be entirely extirpated. Power will sometime or other be abused unless men are well watched, and checked by something they cannot remove when they please.

APRIL 29, 1777

At present, nothing but executive business is done, except the Confederation, and on mere executive business there are seldom any debates; (and still more seldom any worth remembering). We have agreed to three articles: one containing the name; the second a declaration of the sovereignty of the States, and an express provision that they be considered as retaining every power not expressly delegated; and the third an agreement mutually to assist each other against every enemy. The first and latter passed without opposition or dissent, the second occasioned two days debate. It stood originally the third article; and expressed only a reservation of the power of regulating the internal police, and consequently resigned every other power. It appeared to me that this was not what the States expected, and, I thought, it left it in the power of the future Congress or General Council to explain away every right belonging to the States and to make their own power as unlimited as they please. I proposed, therefore an amendment which held up the principle that all sovereign power was in the States separately, and that particular acts of it, which should be expressly enumerated, would be exercised in conjunction, and not otherwise; but that in all things else each state would exercise all the rights and power of sovereignty, uncontrolled. This was at first so little understood that it was some time before it was seconded, and South Carolina first took it up. The opposition was made by Mr. Wilson of Pennsylvania, and Mr. R. H. Lee of Virginia. In the end, however, the question was carried for my proposition, eleven ayes, one no, and one divided. The no was Virginia; the divided, New Hampshire. I was much pleased to find the opinion of accumulating powers to Congress so little supported, and I promise myself, in the whole business I shall find my ideas relative thereto nearly similar to those of most of the States. In a word, Sir, I am of opinion the Congress should have power enough to call out and apply the common strength for the common defence, but not for the partial purposes of ambition. . . .

3 · Fairfax County, Virginia · *Resistance to a Stronger Central Government* · 1783

These instructions of May 30, 1783, from Fairfax County to its representatives in the Virginia Legislature, reflect determined opposition to nationalist efforts to strengthen the central government under the Articles of Confederation.

We desire and instruct you strenuously to oppose all encroachments of the American Congress upon the sovereignty and jurisdiction of the sepa-

Kate Mason Rowland, *The Life of George Mason* (New York, 1892), II, pp. 50-51.

rate States; and every assumption of power, not expressly vested in them, by the Articles of Confederation. If experience shall prove that further powers are necessary and safe, they can be granted only by additional articles to the Confederation, duly acceded to by all the States; for if Congress, upon the plea of necessity, or upon any pretence whatever, can arrogate powers not warranted by the Articles of Confederation, in one instance, they may in another, or in an hundred; every repetition will be strengthened and confirmed by precedents.

And in particular we desire and instruct you to oppose any attempts which may be made by Congress to obtain a perpetual revenue, or the appointment of revenue officers. Were these powers superadded to those they already possess, the Articles of Confederation, and the Constitutions of Government in the different States would prove mere parchment bulwarks to American liberty.

We like not the language of the late address from Congress to the different States, and of the report of their committee upon the subject of revenue, published in the same pamphlet. If they are carefully and impartially examined, they will be found to exhibit strong proofs of lust of power. . . . After having reluctantly given up part of what they found they could not maintain, they still insist that the several States shall invest *the United States in Congress assembled with a power to levy,* for the use of the United States, the following duties, &c., and that the revenue officers shall be amenable to Congress. The very style is alarming. The proposed duties may be proper, but the separate States only can safely have *the power of levying taxes.* Congress should not have even the appearance of such a power. Forms generally imply substance, and such a precedent may be applied to dangerous purposes hereafter. When the same man, or set of men, holds both the sword and the purse, there is an end of liberty. . . .

4 · Massachusetts Delegates · *Resistance to a Constitutional Convention* · 1785

On September 3, 1785, Massachusetts delegates in Congress made the following reply to instructions from the Massachusetts legislature to introduce a resolution in Congress calling for a constitutional convention.

If an alteration, either temporary or perpetual, of the commercial powers of Congress, is to be considered by a Convention, shall the latter be authorized to revise the Confederation *generally,* or only for express purposes? The great object of the Revolution was the establishment of good government, and each of the states, in forming their own, as well as the federal constitution, have adopted republican principles. Notwithstanding this, plans have been artfully laid, and vigorously pursued, which had they been successful, we think would inevitably have changed our republican governments into baleful aristocracies. Those plans are frustrated, but the same spirit remains in their abettors. And the institution of the Cincinnati, honorable and beneficent as the views may have been of the officers who compose it, we fear, if not totally abolished, will have the same fatal tendency. What the effect then may be of calling a Convention to revise the Confederation generally, we leave with your Excellency and the honorable Legislature to determine. We are apprehensive and it is our duty to declare it, that such a measure would produce thro'out the Union, an exertion of the friends of an aristocracy to send members who would promote a change of government, and we can form some judgment of the plan which such members would report to Congress. But should the members be altogether republican, such have been the declamations of designing men against the Confederation generally; against the rotation of members, which perhaps is the best check to corruption, and against the mode of altering the Confederation by the unanimous consent of the Legislatures, which effectually prevents innovations in the Articles by intrigue or surprise, that we think there is great danger of a report which would invest Congress with powers that the honorable legislature have not the most distant intention to delegate. Perhaps it may be said this can produce no ill effect because Congress may correct the report however exceptionable, or if passed by them, any of the states may refuse to ratify it. True it is that Congress and the states have such powers, but would not such a report affect the tranquility and weaken the government of the Union? We have already considered the operation of the report as it would respect Congress; and if animosities and parties would naturally arise from their rejecting it, how much would these be increased if the report approved by Congress and some of the states, should be rejected by other states? Would there not be danger of a party spirit's being thus more generally diffused and warmly supported? Far distant we know it to be from the honorable legislature of Massachusetts to give up a single principle of republicanism, but when a general revision shall have proceeded from their motion, and a report which to them may be highly offensive, shall have been confirmed by seven states in Congress, and ratified by several Legislatures, will not these be ready to charge Massachusetts with inconsistency in being the first to oppose a measure which the state will be said to have originated? Massachusetts has great weight and is considered as one of the most republican states in the Union; and when it is known that the legislature have proposed a general revision, there can be no doubt that they will be represented as being convinced of the necessity of increasing generally the powers of Congress, and the opinion of the state will be urged with such art as to convince numbers that the Articles of the Confederation are altogether exceptionable. Thus, whilst measures are taken to guard against the evils arising from the want in one or two particulars of power in Congress, we are in great danger of incurring the other extreme. "More power in Congress" has been the cry from all quarters, but especially of those whose views, not being confined to a government that will best promote the happiness of the people, are extended to one that will afford lucrative employments, civil and military. Such a government is an aristocracy, which would require a standing army and a numerous train of pensioners and placemen to prop and support its exalted administration. To recommend one's self to such an administration would be to secure an establishment for life and at the same time to provide for his posterity. These are pleasing prospects, which republican governments do not afford, and it is not to be wondered at that many persons of elevated views and idle habits in these states are desirous of the change. We are for increasing the power of Congress as far as it will promote the happiness of the people, but at the same time are clearly of opinion that every measure should be avoided which would strengthen the hands of the enemies to a free government. And that an administration of the present Confederation with all its inconveniences, is preferable to the risk of general dissensions and animosities which may approach to anarchy and prepare the way to a ruinous system of government.

5 · Louis Otto · *The Annapolis Convention* · 1786

This account of the Annapolis Convention was written on October 10, 1786, by an astute foreign observer, Louis Guillaume Otto, French consul in New York, to Count Vergennes, the French Foreign Minister.

The commissioners appointed by various states to propose a general plan of commerce, and to give to Congress the powers necessary to execute it, assembled at Annapolis in the course of last month. But five states alone being represented, they did not think it best to enter into the main question, and confined themselves to addressing to Congress and the different legislatures a report which characterizes the present spirit of the politics of this country. . . .

For a very long time, my lord, the necessity of imparting to the federal government more energy and vigor has been felt, but it has also been felt that the excessive independence granted to the citizens, as regards the states, and to the states as regards Congress, is too dear to individuals for them to be deprived of it without great precautions.

The people are not ignorant that the natural consequences of an increase of power in the government would be a regular collection of taxes, a strict administration of justice, extraordinary duties on imports, rigor-

George Bancroft, *History of the Formation of the Constitution of the United States* (New York, 1883), II, pp. 399-401.

ous executions against debtors—in short, a marked preponderance of rich men and of large proprietors.

It is, however, for the interest of the people to guard as much as possible the absolute freedom granted them in a time when no other law was known but necessity, and when an English army, as it were, laid the foundations of the political constitution.

In those stormy times it was necessary to agree that all power ought to emanate only from the people; that everything was subject to its supreme will, and that the magistrates were only its servants.

Although there are no nobles in America, there is a class of men denominated "gentlemen," who, by reason of their wealth, their talents, their education, their families, or the offices they hold, aspire to a preeminence which the people refuse to grant them; and, although many of these men have betrayed the interests of their order to gain popularity, there reigns among them a connection so much the more intimate as they almost all of them dread the efforts of the people to despoil them of their possessions, and, moreover, they are creditors, and therefore interested in strengthening the government, and watching over the execution of the laws.

These men generally pay very heavy taxes, while the small proprietors escape the vigilance of the collectors.

The majority of them being merchants, it is for their interest to establish the credit of the United States in Europe on a solid foundation by the exact payment of debts, and to grant to Congress powers extensive enough to compel the people to contribute for this purpose. The attempt, my lord, has been vain, by pamphlets and other publications, to spread notions of justice and integrity, and to deprive the people of a freedom which they have so misused. By proposing a new organization of the federal government all minds would have been revolted; circumstances ruinous to the commerce of America have happily arisen to furnish the reformers with a pretext for introducing innovations.

They represented to the people that the American name had become opprobrious among all the nations of Europe; that the flag of the United States was everywhere exposed to insults and annoyance; the husbandman, no longer able to export his produce freely, would soon be reduced to extreme want; it was high time to retaliate, and to convince foreign powers that the United States would not with impunity suffer such a violation of the freedom of trade, but that strong measures could be taken only with the consent of the thirteen states, and that Congress, not having the necessary powers, it was essential to form a general assembly instructed to present to Congress the plan for its adoption, and to point out the means of carrying it into execution.

The people, generally discontented with the obstacles in the way of commerce, and scarcely suspecting the secret motives of their opponents, ardently embraced this measure, and appointed commissioners, who were to assemble at Annapolis in the beginning of September.

The authors of this proposition had no hope, nor even desire, to see the success of this assembly of commissioners, which was only intended to prepare a question much more important than that of commerce. The measures were so well taken that at the end of September no more than five states were represented at Annapolis, and the commissioners from the northern states tarried several days at New York in order to retard their arrival.

The states which assembled, after having waited nearly three weeks, separated under the pretext that they were not in sufficient numbers to enter on business, and, to justify this dissolution, they addressed to the different legislatures and to Congress a report, the translation of which I have the honor to enclose to you.

In this paper the commissioners employ an infinity of circumlocutions and ambiguous phrases to show to their constituents the impossibility of taking into consideration a general plan of commerce and the powers pertaining thereto, without at the same time touching upon other objects closely connected with the prosperity and national importance of the United States.

Without enumerating these objects, the commissioners enlarge upon the present crisis of public affairs, upon the dangers to which the Confederation is exposed, upon the want of credit of the United States abroad, and upon the necessity of uniting, under a single point of view, the interests of all the states.

They close by proposing, for the month of May next, a new assembly of commissioners, instructed to deliberate not only upon a general plan of commerce, but upon other matters which may concern the harmony and welfare of the states, and upon the means of rendering the federal government adequate to the exigencies of the union.

In spite of the obscurity of this document, you will perceive, my lord, that the commissioners were unwilling to take into consideration the grievances of commerce, which are of exceeding interest for the people, without at the same time perfecting the fundamental constitution of Congress.

It is hoped that new commissioners will be appointed, with ample powers to deliberate on these important objects, and to place Congress in a position not only to form resolutions for the prosperity of the union, but to execute them.

II · TOWARD A MORE PERFECT UNION · 1787

Essay 𓆝

The hard facts of the critical period had undermined the premises on which the Articles of Confederation had been built. Some revision was necessary. No one denied that the central government must have more power. The crucial question was what kind and how much.

Even the Articles conferred on Congress undisputed power to declare war, make peace, and to deal with foreign relations. Its basic infirmity lay in the fact that ultimate sovereignty, the source of Congress' limited authority, rested with the states. Article II, the heart of the Articles, explicitly reserved to each state not only "its sovereignty, freedom and independence," but also "every power, jurisdiction and right" not "expressly delegated" to the Congress.

Obvious inadequacies made it clear that the power distribution would have to be altered in favor of the central authority. This concession emphatically did not imply the scrapping of the Articles or repudiation of the Confederation's cornerstone—state sovereignty. Thus, while the states might revise the Articles, perhaps even approximate a viable federal system, they would retain ultimate sovereignty. In the exercise of powers not delegated to Congress, the states would remain supreme. In effect, a sharp line would separate the two spheres. As long as sovereignty remained with the states, they could grant or withdraw power at their pleasure.

This seems to have been the solution hoped for by opponents of radical overhaul prior to the Convention. In light of the inexorable demands of the critical period, the states were prepared to make concessions.

Antifederalists favored yielding to the center, but always with due restrictions, never going so far as to advocate relinquishing state sovereignty. The Philadelphia newspaper correspondent "Legion" said that the powers of Congress ought to be increased, but only with "great caution and circumspection. . . . Perhaps it would be best to grant the additional powers to Congress for a certain limited time, until it could be observed how they operated and answered the purpose. If they did, continue them —if not sufficient, enlarge them, until found adequate to the government of a great commercial people." [1] "Amicus Patriae" of Boston wrote in the same vein, emphasizing that there was no need to alter the fundamental structure. The situation required only that Congress be given the power to regulate trade and collect duties. No other powers were needed. The new ones could be tried for a few years and repealed if they proved dangerous to liberty.[2]

It is therefore understandable that the resolution adopted at Annapolis in 1786, calling for the Philadelphia Convention, suggested no radical departure from the existing system. The Convention was to ". . . take into consideration the situation of the United States to devise such further provisions as shall appear . . . necessary to render the Constitution of the Federal Government adequate to the exigencies of the Union. . . ." Revisions were to be reported to Congress and would become effective only when agreed to by Congress and by every state legislature.[3] When Congress, the only body authorized under the Articles to propose amendments, finally legitimized the Annapolis resolution, it restricted the forthcoming Convention to "the sole and express purpose of revising the Articles of Confederation. . . ." [4] Six states had already commissioned delegates before Congress acted. None of their mandates exceeded the bounds authorized at Annapolis. Delaware, in fact, specifically forbade any alteration of Article V, which guaranteed each state one vote in Congress. Rhode Island refused to send any delegates. Three states—New York, Connecticut, and Massachusetts—adopted the restrictive provision of Congress' declaration, expressly barring more than revision of the Articles. South Carolina, Maryland, and New Hampshire empowered their delegates in language resembling that of the Annapolis resolution.

Perhaps Jefferson caught both the mood and approach. After reading the proposed Charter, he wrote John Adams on November 13, 1787: "I think all the good of this new Constitution might have been couched in three or four new articles to be added to the good, old, venerable fabric, which should have been preserved, even as a religious relic." Unfortunately, Jefferson did not take the trouble to spell out the contents of the "three or four articles" he had in mind.

None of the delegates had been empowered to strike at the core of state supremacy. "Revise and amend" was the order of the day. Grant Congress more power, limited and restricted; and, even more significantly, let the states grant it, let the Congress under the Articles approve it, and let the states—all of them—ratify it. Uproot state sovereignty? No! Only a few, notably Alexander Hamilton and George Read of Delaware, would have preferred completely to wipe out the states.[5] But, just as adherents of state sovereignty had bowed to the overwhelming need to strengthen the central government, thereby arriving at what they considered "middle ground," so also had the nationalists modified their more extreme goals. Six weeks before the delegates assembled, Madison had written Edmund Randolph that, whereas his preference might have led him to advocate a "consolidation of the states," his view had been tempered by a recognition of the possible. "In truth," he had confessed, "my ideas of reform strike so deeply at the old Confederation, and lead to such a systematic change, that they scarcely admit of the expedient."

> I hold it for a fundamental point, that an individual independence of the States is utterly irreconcilable with the idea of an aggregate sovereignty. I think, at the same time, that a consolidation of the States into one simple republic is not less unattainable than it would be inexpedient. Let it be tried, then, whether any middle ground can be taken, which will at once support a due supremacy of the national authority, and leave in force the local authorities so far as they can be subordinately useful.[6]

In the end considerations of principle and expediency conspired to produce Madison's "middle ground."

The Madison-Randolph plan, while rejecting the idea of "consolidation," was calculated to undercut both cornerstones of state supremacy. Distribution of power between the national and state governments was heavily weighted in favor of the former. As Madison proposed to Randolph: "Let it [the national government] have a negative, in all cases whatsoever, on the Legislative acts of the States, as the King of Great Britain heretofore had."[7] This negative was considered "essential, . . . the least possible abridgement of the State sovereignties." Without it "every positive power that can be given on paper" to the national government would be "unavailing." There would clearly be no line circumscribing national power. More than that, the other cornerstone of state supremacy would be destroyed: state sovereignty as the legitimate source of power would bow to popular sovereignty. "To give the new system its proper energy," Madison declared, "it will be desirable to have it ratified by the authority of the people, and not merely by that of the Legislatures."[8]

Even before the Convention, one notes a lurking suspicion that the states might lose their pre-eminence. Nor were these fears unfounded. For although Madison's plan would have preserved the states so far as they could be "subordinately useful," its nationalizing features contained the potential for effective "consolidation," an implication which did not escape notice at the Convention—or later. But having gone on record in favor of some change, it seemed inconsistent to oppose the elevated objectives of the Convention. Whether more than "revision" could be achieved was at best problematical. The authorization at Annapolis did not extend beyond these bounds. Furthermore, the Convention proposals would have to be submitted to Congress and transmitted to the states. It seemed extremely unlikely that Congress and the states would sign their own death warrants. For revision of the Articles, unanimous approval by the thirteen states was required, and Rhode Island had already expressed its unequivocal disapproval by refusing to send delegates. Thus, strident nationalists would have to run a barrier-studded gauntlet to uproot the existing system.

Perhaps confident—in any case, hopeful—that the results of the impending Convention could not or would not extend beyond a moderate revision of the Articles, certain would-be Antifederalists did not attend the gathering at Philadelphia. Others refusing commissions may not have wished to dignify the assembly by their presence. Prominent opponents of a strong central government, not in attendance, included Samuel Adams of Massachusetts and Richard Henry Lee and Patrick Henry of Virginia. "I smelt a Rat," [9] Henry explained laconically. Those who later became Antifederalists were ably represented by Elbridge Gerry of Massachusetts, Luther Martin of Maryland, and George Mason of Virginia. Robert Yates and John Lansing of New York were also there, probably appointed by Governor Clinton to keep an eye on Alexander Hamilton. Yet Richard Henry Lee later lamented the failure of many Antifederalist leaders to accept commissions to the Convention. "The non-attendance of eight or nine men, who were appointed members of the convention, I shall ever consider as a very unfortunate event to the United States," he wrote. "Had they attended," Lee was "pretty clear" that the Constitution would not have had that "consolidating" effect.[10]

Though slightly outnumbered, delegates enamored of Antifederalism promptly made their presence felt. Hardly had the Virginia Plan, embodying the proposals Madison submitted to Randolph, been presented than state sovereignties were stirred. Charles Pinckney immediately asked whether Randolph "meant to abolish the State Governts. altogether." [11] Randolph explained that he "only meant to give the national government a power to defend and protect itself." His plan would take from the states "no more sovereignty than is competent to this end." [12] On May 30, 1787, the day after the Virginia Plan had been proposed, Gouverneur Morris "explained the distinction between a *federal* and *national* supreme Govt," making it clear that he considered Randolph's answer evasive. Morris thought the Virginia Plan would alter—indeed displace —the basic structure of the Articles of Confederation. The Articles were a "federal" government, whereas Randolph's proposals would establish a "national, supreme" government, resting on the principle that "in all communities there must be one supreme power, and one only." [13] Elbridge Gerry, replying to Morris, quickly challenged the authority of the Convention to effect a revolution:

A distinction has been made between a *federal* and *national* government. We ought not to determine that there is this distinction for if we do, it is questionable not only whether this convention can propose a government totally different or whether Congress itself would have a right to pass such a resolution as that before the house. . . . If we have a right to pass this resolution we have a right to annihilate the confederation.[14]

Charles C. Pinckney also wondered whether the act of Congress recommending the Convention as well as the commissions of the delegates "could authorize a discussion of a system founded on different principles from the federal Constitution." [15]

Authorization or no authorization, the Convention proceeded to debate the Virginia Plan on its merits. If its nationalizing implications were not made clear by the questions Gerry and Pinckney raised, they ought to have been. Indeed, as early as May 20, four days before the delegates assembled, George Mason had written his son: "The most prevalent idea in the principal States seems to be a total alteration of the present federal system. . . ." [16] The next day he expressed the same opinion to Arthur Lee.[17] Writing to James Monroe on May 29, William Grayson declared that the delegates from the East were advocating "a very strong government, & wish to prostrate all ye. state legislature, & form a general system out of ye. whole. . . ." The Virginia Plan, Grayson noted, involved uprooting state sovereignty through the mechanism of popular ratification. Said he: "The people of America don't appear to me to be ripe for any great innovations & it seems they are ultimately to ratify or reject. . . ." [18]

Despite the apparent import of the Virginia Plan, Randolph continued to deny its implications. On May 31, the day after he had equivocally answered Charles Pinckney, Pierce Butler expressed his fear that the Convention was "running into an extreme in taking away the powers of the States, and called on Mr. Randolph for the extent of his meaning." Randolph "disclaimed any intention to give indefinite powers to the national Legislature, declaring that he was entirely opposed to such an inroad on the State jurisdictions, and that he did not think any considerations whatever could ever change his determination. His opinion was fixed on this point." [19] His views could not have been very firmly rooted, for later the same day he "was of opinion that it would be impossible to define the powers and length to which the federal Legislature ought to extend just at this time." More significantly, Wilson and Madison were in agreement:

> Mr. Wilson observed that it would be impossible to enumerate the powers which the federal Legislature ought to have.
>
> Mr. Madison said he had brought with him a strong prepossession for the defining of the limits and powers of the federal Legislature, but he brought with him some doubts about the practicability of doing it:—at present he was convinced it could not be done.[20]

If the delegates needed any further evidence that the Virginia Plan would establish a national government and accord it supremacy, both as to broad areas of power as well as to sovereignty, the discussion on June 6 and 7—particularly the pointed comments of Read, Wilson, and Dickinson—must have set them straight. George Read's speech of June 6 makes his position unmistakably clear:

Too much attachment is betrayed to the State Govermts. We must look beyond their continuance. A national Govt. must soon of necessity swallow all of them up. They will soon be reduced to the mere office of electing the national Senate. He [Read] was agst. patching up the old federal System: he hoped the idea would be dismissed. It would be like putting new cloth on an old garment. The confederation was founded on temporary principles. It cannot last: it cannot be amended. If we do not establish a good Govt. on new principles, we must either go to ruin, or have the work to do over again. . . .[21]

While Read's position is distinguishable from that of other nationalists (Wilson and Madison, for example, never suggested abolishing the states), the two positions are enough alike to make it not unreasonable to equate the Virginia Plan with "consolidation." Apparently fearful of the possible repercussions of Read's forthright speech, Wilson went to great lengths to disassociate "consolidation" from the Virginia Plan. Immediately following Read's bold expression of nationalist conviction, Madison records: "Mr. Wilson would not have spoken again but for what had fallen from Mr. Read; namely, that the idea of preserving the State Govts. ought to be abandoned." Wilson, a fervent nationalist, "saw no incompatibility between the national & State Govts. provided the latter were restrained to certain local purposes; nor any probability of their being devoured by the former." The real danger was not from the national government but from the states. "In all confederated systems ancient & modern the reverse had happened; the Generality being destroyed gradually by the usurpations of the parts composing it." [22]

Refusing to be silenced, Read continued to press for annihilation of the state governments.[23] Once again Wilson disclaimed any intent to "swallow up" the states.[24] Yet Read's image of "consolidation" was hard to erase. The next day John Dickinson accused Wilson of wanting to "extinguish" the states. "The preservation of the States in a certain degree of agency is indispensable," Dickinson contended. "It will produce that collision between the different authorities which should be wished for in order to check each other. To attempt to abolish the States altogether, would degrade the Councils of our Country, would be impracticable, would be ruinous." Dickinson likened "the proposed National System to the Solar System, in which the States were the planets, and ought to be left to move freely in their proper orbits." Wilson, he said, "wished to extinguish these planets" by excluding the states "from all agency" in the national government and by drawing "all power . . . from the people at large. . . ." [25] Wilson, of course, denied the charge:

. . . He did not see the danger of the States being devoured by the Nationl. Govt. On the contrary, he wished to keep them from devouring the national Govt. He was not however for extinguishing these planets as was supposed by Mr. D.—neither did he on the other hand, believe that they would warm or enlighten the Sun. Within their proper orbits they must still be suffered to act for subordinate purposes (for which their existence is made essential by the great extent of our Country). . . .[26]

Discussion of the Virginia Plan brought more and more into focus the threats it embodied to the continued existence of the states. Two features in particular raised valid questions as to the survival of the states as viable units in the proposed scheme of government. Dickinson, among others, had chided Wilson for failure of the Virginia Plan to provide for state representation. The legislative negative on state laws also came under attack. Persistent requests for a precise definition of national power under the Virginia Plan were met by dogged refusals to be committed. On June 8, Madison "could not but regard an indefinite power to negative legislative acts of the States as absolutely necessary to a perfect system." "Experience," he argued, "had envinced [sic] a constant tendency in the States to encroach on the federal authority; to violate national Treaties, to infringe the rights & interests of each other; to oppress the weaker party within their respective jurisdictions." National power to negative all state laws deemed improper was "the mildest expedient that could be devised for preventing these mischiefs." "Appeal to coercion" would be the only alternative. Thus, a national negative, extending to "all cases," would "render the use of force unnecessary." [27]

Madison's unequivocal stand for "indefinite" national power did not go unchallenged. Hugh Williamson of North Carolina objected that the effect might be to "restrain the States from regulating their internal" affairs.[28] Gerry feared that such power would "enslave the States." [29] Roger Sherman of Connecticut "thought the cases in which the negative ought to be exercised, might be defined." [30] In defense of Madison's position, Wilson explained that it was impossible to draw a line dividing state and national powers. Some national powers might be defined, he conceded, "but when we come near the line it cannot be found." [31] "A definition of the cases in which the Negative should be exercised," Wilson added, "is impracticable. A discretion must be lodged on one side or the other. Will it not be most safely lodged on the side of the Natl. Govt.? . . . What danger is there that the whole will unnecessarily sacrifice a part? But reverse the case, and leave the whole at the mercy of each part, and will not the general interest be continually sacrificed to local interests?" [32]

Wilson's compelling logic, anticipating Hamilton in *The Federalist* and John Marshall in *McCulloch* v. *Maryland,* [33] convinced Dickinson. Having accused Wilson the previous day of wanting to "extinguish" the states, the delegate from Delaware now argued for indefinite national power:

Mr. Dickinson deemed it impossible to draw a line between the cases proper & improper for the exercise of the negative. We must take our choice

of two things. We must either subject the States to the danger of being injured by the power of the Natl. Govt. or the latter to the danger of being injured by that of the States. He thought the danger greater from the
States. . . .[34]

Pierce Butler, however, was not persuaded. In fact, he "was vehement
agst. the Negative. . . ."[35] "Will a man," he queried, "throw afloat his
property & confide it to a government a thousand miles *distant?*"[36]

Opposition to "indefinite" national power erupted again in the discussion of the provision for proportional representation. Paterson's elaborate
argument of June 9 reflected the fear of small states that they would be
dominated by the superior voting power of the larger states. Proportional
representation would strike "at the existence of the lesser States." Paterson argued for a guarantee to each state of an equal vote in the new
Congress, premising his reasoning on the absence of the Convention's
authority to alter the basic structure of the Articles of Confederation.
"We ought to keep within its limits," he warned, "or we should be
charged by our constituents with usurpation." More than that, the commissions of the delegates were not only the measure of their power; "they
denoted also the sentiments of the States on the subject of our delibera-
tion."

> The idea of a national Govt. as contradistinguished from a federal one, never
> entered into the mind of any of them, and to the public mind we must ac-
> commodate ourselves. We have no power to go beyond the federal scheme,
> and if we had the people are not ripe for any other. We must follow the
> people; the people will not follow us. *The proposition* [proportional repre-
> sentation] could not be maintained whether considered in reference to us
> as a nation, or as a confederacy. A confederacy supposes sovereignty in the
> members composing it & sovereignty supposes equality. If we are to be con-
> sidered as a nation, all State distinctions must be abolished, the whole must
> be thrown into hotchpot, and when an equal division is made, then there
> may be fairly an equality of representation. . . .

Paterson vowed that New Jersey would "never confederate on the plan"
proposed; the state "would be swallowed up." He would not only "oppose
the plan here but, on his return home, do everything in his power to
defeat it there."[37] At this juncture, Wilson sharply challenged: "If N.J.
will not part with her Sovereignty it is in vain to talk of Govt."[38]

The impending impasse came to a head on June 15, when Paterson
brought forward a plan founded on principles diametrically opposed to
those on which the Virginia Plan rested. Alluding to his alternative on
June 9, he confessed strong attachment "to the plan of the existing confederacy." "No other amendments were wanting," he had declared, "than
to mark the orbits of the States with due precision, and provide for the
use of coercion. . . ."[39] In short, the Articles of Confederation would be
the foundation of the New Jersey Plan.

Both the Virginia and New Jersey Plans presumed to alter the Articles of Confederation so as to render it "adequate to the exigencies" of the union.[40] There the similarity ends. The chasm dividing the advocates of a strong national government and their opponents before the Convention now reappeared in stark clarity. That the New Jersey Plan reflected much more than fear for the future position of the *small* states is evidenced by the differences between Paterson's proposals and those of Randolph on issues other than representation.

Under the Virginia Plan[41] the national legislature would have been empowered "to legislate in all cases to which the separate States are incompetent, or in which the harmony of the United States may be interrupted by the exercise of individual Legislation"; it would negate any state law deemed contrary to the national constitution. By implication, the national legislature itself would decide the cases "to which the separate States are incompetent." The Virginia Plan also called for a national executive and a national judiciary whose execution and enforcement of national laws would have been brought directly to bear on individuals. No longer could the states, through failure to heed the laws of Congress and the authority of their courts, shield individuals from the coercive power of the national government. Finally, the Virginia Plan contemplated popular ratification, a device calculated to destroy state sovereignty and enthrone national supremacy.

The New Jersey Plan,[42] on the other hand, would have perpetuated the twin keystones of state supremacy: state power and state sovereignty. Throughout, it sought to protect the states as the dominant centers of authority. Although additional legislative powers were to be vested in the national Congress, all violations were first to be "adjudged by the Common law Judiciarys" of the several states. It not only declared that "none of the [legislative] powers . . . vested in the United States in Congress shall be exercised without the consent" of an unspecified number of states, but also provided that the national executive should be removable by Congress on the application of a majority of the state governors. Representation in Congress would, of course, have remained the same. Article XIII, requiring unanimous approval of amendments by the thirteen states, would also remain unaltered.

Oddly enough, the sixth resolution of the New Jersey Plan contained the substance of what later became the cornerstone of national supremacy—Article VI, Paragraph 2, of the Constitution. Paterson's version read:

> Resolved that all Acts of the United States in Congress, made by virtue and in pursuance of the powers hereby and by the articles of confederation vested in them, and all treaties made and ratified under the authority of the United States shall be the supreme law of the respective States so far forth as those Acts or Treaties shall relate to the said States or their Citizens, and that the

Judiciary of the several States shall be bound thereby in their decisions, any thing in the respective laws of the Individual States to the contrary notwithstanding. . . .

It is noteworthy, however, that even this otherwise nationalistic provision was weakened by the assertion that the supremacy of Congressional acts applied only "so far as those Acts or Treaties shall relate to the said States or their Citizens." If the resolution bound state judges to observe such acts, it also permitted them to decide how far those very acts related to the states and to their citizens. It is true that the second and fifth resolutions of the New Jersey Plan provided for an appeal from the state courts to the federal judiciary. Nevertheless, even *national* enforcement of national law through the federal courts was necessarily limited by the extent of national *power*. As national power would be augmented to a very limited extent—only a commerce power and a limited revenue power would be added—the supremacy of national law would be similarly confined. In effect, a sharp line would continue to define, delimit, and circumscribe national power.

The New Jersey Plan, then, was much more than an expression of the small states' desire to maintain equal footing with the larger states in the national legislature. Paterson's resolutions were grounded in mixed principles and inspired by mixed motives. Said Madison:

> This plan had been concerted among the deputations or members thereof, from Cont. N.Y. N.J. and perhaps Mr. Martin from Maryd. who made with them a common cause on different principles. Cont. and N.Y. were agst. a departure from the principle of the Confederation, wishing rather to add a few new powers to Congs. than to substitute, a National Govt. The States of N.J. and Del. were opposed to a National Govt. because its patrons considered a proportional representation of the States as the basis of it. The eagourness displayed by the Members opposed to a National Govt. from these different [motives] began now to produce serious anxiety for the result of the Convention.—Mr. Dickinson said to Mr. Madison you see the consequence of pushing things too far. . . .[43]

Mixed motives did not, however, blunt the sure sense of direction that welded the plan into a consistent whole. Madison was also acutely aware that prior accord on the representation issue would greatly facilitate settlement of the dispute over allocation of power between the national and state governments. Elbridge Gerry later suggested that before proceeding to the question of representation the delegates should settle the issue of the nature and scope of national power. Madison objected, insisting that representation be first considered.

> It wd. be impossible to say what powers could be safely & properly vested in the Govt. before it was known, in what manner the States were to be represented in it. He was apprehensive that if a just representation were not the

basis of the Govt. it would happen, as it did when the Articles of Confederation were depending, that every effectual prerogative would be withdrawn or withheld, and the New Govt. wd. be rendered as impotent and as short lived as the old.[44]

"The great difficulty lies in the affair of Representation; and if this could be adjusted, all others would be surmountable," Madison had remarked.[45] The logic of Madison's insight would be borne out, but not before deadlock over representation almost stalemated the Convention. For a whole month, from June 15 when Paterson proposed the New Jersey Plan until July 16 when the Connecticut Compromise was consummated, the issue of representation dominated the discussion. Both sides, it should be emphasized, tightly bound the question of state equality in the national legislature to the related issues of national power and state sovereignty. Paterson virtually equated state sovereignty with equal state representation. "If the sovereignty of the States is to be maintained," he contended in his speech of June 16, "the Representatives must be drawn immediately from the States, not from the people: and we have no power to vary the idea of equal sovereignty." [46] The Convention was powerless, he maintained, to alter Article V of the Confederation. By giving each state an equal vote, it had provided the "basis" of the Confederation: "equal Sovereignty." Article XIII, moreover, required the unanimous consent of the thirteen equal states to alter the Confederation. "If the confederacy was radically wrong, let us return to our States, and obtain larger powers, not assume them of ourselves. What is unanimously done, must be unanimously undone." [47] Paterson strongly implied that any other procedure would be revolutionary.

Lansing agreed that the Convention had no power even to consider abridging state sovereignty by revising the mode of representation. He was sure that "N. York would never have concurred in sending deputies to the convention, if she had supposed the deliberations were to turn on a consolidation of the States, and a National Government." [48] Completely unimpressed, Wilson remarked: "With regard to the *power of the Convention,* he conceived himself authorized to *conclude nothing,* but to be at liberty to *propose anything.* . . ." [49] Charles Pinckney also thought that the Convention's recommendatory powers were unlimited. Questioning Paterson's motives, Pinckney suggested: "Give N. Jersey an equal vote, and she will dismiss her scruples, and concur in the Natil. system." [50] Randolph admitted that *he* "was not scrupulous on the point of power." For him, "the salvation of the Republic was at stake," and "it would be treason to our trust, not to propose what we found necessary." Randolph tied the question of representation to the broader issue. "The true question," he insisted, "is whether we shall adhere to the federal plan, or introduce the national plan." [51]

Madison records that Hamilton, "hitherto silent on the business before the Convention," [52] seized this moment flatly to reject both plans. So "serious" was the "crisis which now marked our affairs" that the delegates could not "permit any scruples whatever to prevail" over their duty to "contribute" their "efforts for the public safety & happiness." Their task was "to provide for the exigencies of the Union." To refrain from proposing a plan adequate to those exigencies, "merely because it was not clearly within our powers, would be to sacrifice the means to the end." Perhaps the states could not ratify a plan which extended beyond the purview of the Articles. "But," he suggested, "may not the States themselves in which no constitutional authority equal to this purpose exists in the Legislatures, have had in view a reference to the people at large?"

Paterson's proposals, Hamilton contended, were clearly inadequate to the great purposes of the Convention—purposes which could not possibly be answered by mere "amendment of the confederation, leaving the States in possession of their sovereignty. . . ." Indeed, state sovereignty was the very evil requiring remedy. It was the multiplicity of state legislatures wielding virtually uncontrolled authority which had produced the crisis. Whatever the form of government proposed, Hamilton warned, the real danger would always come from the states, not the national government. Experience had proved this. "The States," he explained, "have constantly shown a disposition rather to regain the powers delegated by them than to part with more, or to give effect with what they had parted with." The states, like men, "love power" and are no less reluctant to part with it. More than that, the states were fortified by "an habitual attachment of the people." "The whole force of this tie is on the side of the State Govt." It followed that the states "will generally be an overmatch for the Genl. Govt. and render any confederacy, in its very nature precarious."

Hamilton could find no practical "middle ground." His was an either/ or dilemma: "The general power whatever be its form if it preserves itself, must swallow up the State powers. Otherwise it will be swallowed up by them." From the premise that "two Sovereignties can not co-exist within the same limits," Hamilton was led to the inevitable conclusion—extinguish the States.

> . . . If they [the state governments] were extinguished, he [Hamilton] was persuaded that great economy might be obtained by substituting a general Govt. He did not mean however to shock the public opinion by proposing such a measure. On the other hand he saw no *other* necessity for declining it. They are not necessary for any of the great purposes of commerce, revenue, or agriculture. Subordinate authorities he was aware would be necessary. There must be district tribunals: corporations for local purposes. . . .[53]

Even Hamilton's disclaimer the next day (June 19) does not vitiate his preference for a "great Federal Republic":

> He [Hamilton] had not been understood yesterday. By an abolition of the States, he meant that no boundary could be drawn between the National &

State Legislatures; that the former must therefore have indefinite authority. If it were limited at all, the rivalship of the States would gradually subvert it. Even as Corporations the extent of some of them as Va. Massts. &c. would be formidable. *As States,* he thought, they ought to be abolished. But he admitted the necessity of leaving in them, subordinate jurisdictions. . . .[54]

Hamilton's plan, modeled on the British, was never seriously considered. Though his *expressed* views were atypical, they differed only in degree from other strong nationalists at the Convention. Hamilton's plan shared one crucial characteristic with Randolph's: the national government would have to be endowed with indefinite power; there could be no line circumscribing national power *vis-à-vis* the states. Hamilton's candor led him openly to confess his preference for the outright abolition of the state governments; proponents of the Virginia Plan—restrained by their sense of the possible—had proposed a system which, while preserving the states, contained the potential for effective "consolidation."

After Hamilton's speech, if not before, it was clear that the issue of state representation in *any* new form of government could not be divorced from the broader questions of state power and state sovereignty. Immediately following Hamilton's attempted disclaimer of his desire to liquidate the states—a preference which even Madison shared in his letter to Randolph—the delegates turned their attention to the question of whether the states ever had a *right* to aspire to sovereignty. Rufus King contended that the states "did not possess the peculiar features of sovereignty"; they "could not make war, nor peace, nor alliances, nor treaties," powers belonging to the Congress, even under the Articles. It followed that since the states had already divested themselves of "essential portions" of sovereignty, the Convention could propose alterations in the Articles which further divested them—including their claim to equal representation. King concluded by doubting the "practicability of annihilating the States" but favoring the idea "that much of their power ought to be taken from them." [55]

King had tried to clarify the terms "states," "sovereignty," "national," and "federal"—words "often used & applied in the discussion inaccurately & delusively." [56] But his explanation had served only further to confuse such words as "power" and "sovereignty." His contention that the states, having never possessed certain "peculiar features of sovereignty," could therefore be divested of other portions of it, really was an argument "that much of their [the states'] *power* ought to be taken from them." It left unanswered the question of whether the states were sovereign in the sense of being the only legitimate *source* of power, or whether they—and only they—could divest themselves of power by delegating portions of it to a central government. If the states were sovereign, then Congress' war power under the Articles indicated only that the states had delegated Congress a certain portion of power. It did not indicate that Congress was entitled

—as a sovereign prerogative—to *more* power. Indeed, if original sovereignty were vested in the states, then the possession of *any* power by Congress could only confirm the dependence of Congress on the sovereign states.

The question, then, turned on the original sovereignty of the states. Luther Martin, replying to King, went to the heart of the matter:

> Mr. Martin, said he considered that the separation from G. B. placed the 13 states in a state of nature towards each other; that they would have remained in that state till this time, but for the confederation; that they entered into the confederation on the footing of equality; that they met now to amend it on the same footing, and that he could never accede to a plan that would introduce an inequality and lay 10 States at the mercy of Va. Massts. and Penna.[57]

Grant the premise, and the conclusion follows irresistibly: when "the states threw off their allegiance to Great Britain, they became independent of her and each other";[58] therefore any disruption of the Confederation by means other than those sanctioned by the Articles would be revolutionary.

Of course Wilson could not agree. He "could not admit the doctrine that when the Colonies became independent of G. Britain, they became independent also of each other."

> He read the declaration of Independence, observing thereon that the *United Colonies* were declared to be free & independent States; and inferring that they were independent, not *Individually* but *Unitedly* and that they were confederated as they were independent, States.[59]

Hamilton concurred.[60] But, quite understandably, neither Hamilton nor Wilson pushed the argument one step further—that when the colonies revolted not as thirteen sovereign states but as a united people, the Articles of Confederation, resting on state sovereignty, represented a usurpation of "the Right of the People," as Jefferson wrote in the Declaration, to alter or abolish government and institute a new one.

Still to be faced in connection with the representation issue were the questions of whether the national legislature ought to consist of two branches and, if so, whether the first branch ought to be elected by the people instead of the states. Opposing popular election, Luther Martin elaborated the significance of state representation. He agreed that the legislative branch ought to be bicameral. This would be an effective means of checking the "dangerous" potentialities of concentrated power. Martin also confessed that "when the confederation was made, congress ought to have been invested with more extensive powers. . . ." "The time is now come," he conceded, "that we can grant them not only new powers, but to modify their government, so that the state governments are not endangered." To be acceptable, however, changes must be consistent with the basic character of the Articles. Thus, Martin concluded: "But whatever we have now in our power to grant, the grant is a state grant, and therefore it must be so organized that the state governments are interested in supporting the union." [61]

Popular election of the first branch, a condition which James Wilson regarded "not only [as] the cornerstone, but as the foundation of the fabric," [62] was agreed to on June 21. On June 27, the Convention voted unanimously to proceed to "the most fundamental points; the rules of suffrage in the two branches. . . ." [63] Martin spoke for three hours "with much diffuseness and considerable vehemence" [64] in defense of the smaller states against the large, and in defense of all the states against the proposed national government. "[T]he Genl. Govt. ought to be formed for the States, not for individuals," he contended. "[I]f the States were to have votes in proportion to their numbers of people, it would be the same thing whether their representatives were chosen by the Legislatures or the people. . . ." [65] Equal state representation must be preserved in both branches, this being prerequisite to the maintenance of state sovereignty.

Martin and his supporters lost this battle. The next day the Convention decided "that the right of suffrage in the first branch . . . ought not to be according to the rule established in the articles of confederation but according to some equitable ratio of representation." [66] Then came the matter of the upper house; it took the form of a motion to give each state an equal vote. The germ of compromise was planted the same day, when Doctor Johnson of Connecticut suggested:

> . . . On the whole he thought that as in some respects the States are to be considered in their political capacity, and in others as districts of individual citizens, the two ideas embraced on different sides, instead of being opposed to each other, ought to be combined; that in *one* branch the *people,* ought to be represented; in the *other,* the *States.*[67]

The seeds planted on June 29 bore fruit after more than two weeks of bitter debate. Madison agreed with Dr. Johnson that "the mixed nature of the Govt. ought to be kept in view," but he "thought too much stress was laid on the rank of the States as political societies." [68] Madison saw the issue of proportional versus equal representation in the second branch more in terms of the position of the states in the union than as a meaningful struggle between large and small states. He therefore entreated the small states "to renounce a principle wch. was confessedly unjust, which could never be admitted, & if admitted must infuse mortality into a Constitution which we wished to last forever." [69]

Hamilton was equally adamant. ". . . [A]s States are a collection of individual men," he queried, "which ought we to respect most, the rights of the people composing them, or of the artificial beings resulting from the composition?" [70] Even Elbridge Gerry urged that "we never were independent States, were not such now, & never could be even on the princi-ples of the Confederation." The advocates of states rights, he charged, were "intoxicated with the idea of their *sovereignty*." [71] Finally, on that fateful June 29, Ellsworth of Connecticut formally moved his colleague's suggestion, trusting that "on this middle ground a compromise would take place." [72] Ahead was long and acrimonious debate. Involved was the accuracy of Ellsworth's famous aphorism: "We were partly national; partly federal." [73]

So vital did Madison, Wilson, and Hamilton consider representation in the upper house that it could not be divorced from the related ques-tions of power and sovereignty. Equal state representation would embrace a principle inconsistent with the underlying theory of the new govern-ment. "I would always exclude inconsistent principles in framing a sys-tem of government," Madison emphasized. "I would compromise on this question, if I could do it on correct principles, but otherwise not—if the old fabric of the confederation must be the ground-work of the new, we must fail." [74] His meaning could hardly be clearer.

"Can we forget for whom we are forming a Government?" Wilson pleaded. "Is it for *men,* or for the imaginary beings called States? Will our honest Constituents be satisfied with metaphysical distinctions?" Echoing Madison's warning, Wilson insisted that inconsistent principles would crumble the whole structure. "The rule of suffrage ought on every principle to be the same in the 2d. as in the 1st. branch. If the Govern-ment be not laid on this foundation, it can neither be solid nor lasting, any other principle will be local, confined & temporary. . . . We talk of States, till we forget what they are composed of." [75]

Rufus King was "filled with astonishment" that the Convention should consider sacrificing the "substantial good" of the new system to "the phantom of *State* sovereignty." [76] Refusal to compromise seemed to mean, as Bedford put it, that "there was no middle way between a perfect con-solidation and a mere confederacy of the States." [77] Reluctantly Madison had reached the same conclusion. "[T]he two extremes before us," he had declared grimly, "are a perfect separation & a perfect incorporation, of the 13 States." [78]

The Convention seemed hopelessly deadlocked. Stalemate was formally confirmed on July 2, when the Convention divided 5-5-1 on the resolution to accord each state an equal vote in the upper house. General C. C. Pinckney now proposed that a committee be formed to attempt a com-promise. On July 5, the committee presented its report; two proposals, embodying the "partly national, partly federal" principle, were recom-mended, "on condition that both shall be generally adopted." [79] The first branch of the legislature would be popularly elected and based on pro-portional representation. It would also have the exclusive power of orig-inating money bills. In the second branch each state would have an equal vote.

The committee's proposals—except for the one according the first branch exclusive authority for originating money bills—embraced no new middle ground. Nationalists had already rejected the very notion of state equality in the second branch as destructive of effective government. Understandably, they continued to oppose this presumably vital concession to the advocates of state sovereignty. Deeply incensed, Madison was "not only fixed in his opposition to the Report of the Comme. but was prepared for any want that might follow a negative of it." [80] He "could not regard the exclusive privilege of originating money bills as any concession," since it "left in force all the objections which had prevailed agst. allowing each State an equal voice." [81] Gouverneur Morris was no less emphatic. "He conceived the whole aspect of it to be wrong. . . . State attachments, and State importance have been the bane of this Country," he exclaimed. "We cannot annihilate; but we may perhaps take out the teeth of the serpents. . . . This Country must be united," Morris entreated. "If persuasion does not unite it, the sword will," [82] he warned ominously.

So the debate on representation continued. On July 7, Madison again objected to state equality in the second branch. "If a just representation were not the basis of the Govt.," he reiterated, "the New Govt. wd. be rendered as impotent and as short lived as the old." [83] Gouverneur Morris persisted in his opposition; the committee's report "maintained the improper Constitution of the 2d. branch. It made it another Congress, a mere whisp of straw." Elbridge Gerry, Morris recalled, had said that the new government would be "partly national, partly federal; that it ought in the first quality to protect individuals; in the second, the States." "But," Morris asked, "in what quality was it to protect the aggregate interest of the whole." Surely, he argued, the only rationale behind state equality was "to keep the majority of the people from injuring particular States. But particular States ought to be injured for the sake of a majority of the people, in case their conduct should deserve it." [84]

Four days later Edmund Randolph spoke out against state representation: "If a fair representation of the people be not secured, the injustice of the Govt. will shake it to its foundations." [85] On July 14, the searing issue erupted again as opponents of state equality in the second branch made a concerted effort to defeat the committee's proposal. Luther Martin brought matters to a head by calling for a vote on the whole report. "He did not like many parts of it," he confessed. "He did not like having two branches, nor the inequality of votes in the 1st. branch." He was, however, willing to give the plan a trial.[86] Wilson hoped to delay the vote. "The equality of votes was a point of such critical importance that every opportunity ought to be allowed, for discussing and collecting the mind of the Convention on it." [87]

Wilson's suggestion that the report be reconsidered was "tacitly agreed to." As the nationalists prepared to take their last stand, Charles Pinckney, attempting to salvage a measure of proportional representation in the second branch, moved that:

> . . . instead of an equality of votes the States should be represented in the 2d. branch as follows: N.H. by 2. members. Mas 4. R.I. 1. Cont. 3. N.Y. 3. N.J. 2. Pa. 4. Del. 1. Md. 3. Virga. 5. N.C. 3. S.C. 3. Geo. 2. making in the whole 36.[88]

Wilson seconded the motion, and Madison "concurred" in it "as a reasonable compromise." [89] But Jonathan Dayton and Roger Sherman lodged protests which effectively pinpointed the dual motives driving the promoters of equal state representation. "The smaller States," Dayton insisted, "can never give up their equality." He would "in no event yield that security for their rights." Sherman favored "the equality of votes not so much as a security for the small States; as for the State Govts. which could not be preserved unless they were represented & had a negative in the Genl. Government." [90]

King, Madison, and Wilson made final pleas in favor of Pinckney's "compromise" motion. Their speeches read like the grim protests of men forced to swallow a bitter pill. King "was sure that no Govt. could last that was not founded on just principles." The delegate from Maryland "preferred the doing of nothing, to an allowance of an equal vote to all the States." "It would be better," he thought, "to submit to a little more confusion & convulsion, than to submit to such an evil." [91] Madison, no less apprehensive for the future of the new government, reminded the Convention of "the consequences of laying the existing confederation on improper principles." "If the proper foundation of Government was destroyed," he warned, "by substituting an equality in place of a proportional Representation, no proper superstructure would be raised." The "partly national, partly federal" formula, the basis of the so-called compromise, was internally inconsistent and inherently defective:

> . . . it had been said that the Governt. would in its operation be partly federal, partly national; that altho' in the latter respect the Representatives of the people ought to be in proportion to the people: yet in the former it ought to be according to the number of the States. If there was any solidity in this distinction he [Madison] was ready to abide by it, if there was none it ought to be abandoned. In all cases where the Genl. Governt. is to act on the people, let the people be represented and the votes be proportional. In all cases where the Governt. is to act on the States as such, in like manner as Congs. now act on them, let the States be represented & the votes be equal. This was the true ground of compromise if there was any ground at all. But he denied that there was any ground. He called for a single instance in which the Genl. Govt. was not to operate on the people individually. . . .

Madison proceeded to enumerate "the objections agst. an equality of votes in the 2d. branch, notwithstanding the proportional representation in the first":

> 1. the minority could negative the will of the majority of the people. 2. they could extort measures by making them a condition of their assent to other necessary measures. 3. they could obtrude measures on the majority by virtue of the peculiar powers which would be vested in the Senate. 4. the evil instead of being cured by time, would increase with every new State that should be admitted, as they must all be admitted on the principle of equality. 5. the perpetuity it would give to the (preponderance of the) Northn. agst. the Southn. Scale [sic] was a serious consideration. It seemed now to be pretty well understood that the real difference of interests lay, not between the large & small but between the N. and Southn. States. The institution of slavery & its consequences formed the line of discrimination. . . .[92]

To the speeches of King and Madison, James Wilson "would add a few words only." State equality in the second branch was "a fundamental and perpetual error" which "ought by all means to be avoided." In response to the argument that "an equal vote in one branch of the Legislature is essential to their [the states'] preservation," Wilson admitted that the states "ought to be preserved." "But does it follow that an equality of votes is necessary for the purpose?" [93] In the minds of a bare majority of the Convention, the answer, apparently, was affirmative. For Pinckney's motion, which aimed at persuading the Convention to accept what Madison had called "a reasonable compromise," failed to pass, confirming Elbridge Gerry's prediction that it had "no hope of success." [94] The next day, July 16, the Convention approved "the whole of the report from the grand Committee" by a vote of 5-4-1. The so-called Connecticut Compromise had been accepted, but not before the die-hard nationalists tried unsuccessfully to undo it.

As if to record for posterity their unremitting opposition, Randolph and King—supported by others who felt that the people instead of the states ought to be represented in the second branch of the legislature—attempted to reopen the representation issue. "It will probably be in vain to come to any final decision with a bare majority on either side," Randolph declared shortly after the vote was taken. He therefore felt that the subject ought to be considered further and moved for an overnight adjournment.[95] The motion failed. Elbridge Gerry, who opposed it, explained that although he could see "no new ground of compromise," he would now concur in a temporary adjournment. John Rutledge of South Carolina thought an adjournment was unnecessary, since there was "no chance of a compromise." The views of the small states being "fixt," the large states had no choice but to decide "whether they would yield or not." He hoped that "another Convention will supply our omissions. . . ." [96]

Buoyed perhaps by Gerry's reversal, Randolph and King renewed the motion to adjourn until the next day, and this time it carried.[97] The temporary respite, however, undid nothing. According to Madison's account, the opponents of equal state representation in the second branch could not unite on whether to continue the fight or to yield reluctantly:

> . . . Several of them supposing that no good Governnt could or would be built on that foundation, and that as a division of the Convention into two opinions was unavoidable, it would be better that the side comprising the principal States, and a majority of the people of America, should propose a scheme of Govt. to the States, than that a scheme should be proposed by the other side, would have concurred in a firm opposition to the smaller States, and in a separate recommendation, if eventually necessary. Others seemed inclined to yield to the smaller States, and to concur in such an Act however imperfect & exceptionable, as might be agreed on by the Convention as a body, tho' decided by a bare majority of States and by a minority of the people of the U. States. . . .[98]

Thus the curtain came down on the most hotly contested issue before the Convention.

Enemies of a strong national government, as well as friends of the small states, had good reason to hail the Connecticut Compromise as a victory. The term "compromise" is a misnomer. Notwithstanding the implications of Luther Martin's remarks of July 10—that adherents of equal state representation, having lost their battle in the first branch of the legislature, were entitled to equal representation in the second branch[99]— the Connecticut Compromise bears no earmarks of compromise. Proportional representation in the first branch had been determined prior to the struggle over representation in the second, prior to the "partly national, partly federal" formula suggested by Dr. Johnson, formalized by Ellsworth's motion, and acted on by the committee. Strong national government men had lost a battle, but not the war.

For over a month supporters of the Virginia Plan, embodying the essence of Madison's "middle ground," had fought to stave off what they thought would vitiate the nationalizing features of the new system. Repeatedly the nationalists had insisted that equal state representation would infect the new government with the same disease that plagued the Articles. National supremacy would be undermined in two ways: (1) equal representation would make the states a constituent part of the national government, thereby creating the likelihood that the states would defeat the exercise of national power; and (2) state representation—instead of popular representation—in the second branch would taint the principle of popular sovereignty, denying the people proper representation in their government. Thus, state supremacy, state power, and state sovereignty—the very infirmity which the new system was designed to correct—would permeate the new government.

It is understandable that opponents of the Virginia Plan were inflexible on the issue of state representation. No less understandable is the desperate struggle of those who, fearful that even their "middle ground" would be seriously undermined, refused to accept the finality of that fateful vote on July 16, until convinced that hopeless stalemate would otherwise result.

When the Convention met on July 17, Gouverneur Morris still entertained hope that the representation issue might be reopened. His motion to reconsider the Connecticut Compromise, however, was not even seconded.[100] Instead, the Convention proceeded to reject the provision in the Virginia Plan calling for a legislative negative on state laws which, in the opinion of the national legislature, contravened the new constitution. On May 31, the nationalists had won an easy victory on this issue.[101] They had failed on June 8 to strengthen the negative by endowing the legislature with a veto over state laws deemed merely "improper." [102] Now it was urgent that the original resolution be retained. Madison had written Randolph before the Convention assembled that he conceived a national veto power the least possible abridgement of the State sovereignties.[103] On June 8, he still believed ". . . indefinite power to negative legislative acts of the States absolutely necessary to a perfect system." [104] During the debate on July 17, he reiterated his conviction that "nothing short of a negative" would control "the propensity of the States to pursue their particular interests in opposition to the general interest." To the very end Madison continued to support the negative as "the most mild & certain means of preserving the harmony of the system." [105]

Only Charles Pinckney, who had moved to strengthen the negative on June 8, spoke in Madison's support.[106] Gouverneur Morris thought the negative would be "terrible to the States," that "it would disgust all the States." Luther Martin considered "the power as improper & inadmissable." Roger Sherman felt it involved "a wrong principle"—"that a law of a State contrary to the articles of the Union, would if not negatived, be valid & operative." Most important, Sherman and Morris thought the negative was not necessary. "A law that ought to be negatived," Morris declared, "will be set aside in the Judiciary department. . . ." Sherman "thought it unnecessary, as the Courts of the States would not consider as valid any law contravening the authority of the Union. . . ." [107]

Thus, only a day after the nationalists had suffered a major defeat, making all the more necessary the preservation and strengthening, if possible, of the legislative negative, the Convention voted against Madison's "mildest expedient." Madison's "middle ground," that solid foundation on which an effective national government was supposed to rest, was beginning to resemble quicksand into which the underpinnings of national supremacy were rapidly sinking.

But appearances are often deceptive. Immediately following rejection of the legislative negative, the Convention unanimously adopted the substance of the supremacy clause.[108] The version adopted as Article VI, paragraph 2, initially written into the New Jersey Plan, was virtually the same as that Luther Martin presented to the Convention on July 17. Rejection of the legislative negative in favor of the supremacy clause closely parallels Jefferson's approach to ways of controlling unbridled state legislative power. Writing Madison from Paris, June 20, 1787, he queried the wisdom of so drastic a check as the legislative negative:

> The negative proposed to be given them [Congress] on all the acts of the several legislatures is now for the first time suggested to my mind. Prima facie, I do not like it. It fails in an essential character that the hole and the patch should be commensurate. But this proposes to mend a small hole by covering the whole garment. Not more than one out of one hundred state-acts concern the confederacy. This proposition, then, in order to give them one degree of power, which they [Congress] ought to have, gives them ninety-nine more, which they ought not to have, upon the presumption that they will not exercise the ninety-nine.

Jefferson went on to suggest judicial review as the proper remedy, a function plainly implied in the supremacy clause. "Would not appeal," he asked, "from the state judicature to a federal court, in all cases where the act of Confederation controuled the question, be as effectual a remedy, and exactly commensurate to the defect?" [109] Gouverneur Morris and Roger Sherman used much the same reasoning. On July 17, they agreed that judicial review, operating under the supremacy clause, was an effective substitute for the onerous legislative negative.[110]

The nationalists had won an unwitting victory. At the time, however, it seemed like another defeat. In the minds of nationalists, judicial review did not compensate for the loss of a legislative negative. Accordingly, they attempted to reinstate it. On August 23, Charles Pinckney, considering the precaution as essentially necessary, so moved. Still smarting from the nationalists' defeat of July 16, when the Connecticut Compromise was finally approved, Pinckney added that the victory of the small states ought to obviate any objection on their part to endowing the Congress with the negative.[111]

Pinckney's motion met with much the same opposition as that leveled against it on June 8 and July 17. Sherman thought it "unnecessary," especially in light of the supremacy clause. Williamson agreed and added that "a revival of the question was a waste of time." Rutledge felt that the negative "alone would damn and ought to damn the Constitution." It would be "worse than making mere corporations" of the states. Ellsworth queried the efficacy of the negative, and Gouverneur Morris could not see its "utility or practicability." George Mason was "apprehensive that great objections would lie agst." the negative.[112] Reminding the Convention that he "had been from the beginning a friend to the principle" behind the negative, Madison refused to accept the supremacy clause and judicial review as an effective substitute.[113] Wilson explicitly denied the efficacy of judicial review alone to harness the "powerful tendency in the Legislature [of the states] to absorb all power into its vortex." [114] The "key-stone wanted to compleat the wide arch of Government we are raising" was the negative. Said Wilson:

> The power of self-defence had been urged as necessary for the State Governments. It was equally necessary for the General Government. The firmness of Judges is not of itself sufficient. Something further is requisite. It will be better to prevent the passage of an improper law, than to declare it void when passed.[115]

To the very end, Madison lamented the Convention's failure. Asked how a certain commercial problem would be handled, Madison replied on September 12:

> There will be the same security as in other cases. The jurisdiction of the supreme Court must be the source of redress. So far only had provision been made in the plan against injurious acts of the States. His own opinion was, that this was insufficient,—A negative on the State laws alone could meet all the shapes which these could assume. But this had been overruled.[116]

Madison's and Wilson's relentless protests clearly imply that the opposition had, in their judgment, once again undercut the foundations of Madison's "middle ground." Neither side anticipated that judicial review, operating through the supremacy clause and controlling state laws contravening the Constitution, might become a formidable check on any state action threatening national supremacy.

Unwittingly, the nationalists had partially recovered the losses they had incurred by the Connecticut Compromise. The sapping of national power by the state legislatures had been potentially curbed, but the exercise of sufficient power by the national government had not yet been assured. Even the supremacy clause could not ensure the operation of supreme national law beyond the confines of national power, constitutionally granted. Thus, unless the national government were endowed with *indefinite* power, as the nationalists had earlier insisted, the existence of state power would still pose a serious threat to national supremacy. In effect, a sharp line, dividing national and state power, would continue to circumscribe national authority.

When, on August 20, the Convention unanimously adopted the necessary and proper clause, granting Congress the power "to make all laws necessary-and-proper for carrying into execution the foregoing powers, and all other powers vested, by this Constitution, in the Government of the U.S. or any department or officer thereof," [117] it took a giant step toward conversion of the "foregoing" enumerated powers into powers of indefinite scope. "Let the end be legitimate," John Marshall later wrote in his classic opinion in *McCulloch* v. *Maryland;* "let it be within the scope of the Constitution, and all means which are appropriate, which are plainly adapted to that end, which are not prohibited, but consist within the letter and the spirit of the Constitution, are constitutional." [118] The end still had to be "within the scope of the Constitution," but it was clear that the ends could be enlarged by recourse to the necessary-and-proper clause. National power could be interpreted as indefinite in relation to state power. No precise line dividing the two spheres had been drawn.

National power and its supremacy—ingredients which both nationalists and their opponents thought had been undermined by the Connecticut Compromise—were restored by the combined operation of the supremacy clause, the necessary-and-proper clause, and judicial review. Both sides, still influenced by the implications of the Connecticut Compromise, seemed generally unaware of the restoration of national supremacy which took place after July 16. The necessary-and-proper clause passed unanimously, without debate. Despite the necessary-and-proper clause, Mason and Ellsworth believed, the Constitution drew a line between national and state power. "The United States will have a qualified sovereignty only," Mason declared. "The individual States will retain a part of the Sovereignty." [119] Ellsworth was even more specific: "The U.S. are sovereign on one side of the line dividing the jurisdictions—the States on the other—each ought to have power to defend their respective Sovereignties." [120]

Notwithstanding these apparent disclaimers, the Convention had provided for national supremacy. It remained to undercut the other denationalizing effect of the Connecticut Compromise: the claim of state sovereignty based on representation in the Senate. The question of whether ultimate sovereignty—the legitimate *source* of power allocated in the Constitution—would rest with the states or with the people came before the delegates for final decision on July 23. Resolution 15 of the Virginia Plan, providing for popular rather than state ratification of the proposed constitution, after only brief debate had been approved on June 12.[121] At that time, Madison and Wilson favored popular ratification on principle. Madison called the provision "essential." It was "indispensable that the new Constitution should be ratified in the most unexceptionable form and by the supreme authority of the people themselves." Sherman and Gerry, sensing the revolutionary implications, favored ratification by the state legislatures. The Articles of Confederation, Sherman pointed out, prescribed the proper method of ratification.[122]

It was now nearly two months since the Convention had begun. Passage of the Connecticut Compromise had rendered the issue of ratification more crucial than ever. Debate revealed the nationalists' sense of urgency. Ellsworth's motion, seconded by Paterson, took the form of reversing the prior decision. The New Jersey delegate moved that the proposed Constitution be referred to the state legislatures for ratification. George Mason—on most counts an Antifederalist—immediately objected. Popular ratification was one of "the most important and essential" parts of the new Constitution. Popular sovereignty, the doctrine that all legitimate power derives from the people, Mason asserted, "should be cherished as the basis of free Government." [123] Invoking considerations of expediency, Randolph pointed out that some states "will not take the requisite steps, unless expressly called upon to refer the question to the people." [124] Ghorum, Williamson, and King sided with Randolph, declaring that it would be much more difficult to obtain ratification by state legislatures than by popularly elected conventions.[125] Elbridge Gerry, however, "could not see any ground to suppose that the people will do what their rulers will not." [126]

Oliver Ellsworth rose to defend his motion and to refute the notion of popular sovereignty. It had been contended, he declared, "1. that the Legislatures have no authority in this case. 2. that their successors having equal authority could rescind their acts." Both propositions were untenable:

> As to the 2d. point he could not admit it to be well founded. An Act to which the States by their Legislatures, make themselves parties, becomes a compact from which no one of the parties can recede of itself. As to the 1st. point, he observed that a new set of ideas seemed to have crept in since the articles of Confederation were established. Conventions of the people, or with power expressly derived from the people, were not then thought of. The Legislatures were considered as competent. Their ratification has been acquiesced in without complaint. To whom have Congs. applied on subsequent occasions for further powers? To the Legislatures; not to the people. The fact is that we exist at present, and we need not enquire how, as a federal Society, united by a charter one article of which is that alterations therein may be made by the Legislative authority of the States. . . .[127]

Reverting to the fundamentals of 1776, Gouverneur Morris pointed out: "The amendmt. moved by Mr. Ellsworth erroneously supposes that we are proceeding on the basis of the Confederation. This Convention is unknown to the Confederation." Recognizing the revolutionary nature of popular ratification, Morris explained:

> . . . If the Confederation is to be pursued no alteration can be made without the unanimous consent of the Legislatures: Legislative alterations not conformable to the federal compact, would clearly not be valid. The Judges would consider them as null & void. Whereas in case of an appeal to the people of the U.S., the supreme authority, the federal compact may be altered by a *majority of them;* in like manner as the Constitution of a particular State may be altered by a majority of the people of the State. . . .[128]

After Morris' bold assertion of the *right* of peaceful revolution—the right of the people to alter or abolish an existing government and establish a new one—Madison spelled out the case for popular sovereignty.

Involved was the distinction between a mere confederation and a constitution. He considered "the difference between a system founded on the
Legislatures only, and one founded on the people, to be the true difference between a *league* or *treaty,* and a *Constitution.*" [129]

Surprisingly—or perhaps understandably, in light of what advocates of
state sovereignty thought they had won in the Connecticut Compromise
—the sentiment in favor of popular ratification was much greater on this
July 23 than it had been on June 12, when the provision was originally
approved. Then the vote had been 6-3-2.[130] Now the delegates turned
down Ellsworth's motion for state ratification by a vote of 7-3. By the
overwhelming margin of 9-1 it was agreed to "refer the Const. after the
approbation of Congs. to assemblies chosen by the people." [131] Nationalists had won a great victory. Notwithstanding equal state representation
in one branch of the national legislature, ultimate sovereignty by virtue
of popular ratification would rest with the people.

Advocates of state ratification made a last attempt to recover. In the
discussion concerning the number of affirmative votes necessary to ratify
the Constitution, Luther Martin "insisted on a reference to the State
Legislatures," and warned of "the danger of commotions from a resort to
the people & to first principles in which the Governments might be on
one side & the people on the other. . . ." [132] Madison brushed the Mary-
lander's objections lightly aside: "The people were in fact, the fountain
of all power, and by resorting to them, all difficulties were got over."
The people ". . . could alter constitutions as they pleased. It was a principle in the Bills of Rights, that first principles might be resorted to." [133]

The Convention's decision to resort to "first principles" helped to
neutralize the disabling effects of the Connecticut Compromise. States
had not been abolished, but their role as constituent parts of the national
government was reduced. National power had been strengthened and
national supremacy provided for in the supremacy clause, judicial review,
and the necessary-and-proper clause. Representation by states tainted the
principle of popular representation, but ratification by the people firmly
imbued the government with popular sovereignty. The dual foundations
of state supremacy under the Articles—state power and state sovereignty
—had been considerably shaken. In their place the Constitution set the
twin cornerstones of national supremacy—indefinite national power and
popular sovereignty. Absence of any precise line circumscribing national
power created the possibility that national supremacy *could* lead to an
effectively "consolidated" system. With the notable exception of Yates
and Lansing who left Philadelphia on July 10, Antifederalists were slow
to realize these ominous possibilities, nor were the nationalists more than
dimly aware of them.

That neither side was completely satisfied with the finished document
is quite understandable. Starting from positions poles apart, both sides
seemed blind to the significance of the Convention's actions following

the July 16 decision to endorse the Connecticut Compromise. Alert to the denationalizing effects of equal state representation, nationalists had opposed it. And, ironically, their strenuous effort to safeguard national power by the legislative veto met with ignominious defeat the day after the Connecticut Compromise was adopted. If July 16, a Monday, seemed like "Black Monday," the next day must have appeared even gloomier. Madison, Hamilton, Wilson, *et al.* had already tempered their more extreme desires. Now even Madison's "middle ground" seemed in jeopardy. A vital principle had, apparently, been vitiated. The nationalists never recovered from the shocks of July 16 and 17. The remainder of the Convention abounds with sentiments of their despair. The supremacy clause and judicial review, as a kind of substitute for the legislative negative, left much to be desired. Gloom pervades the letter Madison wrote to Jefferson on September 6, 1787:

> . . . The extent of them [the resolutions comprising the new Constitution] may perhaps surprise you. I hazard an opinion nevertheless that the *plan, should* it *be adopted,* will neither effectually *answer* its *national object,* not [nor] prevent the local *mischiefs* which everywhere *excite disgusts* agst. the *State Governments.* . . .[134]

Madison was not the only pessimist. Others looked hopefully to a second Convention to undo the Connecticut Compromise and reinstate the legislative negative. Charles Pinckney, who had earlier failed in his attempt to build up Randolph's original version of the negative, tried on August 23 to restore it. Failing, he also favored a second Convention.[135] On August 31, Gouverneur Morris and Edmund Randolph voiced similar hopes. Morris was "ready for a postponement. He had long wished for another Convention, that will have the firmness to provide a vigorous Government, which we are afraid to do." Randolph agreed.[136] Morris was simply reiterating his candid judgment of August 17, when he declared: "We are acting a very strange part. We first form a strong man to protect us, and at the same time wish to tie his hands behind him." [137] On the last day of the Convention, Hamilton confessed that:

> . . . No man's ideas were more remote from the plan than his own were known to be; but is it possible to deliberate between anarchy and Convulsion on one side, and the *chance* of good to be expected from the plan on the other.[138]

It seems odd that such profound disappointment should have engendered so little hope in the camp of the opposition. So deep was the cleavage that even modified positions, the more moderate stances involving concessions to the other side, were fundamentally opposed. If "consolidation" envisioned no states in effect, and if the Articles barely conceived of a national government, then these polar opposites were not much farther apart than were the Virginia and New Jersey Plans. Just as

THE UNRESOLVED POTENTIALITIES

(1) CONSOLIDATION	(2) NATIONAL SUPREMACY	(3) DUAL SOVEREIGNTY	(4) ARTICLES OF CONFEDERATION
States, as *States*, abolished	(Virginia Plan) No line separating national and state powers	(New Jersey Plan) Sharp line separating national and state powers	States are sovereign
These positions differ in *degree*, both being premised on (a) popular sovereignty, and (b) "indefinite" national authority, making it possible for the Virginia Plan to *become* consolidation.		These differ in *degree*, both being based on (a) sharp boundary between national and state powers, and (b) state sovereignty, making it possible for the New Jersey Plan to revert to the original power distribution under the Articles.	

Positions (1) and (2) differ in *kind* from (3) and (4).

Federalist $\left\{ \begin{array}{l} \text{(1) Consolidation} \\ \text{(2) National supremacy} \end{array} \right.$

⟶ The Constitution is *ambiguous*. Through constitutional interpretation, it has fluctuated between national supremacy and dual sovereignty, sometimes moving both ways simultaneously.

Antifederalist $\left\{ \begin{array}{l} \text{(3) Dual sovereignty} \\ \text{(4) Articles of Confederation} \end{array} \right.$

(By courtesy of Mr. Sanford B. Gabin)

"consolidation" differed only in degree from the Virginia Plan, so the Articles differed only in degree from the New Jersey Plan.

In essence, then, the Virginia and New Jersey plans diverged as sharply as did "consolidation" and the Articles. Both the Virginia Plan and "consolidation" were rooted in the notion of popular sovereignty, whereas the New Jersey Plan and the Articles were based on state sovereignty. Beyond this crucial difference, the Virginia Plan and "consolidation" would have endowed the national government with indefinite, rather than limited, power. The presence or absence of a line delimiting national power in relation to state power constituted, therefore, the core of the difference between the competing positions. The very absence of this line in both the Virginia Plan and "consolidation" made for differences only of degree. National supremacy, based on indefinite national power, could become "consolidation." By the same token, the New Jersey Plan, premised on a line limiting national power *vis-à-vis* the states, could revert to the state supremacy under the Articles.

If these fundamental differences between the nationalists and the would-be Antifederalists appeared less than obvious after the fateful days of July 16 and 17, they were blurred by the effects of the Connecticut Compromise and the substitution of the supremacy clause for the legislative negative. Before the resolution of these issues, debate on equal state representation and on the legislative negative had brought into relatively clear focus basic cleavages—state sovereignty versus popular sovereignty; state supremacy versus national supremacy. The events of July 16 and 17 colored profoundly the rest of the Convention's work. The nationalists were convinced that they had suffered fatal defeats; the opposition, buoyed perhaps by the nationalists' disappointment and flushed by their apparent victories, were lulled into acceptance of the Constitution's most nationalizing provisions.

What emerged from this often ambiguous interplay was a document no less ambiguous. The Constitution reflects the conflicting influences and drives of latter-day Federalists and Antifederalists alike. History abundantly demonstrates the Constitution's incredible flexibility, lending itself to widely divergent interpretations, differences which always seem to turn on the presence or absence of that ubiquitous line purporting to delineate the spheres of national and state power. Antifederalists in the Convention at Philadelphia did not succeed in drawing that line. But their successors have contributed immeasurably to the seemingly endless dispute over its presence.

Notes 🪶

1. *Independent Gazetteer* (Philadelphia), April 13, 1787. Quoted in Main, *op. cit.*, p. 115.

2. *Continental Journal* (Boston), May 31, 1787. Quoted in Main, *ibid.*

3. Max Farrand, *The Framing of the Constitution of the United States* (New Haven, Conn.: Yale University Press, 1913), II, 10.

4. *Id.*, 28.

5. George Read did not conceal his preference for a "consolidated" government at the Convention. See *infra*, notes 21 and 23. For Hamilton's position, see *infra*, note 54.

6. Madison to Randolph, April 8, 1787, in Hunt, *The Writings of James Madison*, II, pp. 336-40.

7. *Ibid.*

8. *Ibid.*

9. Max Farrand, *The Framing of the Constitution of the United States* (New Haven, Conn.: Yale University Press, 1913), p. 15.

10. Richard Henry Lee, "Letters from the Federal Farmer to the Republican," Letter I, October 8, 1787; cited in Paul Leicester Ford, ed., *Pamphlets on the Constitution of the United States* (Brooklyn, N.Y., 1888), p. 285.

11. Farrand, *The Records of the Federal Convention* (New Haven, Conn.: Yale University Press, 1911), I, pp. 33-34. Cited hereafter as Farrand.

12. *Id.*, 42.

13. *Id.*, 34.

14. *Id.*, 42-43.

15. *Id.*, 34.

16. Farrand, III, 23.

17. *Id.*, 24.

18. *Id.*, 30.

19. Farrand, I, 53.

20. *Id.*, 60.

21. *Id.*, 136.

22. *Id.*, 137.

23. *Id.*, 141.

24. *Id.*, 143.

25. *Id.*, 152-53.

26. *Id.*, 153-54.

27. *Id.*, 164-65.

28. *Id.*, 165.

29. *Id.*

30. *Id.*, 166.

31. *Id.*, 170.

32. *Id.*, 166-67.

33. 4 Wheat. 316 (1819).

34. Farrand, I, 167.

35. *Id.*, 168.

36. *Id.*, 173.

37. *Id.*, 177-79.

38. *Id.*, 180.

39. *Id.*, 179.

40. For a comparison of the purpose of the two plans, see *id.*, 20 (Virginia Plan), and *id.*, 242 (New Jersey Plan).

41. *Id.*, 20-22.

42. *Id.*, 242-44. For James Wilson's point-by-point comparison of the two plans, see *id.*, 252-53.

43. *Id.*, 242.

44. *Id.*, 551.

45. *Id.*, 321.

46. *Id.*, 251.

47. *Id.*, 250.

48. *Id.*, 249.

49. *Id.*, 253.

50. *Id.*, 255.

51. *Id.*

52. *Id.*, 282. The other quotations from Hamilton's speech are from *id.*, 282-93.

53. *Id.*, 287.

54. *Id.*, 323. For other evidence that Hamilton preferred abolition of the state governments, see James Wilson's understanding of Hamilton's speech, *id.*, 322, and Dr. Johnson's comments, *id.*, 355. Hamilton's speech itself seems to leave little room for misunderstanding. By "subordinate jurisdictions," he means "corporations." Further, if Hamilton means only to give the national government indefinite power and maintain the states as states, why didn't he simply support the Virginia Plan? Yates reports him as casting it aside disdainfully: "Whatever is the Virginia plan, but pork still, with a little change of sauce."

55. *Id.*, 323-24.

56. *Id.*, 323.

57. *Id.*, 324.

58. *Id.*, 329.

59. *Id.*, 324.

60. *Id.*

61. *Id.*, 347.
62. *Id.*, 359.
63. *Id.*, 436.
64. *Id.*, 445.
65. *Id.*, 444.
66. *Id.*, 460.
67. *Id.*, 461-62.
68. *Id.*, 463.
69. *Id.*, 464.
70. *Id.*, 466.
71. *Id.*, 467.
72. *Id.*, 468.
73. *Id.*
74. *Id.*, 475-76.
75. *Id.*, 483.
76. *Id.*, 489.
77. *Id.*, 490.
78. *Id.*, 449.
79. *Id.*, 526.
80. *Id.*, 529 (note 9).
81. *Id.*, 527.
82. *Id.*, 529-30.
83. *Id.*, 551.
84. *Id.*, 551-52.
85. *Id.*, 580.
86. Farrand, II, 4.
87. *Id.*
88. *Id.*, 5.
89. *Id.*
90. *Id.*
91. *Id.*, 7.
92. *Id.*, 8-10.
93. *Id.*, 10.
94. *Id.*, 5.
95. *Id.*, 18.
96. *Id.*, 19.
97. *Id.*
98. *Id.*, 20.
99. *Supra*, note 87.
100. Farrand, II, 25.
101. Farrand, I, 54.
102. *Id.*, 168.
103. *Supra*, note 6.
104. *Supra*, note 27.
105. Farrand, II, 27-28.
106. *Id.*, 28.
107. *Id.*, 28.
108. *Id.*

109. Jefferson to Madison, June 20, 1787; Boyd, XI, 480-81. Compare "Notes on Virginia," *The Writings of Thomas Jefferson* (H. A. Washington, ed.), VIII, p. 391. Quoted in Mason, *Free Government in the Making, op. cit.*, p. 169.

110. *Supra*, note 108. See also Sherman on August 23, Farrand, II, 390.

111. Farrand, II, 390.
112. *Id.*, 390-91.
113. *Id.*, 390.
114. Madison's language, *id.*, 74.
115. *Id.*, 391.
116. *Id.*, 589.
117. *Id.*, 344-45.
118. 4 Wheat. 316, 420 (1819).
119. Farrand, II, 347.
120. *Id.*, 349.
121. Farrand, I, 214.
122. *Id.*, 122-23.
123. Farrand, II, 88.
124. *Id.*, 89.
125. *Id.*, 90-92.
126. *Id.*, 90.
127. *Id.*, 91.
128. *Id.*, 92.
129. *Id.*, 93.
130. Farrand, I, 214.

131. Farrand, II, 93-94.

132. *Id.*, 476. Gerry also advocated state ratification at this time; see *id.*, 478.

133. *Id.*, 476.

134. Madison to Jefferson, September 6, 1787, in Farrand, III, 77.

135. Farrand, II, 391.

136. *Id.*, 479. Randolph, of course, later suggested a second Convention for precisely the *opposite* reasons. See his speech of September 10, *id.*, 564, where he deplores, among other things, the dangerous extent of national power, including the implied powers.

137. *Id.*, 317.

138. *Id.*, 645-46 (emphasis added).

Documents ॐ

1 · Madison's *"Middle Ground"* · April 8, 1787

Six weeks before the Philadelphia Convention assembled, James Madison formulated "some leading propositions" and submitted them on April 8, 1787, to Edmund Randolph of Virginia. Contained in this letter are the essential ingredients of the so-called Randolph plan.

. . . I am glad to find that you are turning your thoughts towards the business of May next. My despair of your finding the necessary leisure, as signified in one of your letters, with the probability that some leading propositions at least would be expected from Virginia, had engaged me in a closer attention to the subject than I should otherwise have given. I will just hint the ideas that have occurred, leaving explanations for our interview.

I think with you, that it will be well to retain as much as possible of the old Confederation, though I doubt whether it may not be best to work the valuable articles into the new system, instead of engrafting the latter on the former. I am also perfectly of your opinion, that, in framing a system, no material sacrifices ought to be made to local or temporary prejudices. An explanatory address must of necessity accompany the result of the Convention on the main object. I am not sure that it will be practicable to present the several parts of the reform in so detached a manner to the States, as that a partial adoption will be binding. Particular States may view different articles as conditions of each other, and would only ratify them as such. Others might ratify them as independent propositions. The consequence would be that the ratifications of both would go for nothing. I have not, however, examined this point thoroughly. In truth, my ideas of a reform strike so deeply at the old Confederation, and lead to such a systematic change, that they scarcely admit of the expedient.

I hold it for a fundamental point, that an individual independence of the States is utterly irreconcilable with the idea of an aggregate sovereignty. I think, at the same time, that a consolidation of the States into one simple republic is not less unattainable than it would be inexpedient. Let it be tried, then, whether any middle ground can be taken, which will at once support a due supremacy of the national authority, and leave in force the local authorities so far as they can be subordinately useful.

The first step to be taken is, I think, a change in the principle of

Gaillard Hunt, ed., *The Writings of James Madison* (New York, 1904), II, pp. 336-40. The same material is contained in Madison's letter to Washington, April 16, 1787, *ibid.*, II, pp. 344-52.

representation. According to the present form of the Union, an equality of suffrage, if not just towards the larger members of it, is at least safe to them, as the liberty they exercise of rejecting or executing the acts of Congress, is uncontrollable by the nominal sovereignty of Congress. Under a system which would operate without the intervention of the States, the case would be materially altered. A vote from Delaware would have the same effect as one from Massachusetts or Virginia.

Let the national Government be armed with a positive and complete authority in all cases where uniform measures are necessary, as in trade, &c., &c. Let it also retain the powers which it now possesses.

Let it have a negative, in all cases whatsoever, on the Legislative acts of the States, as the King of Great Britain heretofore had. This I conceive to be essential and the least possible abridgement of the State sovereignties. Without such a defensive power, every positive power that can be given on paper will be unavailing. It will also give internal stability to the States. There has been no moment since the peace at which the Federal assent would have been given to paper-money, &c., &c.

Let this national supremacy be extended also to the Judiciary department. If the Judges in the last resort depend on the States, and are bound by their oaths to them and not to the Union, the intention of the law and the interests of the nation may be defeated by the obsequiousness of the tribunals to the policy or prejudices of the States. It seems at least essential that an appeal should lie to some national tribunals in all cases which concern foreigners, or inhabitants of other States. The admiralty jurisdiction may be fully submitted to the National Government.

A Government formed of such extensive powers ought to be well organized. The Legislative department may be divided into two branches. One of them to be chosen every _____ years by the Legislatures or the people at large; the other to consist of a more select number, holding their appointments for a longer term, and going out in rotation. Perhaps the negative on the State laws may be most conveniently lodged in this branch. A Council of Revision may be superadded, including the great ministerial officers.

A national Executive will also be necessary. I have scarcely ventured to form my own opinion yet, either of the manner in which it ought to be constituted, or of the authorities with which it ought to be clothed.

An article ought to be inserted expressly guaranteeing the tranquility of the States against internal as well as external dangers.

To give the new system its proper energy, it will be desirable to have it ratified by the authority of the people, and not merely by that of the Legislatures.

I am afraid you will think this project, if not extravagant, absolutely unattainable and unworthy of being attempted. Conceiving it myself to go no further than is essential, the objections drawn from this source are to be laid aside. I flatter myself, however, that they may be less formidable on trial than in contemplation. The change in the principle of representation will be relished by a majority of the States, and those too of most influence. The northern States will be reconciled to it by the actual superiority of their populousness; the Southern by their expected superiority on this point. This principle established, the repugnance of the large States to part with power will in a great degree subside, and the smaller States must ultimately yield to the predominant will. It is also already seen by many, and must by degrees be seen by all, that, unless the Union be organized efficiently on republican principles, innovations of a much more objectionable form may be obtruded, or, in the most favorable event, the partition of the Empire, into rival and hostile confederacies will ensue. . . .

2 · *The Virginia or Randolph Plan* · Presented to the Federal Convention May 29, 1787

1. Resolved that the articles of Confederation ought to be so corrected & enlarged as to accomplish the objects proposed by their institution; namely. "common defence, security of liberty and general welfare."

2. Resd. therefore that the rights of suffrage in the National Legislature ought to be proportioned to the Quotas of contribution, or to the number of free inhabitants, as the one or the other rule may seem best in different cases.

3. Resd. that the National Legislature ought to consist of two branches.

4. Resd. that the members of the first branch of the National Legislature ought to be elected by the people of the several States every   for the term of   ; to be of the age of   years at least, to receive liberal stipends by which they may be compensated for the devotion of their time to public service; to be ineligible to any office established by a particular State or under the authority of the United States, except those peculiarly belonging to the functions of the first branch, during the term of service, and for the space of   after its expiration; to be incapable of re-election for the space of   after the expiration of their term of service, and to be subject to recall.

5. Resold. that the members of the second branch of the National Legislature ought to be elected by those of the first, out of a proper number of persons nominated by the individual Legislatures, to be of the age of   years at least; to hold their offices for a term sufficient to ensure their independency, to receive liberal stipends, by which they may be compensated for the devotion of their time to public service; and to be ineligible to any office established by a particular State, or under the authority of the United States, except those peculiarly belonging to the

functions of the second branch, during the term of service, and for the space of   after the expiration thereof.

6. Resolved that each branch ought to possess the right of originating Acts; that the National Legislature ought to be impowered to enjoy the Legislative Rights vested in Congress by the Confederation & moreover to legislate in all cases to which the separate States are incompetent, or in which the harmony of the United States may be interrupted by the exercise of individual Legislation; to negative all laws passed by the several States, contravening in the opinion of the National Legislature the articles of Union; and to call forth the force of the Union agst. any member of the Union failing to fulfill its duty under the articles thereof.

7. Resd. that a National Executive be instituted; to be chosen by the National Legislature for the term of   years, to receive punctually at stated times, a fixed compensation for the services rendered, in which no increase or diminution shall be made so as to affect the Magistracy, existing at the time of increase or diminution, and to be ineligible a second time; and that besides a general authority to execute the National laws, it ought to enjoy the Executive rights vested in Congress by the Confederation.

8. Resd. that the Executive and a convenient number of the National Judiciary, ought to compose a council of revision with authority to examine every act of the National Legislature before [it shall operate, & every act of a particular Legislature before] a Negative thereon shall be final; and that the dissent of the said Council shall amount to a rejection, unless the Act of the National Legislature be again passed, or that of a particular Legislature be again negatived by   of the members of each branch.

9. Resd. that a National Judiciary be established to consist of one or more supreme tribunals, and of inferior tribunals to be chosen by the National Legislature, to hold their offices during good behaviour; and to receive punctually at stated times fixed compensation for their services, in which no increase or diminution shall be made so as to affect the persons actually in office at the time of such increase or diminution. that the jurisdiction of the inferior tribunals shall be to hear & determine in the first instance, and of the supreme tribunal to hear and determine in the dernier resort, all piracies & felonies on the high seas, captures from an enemy; cases in which foreigners or citizens of other States applying to such jurisdictions may be interested, or which respect the collection of the National revenue; impeachments of any National officers, and questions which may involve the national peace and harmony.

10. Resolvd. that provision ought to be made for the admission of States lawfully arising within the limits of the United States, whether from a voluntary junction of Government & Territory or otherwise, with the consent of a number of voices in the National legislature less than the whole.

11. Resd. that a Republican Government & the territory of each State, except in the instance of a voluntary junction of Government & territory, ought to be guaranteed by the United States to each State.

12. Resd. that provision ought to be made for the continuance of Congress and their authorities and privileges, until a given day after the reform of the articles of Union shall be adopted, and for the completion of all their engagements.

13. Resd. that provision ought to be made for the amendment of the Articles of Union whensoever it shall seem necessary, and that the assent of the National Legislature ought not to be required thereto.

14. Resd. that the Legislative Executive & Judiciary powers within the several States ought to be bound by oath to support the articles of Union.

15. Resd. that the amendments which shall be offered to the Confederation, by the Convention ought at a proper time, or times, after the approbation of Congress to be submitted to an assembly or assemblies of Representatives, recommended by the several Legislatures to be expressly chosen by the people, to consider & decide thereon.

3 · *The New Jersey or Paterson Plan* · Presented to the Federal Convention June 15, 1787

1. Resd. that the articles of Confederation ought to be so revised, corrected & enlarged, as to render the federal Constitution adequate to the exigences of Government, & the preservation of the Union.

2. Resd. that in addition to the powers vested in the U. States in Congress, by the present existing articles of Confederation, they be authorized to pass acts for raising a revenue, by levying a duty or duties on all goods or merchandizes of foreign growth or manufacture, imported into any part of the U. States, by Stamps on paper, vellum or parchment, and by a postage on all letters or packages passing through the general post-Office, to be applied to such federal purposes as they shall deem proper & expedient; to make rules & regulations for the collection thereof; and the same from time to time, to alter & amend in such manner as they shall think proper: to pass Acts for the regulation of trade & commerce as well with foreign nations as with each other: provided that all punishments, fines, forfeitures & penalties to be incurred for contravening such acts rules and regulations shall be adjudged by the Common law Judiciarys of the State in which any offence contrary to the true intent & meaning of such Acts rules & regulations shall have been committed or perpetrated, with liberty of commencing in the first instance all suits & prosecutions for that purpose in the superior Common law Judiciary in such State, subject nevertheless, for the correction of all errors, both in law & fact in rendering judgment, to an appeal to the Judiciary of the U. States.

Farrand, I, 242-45.

3. Resd. that whenever requisitions shall be necessary, instead of the rule for making requisitions mentioned in the articles of Confederation, the United States in Congs. be authorized to make such requisitions in proportion to the whole number of white & other free citizens & inhabitants of every age sex and condition including those bound to servitude for a term of years & three fifths of all other persons not comprehended in the foregoing description, except Indians not paying taxes; that if such requisitions be not complied with, in the time specified therein, to direct the collection thereof in the non complying States & for that purpose to devise and pass acts directing & authorizing the same; provided that none of the powers hereby vested in the U. States in Congs. shall be exercised without the consent of at least   States, and in that proportion if the number of Confederated States should hereafter be increased or diminished.

4. Resd. that the U. States in Congs. be authorized to elect a federal Executive to consist of   persons, to continue in office for the term of   years, to receive punctually at stated times a fixed compensation for their services, in which no increase or diminution shall be made so as to affect the persons composing the executive at the time of such increase or diminution, to be paid out of the federal treasury; to be incapable of holding any other office or appointment during their time of service and for   years thereafter; to be ineligible a second time, & re moveable by Congs. on application by a majority of the Executives of the several States; that the Executives besides their general authority to execute the federal acts ought to appoint all federal officers not otherwise provided for, & to direct all military operations; provided that none of the persons composing the federal Executive shall on any occasion take command of any troops, so as personally to conduct any enterprise as General, or in other capacity.

5. Resd. that a federal Judiciary be established to consist of a supreme Tribunal the Judges of which to be appointed by the Executive, & to hold their offices during good behaviour, to receive punctually at stated times a fixed compensation for their services in which no increase or diminution shall be made, so as to affect the persons actually in office at the time of such increase or diminution; that the Judiciary so established shall have authority to hear & determine in the first instance on all impeachments of federal officers, & by way of appeal in the dernier resort in all cases touching the rights of Ambassadors, in all cases of captures from an enemy, in all cases of piracies & felonies on the high seas, in all cases in which foreigners may be interested, in the construction of any treaty or treaties, or which may arise on any of the Acts for regulation of trade, or the collection of the federal Revenue: that none of the Judiciary shall during the time they remain in Office be capable of receiving or holding any other office or appointment during their time of service, or for thereafter.

6. Resd. that all Acts of the U. States in Congs. made by virtue & in pursuance of the powers hereby & by the articles of confederation vested in them, and all Treaties made & ratified under the authority of the U. States shall be the supreme law of the respective States so far forth as those Acts or Treaties shall relate to the said States or their Citizens, and that the Judiciary of the several States shall be bound thereby in their decisions, any thing in the respective laws of the Individual States to the contrary notwithstanding; and that if any State, or any body of men in any State shall oppose or prevent ye. carrying into execution such acts or treaties, the federal Executive shall be authorized to call forth ye power of the Confederated States, or so much thereof as may be necessary to enforce and compel an obedience to such Acts, or an Observance of such Treaties.

7. Resd. that provision be made for the admission of new States into the Union.

8. Resd. the rule for naturalization ought to be the same in every State.

9. Resd. that a Citizen of one State committing an offence in another State of the Union, shall be deemed guilty of the same offence as if it had been committed by a Citizen of the State in which the Offence was committed.

4 · Hamilton's *Plan of Union* · Presented to the Federal Convention June 18, 1787

I. The Supreme Legislative power of the United States of America to be vested in two different bodies of men; the one to be called the Assembly, the other the Senate who together shall form the Legislature of the United States with power to pass all laws whatsoever subject to the Negative hereafter mentioned.

II. The Assembly to consist of persons elected by the people to serve for three years.

III. The Senate to consist of persons elected to serve during good behaviour; their election to be made by electors chosen for that purpose by the people: in order to this the States to be divided into election districts. On the death, removal or resignation of any Senator his place to be filled out of the district from which he came.

IV. The supreme Executive authority of the United States to be vested in a Governour to be elected to serve during good behaviour—the election to be made by Electors chosen by the people in the Election Districts aforesaid— The authorities & functions of the Executive to be as follows: to have a negative on all laws about to be passed, and the execution of all laws passed, to have the direction of war when authorized or begun; to have with the advice and approbation of the Senate the power of making

Farrand, I, 291-93.

all treaties; to have the sole appointment of the heads or chief officers of the departments of Finance, War and Foreign Affairs; to have the nomination of all other officers (Ambassadors to foreign Nations included) subject to the approbation or rejection of the Senate; to have the power of pardoning all offences except Treason; which he shall not pardon without the approbation of the Senate.

V. On the death resignation or removal of the Governour his authorities to be exercised by the President of the Senate till a Successor be appointed.

VI. The Senate to have the sole power of declaring war, the power of advising and approving all Treaties, the power of approving or rejecting all appointments of officers except the heads or chiefs of the departments of Finance War and foreign affairs.

VII. The Supreme Judicial authority to be vested in Judges to hold their offices during good behaviour with adequate and permanent salaries. This Court to have original jurisdiction in all causes of capture, and an appellative jurisdiction in all causes in which the revenues of the general Government or the citizens of foreign nations are concerned.

VIII. The Legislature of the United States to have power to institute Courts in each State for the determination of all matters of general concern.

IX. The Governour Senators and all officers of the United States to be liable to impeachment for mal— and corrupt conduct; and upon conviction to be removed from office, & disqualified for holding any place of trust or profit—all impeachments to be tried by a Court to consist of the Chief   or Judge of the Superior Court of Law of each State, provided such Judge shall hold his place during good behavior, and have a permanent salary.

X. All laws of the particular States contrary to the Constitution or laws of the United States to be utterly void; and the better to prevent such laws being passed, the Governour or president of each state shall be appointed by the General Government and shall have a negative upon the laws about to be passed in the State of which he is Governour or President.

XI. No State to have any forces land or Naval; and the Militia of all the States to be under the sole and exclusive direction of the United States, the officers of which to be appointed and commissioned by them.

III · VICTORY AND DEFEAT · 1787-1790

Essay &

In a perceptive article written in 1955, Cecelia Kenyon labeled Antifederalists "men of little faith," wanting in the belief that men can govern wisely and well without falling prey to the corruptive effect of political power.[1] At least one prominent Antifederalist—Tredwell of New York—would have reversed the label. In the New York ratifying convention, Tredwell pointedly hurled the same charge at the Federalists. He was "seriously alarmed" by the Federalist attempt to "shake or corrupt our [the Antifederalists'] faith" in "some of the most essential principles of freedom. . . ." "Have we not been told," Tredwell asked, "that if government is but properly organised, and the powers were suitably distributed among the several members, it is unnecessary to provide any other security against the abuse of its power, that power thus distributed needs no restriction?" "Why are we told," he went on, "that all restrictions of power are found to be inconvenient? That we ought to put unlimited confidence in our rulers? That it is not our duty to be jealous of men in power."

The Federalists, Tredwell maintained, tended "to corrupt our political faith, to take us off guard, and lull to sleep that jealousy which . . . is essentially necessary for the preservation of freedom. . . ." The proposed Constitution, moreover, "departed widely from the principles and political faith of '76, when the spirit of liberty ran high, and danger put a curb on ambition."

> Here we find no security for the rights of individuals—no security for the existence of our state governments—here is no bill of rights, no proper restrictions of power; our lives, our property, and our consciences are left wholly at the mercy of the legislature, and the powers of the judiciary may be extended to any degree short of Almighty. Sir, in this constitution we have not only neglected, we have done worse—we have openly violated our faith, that is, our public faith.[2]

Tredwell was not convinced that the proposed government would be federal. He saw it "as complete a consolidation as the government of this state in which legislative powers, to a certain extent, are exercised by the several towns and corporations." "The sole difference between a state government under this constitution, and a corporation under a state government," he declared, "is, that a state being more extensive than a town, its powers are likewise proportionably extended, but neither of them enjoy the least share of sovereignty. . . ." In short:

> the whole power and sovereignty of our state governments, and with them the liberties of our country are swallowed up by the general government; for it is well worth observing, that while our state governments are held up to us as the great and sufficient security of our rights and privileges, it is carefully provided that they shall be disarmed of all power, and made totally dependent on the bounty of congress for their support, and consequently for their existence, so that we have scarce a right secured under either.[3]

The Federalists had violated "the principles and political faith of '76." In essence, this was the Antifederalist case against the new Constitution: it made for a "consolidated" system of government, lacked a bill of rights, and thereby threatened to extinguish the rights of both individuals and the states. State law would be superseded by supreme national law. Indefinite national power would effectively demolish the states, which would thus become powerless to safeguard individual rights.

If, as Spencer Roane suggested, "a Constitution ought to be like Caesar's wife, not only good, but unsuspected . . . ,"[4] then the proposed Constitution failed to meet the test. It was both bad and suspect: bad because it would destroy the basic rights of the individual and the states; suspect because the new Constitution seemed to be an unauthorized usurpation of the original sovereignty of the states. "The question turns, sir," Patrick Henry declared in the Virginia convention, "on that poor little thing—the expression, We, the people, instead of the states of America."[5] "What right had they to say, *We the people?*" the eloquent Virginian demanded. "Who authorized them to speak the language of, *We the people,* instead of, *We the states?*"[6] If the language, We the people, "does not go to an annihilation of the state governments, and to a perfect consolidation of the whole union," Nason of Massachusetts asserted, "I do not know what does."[7] Taylor of North Carolina was equally disturbed. "This is a consolidation of all the states," he alleged. "Had it said, *We the States,* there would have been a federal intention in it. But, sir, it is clear that a consolidation is intended."[8]

MacLaine thought that Taylor's objection to the preamble was "merely a dispute about words, without any meaning whatever."[9] MacLaine was wrong. The dispute over words had real substance; it went to important issues, the determination of which might settle the supremely significant question: Precisely what type of government did the framers of the proposed Constitution establish and did they have the right to frame that kind of a government? Three little words involved such thorny issues as: Who revolted from Great Britain—the states or the people? Was the Declaration of Independence a formulation of thirteen independent states or of a united people transcending state boundaries? Were the Articles of Confederation a legitimate manifestation of the sovereign right of the several states to establish a confederacy, or did the Articles represent a usurpation of the original sovereignty vested in the people, and expressed in the act of revolution? The nature and legitimacy of the proposed government turned on answers to these questions. Antifederalists vehemently charged that the new government purported to derive its powers from the people, not the states; it was grounded in popular sovereignty, not state sovereignty. Would popular ratification of the Constitution, therefore, constitute a revolutionary act? Would it be a usurpation of state sovereignty or a legitimate revival of the original sovereignty of the people?

These issues were brilliantly illuminated in the debates over ratification in the Pennsylvania convention. Three stalwart Antifederalists—Findley, Smilie, and Whitehill—pitted intellects against the redoubtable James Wilson, who formulated and first expounded the standard arguments used by all supporters of ratification. Wilson, a leading nationalist and Pennsylvania delegate at the Philadelphia Convention, posed the burning question of the day: "Of what description is the constitution before us?" To the inquiry, which continues to vex scholars, Wilson replied:

> In its principles, Sir, it is purely democratical; varying indeed, in its form, in order to admit all the advantages, and to exclude all the disadvantages which are incidental to the known and established constitutions of government. But when we take an extensive and accurate view of the streams of power that appear through this great and comprehensive plan, when we contemplate the variety of their directions, the force and dignity of their currents, . . . we shall be able to trace them all to one great and noble source, THE PEOPLE.[10]

The grandiloquent words "We, the people" are "the fee simple of freedom and government . . . declared to be in the people, . . . an inheritance with which they will not part." [11]

Wilson's unremitting insistence that the people—to the complete exclusion of the states—were the only proper source of sovereignty led to admissions which fed more and more fuel to the fire raging in Antifederalist minds. He confessed that "the Federal convention had exceeded the powers given to them by the several legislatures. . . . The Federal convention did not act at all upon the powers given to them by the States; . . . they proceeded upon original principles, and having framed a constitution which they thought would promote the happiness of their country, they have submitted it to their consideration, who may either adopt or reject it, as they please." [12]

The Pennsylvania debate reached an emotional and intellectual peak when Findley, on December 6, 1787, "delivered an eloquent and powerful speech, to prove that the proposed plan of government amounted to a consolidation, and not a confederation of the states." The Pennsylvania *Packet* reported:

> Mr. Wilson had before admitted that if this was a just objection, it would be strongly against the system; and it seems from the subsequent silence of all its advocates upon the subject (except Dr. Rush, who . . . insinuated that he saw and rejoiced at the eventual annihilation of the state sovereignties) Mr. Findley had established his position. Previous to an investigation of the plan, that gentleman . . . showed that we were in an eligible position to attempt the improvement of the Federal Government, but not so desperately circumstanced as to be obliged to adopt any system, however destructive to the liberties of the people, and the sovereign rights of the states.

Findley went on to argue "that the proposed constitution established a general government and destroyed the individual governments," basing his case on "evidence taken from the system itself." [13]

Findley's speech evoked serious response from James Wilson. "The secret is now disclosed," he replied solemnly, "and it is discovered to be a dread that the boasted state sovereignties will, under this system, be disrobed of part of their power." Mounting a frontal attack, Wilson queried the very foundation of state sovereignty. "Upon what principle," he asked, "is it contended that the sovereign power resides in the state governments?" Findley had contended that "there can be no subordinate sovereignty." Wilson joined issue:

> Now if there can not, my position is, that sovereignty resides in the people. They have not parted with it; they have only dispensed such portions of power as were conceived necessary for the public welfare. This constitution stands upon this broad principle. I know very well, Sir, that the people have hitherto been shut out of the federal government, but it is not meant that they should any longer be dispossessed of their rights. In order to recognize this leading principle, the proposed system sets out with a declaration that its existence depends upon the supreme authority of the people alone. . . .

Here, then, was the crucial point—the people were always sovereign; the states were mere pretenders, perhaps usurpers. How dared the states question the sovereignty of their masters, Wilson asked. "[H]ow comes it, Sir, that these State governments dictate to their superiors?—to the majesty of the people?" [14]

Findley, Whitehill, and Smilie had met a formidable adversary, one who pulled no punches in his defense of the "leading principle"—popular sovereignty. Making crystal clear the unbridgeable gap separating the two positions, Wilson proceeded:

> His position [Findley's] is, that the supreme power resides in the States, as governments; and mine is, that it *resides* in the PEOPLE, as the fountain of government; that the people have not—that the people mean not—and that

the people ought not, to part with it to any government whatsoever. In their hands it remains secure. They can delegate it in such proportions, to such bodies, on such terms, and under such limitations, as they think proper. I agree with the members in opposition, that there cannot be two sovereign powers on the same subject.[15]

To underscore the impasse, Wilson drew on the immortal Declaration, confirming "the inherent and unalienable right of the people . . . to form either a general government, or state governments, in what manner they please. . . ." "The broad basis on which our independence was placed" was that *"governments* are instituted among men, *deriving their just powers from the consent of the governed."* "On the same certain and solid foundation this system is erected." [16] Antifederalists argued that thirteen sovereign states won their independence from Great Britain; Wilson contended that the sovereign people rebelled. Antifederalists contended that the Articles of Confederation constituted a legitimate expression of state sovereignty; Wilson insisted that the Articles were an aberration. Because popular sovereignty underlay the proposed Constitution, Wilson explained, "we are told it is a violation of the present confederation—a CONFEDERATION of SOVEREIGN STATES." But for Wilson this meant only that the Articles were not founded on "the principle of free governments." [17] "The true and only safe principle for a free people, is a practical recognition of their original and supreme authority." [18] There was no middle ground. "I am astonished to hear the ill-founded doctrine," Wilson declared, "that States alone ought to be represented in the federal government. . . ."

> No: let us *reascend* to first principles. That expression is not strong enough to do my ideas justice. Let us RETAIN first principles. The people of the United States are now in the possession and exercise of their original rights, and while this doctrine is known and operates, we shall have a cure for every disease.[19]

Wilson's outspoken defiance of state sovereignty confirmed the Antifederalists' worst fears. Charges that the Convention had produced a "consolidated" system, designed ultimately, if not immediately, to "swallow up" the states, echoed and re-echoed throughout the country. "I confess," lamented Samuel Adams in Massachusetts, "as I enter the Building I stumble at the Threshold. I meet with a National Government, instead of a Federal Union."

> I am not able to conceive why the Wisdom of the Convention led them to give Preference to the former [the national government] before the latter [the sovereign states]. If the several states in the Union are to become one entire Nation, under one Legislature, the powers of which shall extend to every Subject of Legislation, and its laws be Supreme and control the whole, the Idea of Sovereignty in those States must be lost. . . .[20]

In Virginia George Mason, Richard Henry Lee, and Patrick Henry joined the refrain. "Whether the Constitution be good or bad," Mason observed, going to the heart of the matter, "it is a national government, and no longer a Confederation." [21] "The plan proposed," Lee conceded, "appears to be partly federal, but principally however, calculated ultimately to make the states one consolidated government." [22] "This government," Henry declared, "is not a Virginian, but an American government. Is it not, therefore a consolidated government?" [23]

Did it follow, however, that the substitution of a national government for the central government under the Articles amounted to a "consolidated" system? "We have heard much about a consolidated government," James Wilson exclaimed, and challenged Antifederalists to "condescend to give us a definition."

> I think this the more necessary, because I apprehend that the term, in the numerous times it has been used, has not always been used in the same sense. It may be said, and I believe it has been said, that a consolidated government is such as will absorb and destroy the governments of the several States. If it is taken in this view, the plan before us is not a consolidated government. . . . On the other hand, if it is meant that the general government will take from the state governments their power in some particulars, it is confessed and evident that this will be its operation and effect.[24]

Denying that the proposed Constitution would establish a consolidated government, Wilson made clear the intention to preserve the states in a subordinate capacity. Continued existence of the state governments was "one of the most prominent features" of the new system.[25] Madison and Hamilton rallied behind Wilson. The New Yorker insisted that "it can never be the interest or desire of the national legislature to destroy the *state government*." Such a desire would be "madness," "political suicide." Antifederalists had indulged in a "curious sophistry." They argued that since two supreme powers could not coexist over the same subject, the national government, being supreme over the states, would render state power impotent. "That two supreme powers cannot act together is false," Hamilton contended.

> They are inconsistent only when they are aimed at each other, or at one indivisible object. The laws of the United States are supreme, as to all their proper, constitutional objects: the laws of the states are supreme in the same way. These supreme laws may act on different objects, without clashing or they may operate on different parts of the same object, with perfect harmony. Suppose both governments should lay a tax of a penny on a certain article: had not each an independent and uncontrolable power to collect its own tax? The meaning of the maxim, there can not be two supremes, **is** simply this: Two powers cannot be supreme over each other. . . .[26]

Hamilton went so far as to suggest that the Constitution embodied the doctrine later known as "dual sovereignty"—implying that the national and state governments were supreme in their own spheres of operation. To allay Antifederalist fears, Madison was even more ambiguous. The new Constitution was of a "mixed nature," he explained:

> . . . In some respects it is a government of a federal nature; in others it is of a consolidated nature. Even if we attend to the manner in which the constitution is investigated, ratified and made the act of the people of America, I can say . . . that this government is not completely consolidated, nor is it entirely federal. Who are the parties to it? The people—but not the people as composing one great body; but the people as composing thirteen sovereignties. . . .[27]

Going still further, Madison conceded that popular ratification—the keystone of popular sovereignty—was of a "mixed nature." Even the necessary-and-proper clause was "only a superfluity." [28]

Antifederalists were neither convinced, placated, nor pacified. Patrick Henry, in fact, was jollied by Federalist straining.

> We may be amused if we please, by a treatise of political anatomy. In the brain it is national: the stamina are federal—some limbs are federal, others national. The senators are voted for by the state legislatures, so far it is federal. Individuals choose the members of the first branch; here it is national. It is federal in its conferring general powers; but national in retaining them. It is not to be supported by the states—the pockets of individuals are to be searched for its maintenance. What signifies it to me, that you have the most curious anatomical description of it in its creation. To all the common purpose of legislation, it is a great consolidation of government.[29]

Antifederalist misgivings were genuine. Smilie of Pennsylvania predicted that "the shadow of State government may long be retained when the substance is totally lost and forgotten." [30] It was "the silent but certain operation of the *powers,* and not the cautious, but artful tenor of the expressions contained in this system, that can excite terror, or generate oppression." [31]

The prospect of consolidation, if not outright consolidation, arose from the failure of the Constitution to draw a line, circumscribing and sharply defining national power, particularly in relation to state power. The powers of Congress were, to be sure, enumerated; but, as Bodman of Massachusetts complained, they "ought to have been defined." Bodman was "willing to give power to the federal head—but he wished to know what that power was." Without more precise definition, the powers enumerated in Article I, section 8, were "certainly unlimited, and therefore dangerous." [32] Williams of New York agreed that it was perhaps "utterly impossible fully to define" the powers latent in the necessary-and-proper clause.[33] But, he wondered, "Are not the terms, *common defence* and *general welfare,* indefinite, undefinable terms?" [34]

Melancton Smith of New York leveled the same criticism. "It is necessary," he declared soberly, "that the powers vested in government should be precisely defined, that the people may be able to know whether it moves in the circle of the constitution."

> It is the more necessary in governments like the one under examination, because Congress here is to be considered as only a parr [part] of a complex system. The *state governments* are necessary for certain local purposes. The *general government* for national purposes. The latter ought to rest on the former, not only in its form, but in its operations.

It was therefore of "the highest importance that the line of jurisdiction should be accurately drawn." This was necessary "in order to maintain harmony between the governments, and to prevent the constant interference which must either be the cause of perpetual differences, or oblige one to yield, perhaps unjustly, to the other." "The idea that congress ought to have *unlimited powers*" Smith considered "entirely novel," a threat to the very existence of the states.[35] "The constitutional line between the authority of each," he insisted, "should be so obvious, as to leave no room for jealous apprehensions or violent contests." [36]

Antifederalists persisted in the clamor that national power be precisely defined, only to be met by stubborn refusal to do so. Jasper Yeates of Pennsylvania asked: "Is it, indeed, possible to define any power so accurately, that it shall reach the particular object for which it was given, and yet not be liable to perversion and abuse?" [37] The question was not so much whether a line could be drawn with reasonable accuracy, as whether so limiting national power would render it unlikely to reach, as Yeates put it, "the particular object for which it was given." Addressing himself to "the *accuracy* with which the *line is drawn* between the powers of the *general government,* and that of the *particular State governments,*" Wilson would not pretend "that the line is drawn with mathematical precision; the inaccuracy of language must, to a certain degree, prevent the accomplishment of such a desire." "Whoever views the matter in a true light," he urged, "will see that the powers are as minutely enumerated and defined as was possible. . . ." [38] Mincing no words, Wilson declared flatly that national power could not be limited, if it were to reach its national objects.

> We find on an examination of all its parts, that the objects of this government are such as extend beyond the bounds of the particular States. This is the line of distinction between this government and the particular State governments.[39]

Wilson's unequivocal avowal of national supremacy evoked from Antifederalists the not unnatural query: "[W]here is the bill of rights which shall check the power of this congress, which shall say, *thus far shall ye come and no farther?* The safety of the people depends on a bill of rights." [40]

The proposed Constitution seemed to depart from the traditional stress on basic rights. Except for the provisions against bills of attainder, *ex post facto* laws, the guarantee of jury trial in criminal cases, and the injunction against suspending the writ of habeas corpus, it contained no bill of rights. Indeed, it was not until September 12 that George Mason, who a decade earlier had prepared his own state's bill of rights, rose in the Convention at Philadelphia to announce that he "wished the plan had been prefaced with a Bill of Rights." "It would give great quiet to the people," Mason declared.[41] This last-minute effort was to no avail. His motion defeated 10 to 1, Mason returned to Virginia with a "fixed disposition to prevent the adoption of the plan," being convinced that "the want of a Bill of Rights is a fatal objection." [42]

What loomed before George Mason as a "fatal objection" before the Convention adjourned seemed hardly to have occurred to other delegates during the entire summer. "I cannot say," James Wilson remarked almost casually in the Pennsylvania ratifying convention, "what were the reasons of every member of that convention [at Philadelphia], for not adding a bill of rights; I believe the truth is, that such an idea never entered the mind of many of them." [43] Mason's "fatal objection," Madison noted impatiently, "surely was not brought forward in the Convention. . . . Were it allowed the weight which Col. M. may suppose it deserves, it would remain to be decided whether it be candid to arraign the Convention for omissions which were never suggested to them. . . ." [44]

Mason's objection had, in fact, been only faintly urged and not at the time when it might have been effectively pressed. Apparently confirmed is Wilson's observation that serious consideration of a bill of rights "would have been spurned . . . with the greatest indignation. . . ." [45]

Indicative of the Convention's attitude is the discussion of August 22 on the proposed prohibition of *ex post facto* laws. Gouverneur Morris, Oliver Ellsworth, Samuel Johnson, and Wilson all agreed that barring *ex post facto* laws would be both unnecessary and undesirable. Ellsworth contended that "there was no lawyer, no civilian who would not say that *ex post facto* laws were void of themselves." Why bother to prohibit them? Wilson feared that forbidding them would "bring reflections on the Constitution and proclaim that we are ignorant of the first principles of Legislation, or are constituting a Government which will be so." Johnson agreed that such a clause would imply "an improper suspicion of the National Legislature." When Charles Carroll of Maryland suggested that since the states had passed *ex post facto* laws, the national Constitution ought to incorporate the wisdom of the states' experience, Wilson remarked dryly: "If these prohibitions in the State Constitutions have no effect, it will be useless to insert them in this Constitution." "Besides," he added, "both sides will agree to the principle & will differ as to its application." Hugh Williamson of North Carolina was not convinced. Anticipating the argument for a bill of rights, which Jefferson found so persuasive, Williamson broached the intimate connection between judicial review and a bill of rights:

> Such a prohibitory clause is in the Constitution of N. Carolina, and tho it has been violated, it has done good there & may do good here, *because the judges can take hold of it*.[46]

Bills of rights, including *ex post facto* laws, were "an unnecessary guard as the principles of justice, law, etc. were a perpetual bar to such. To say that the legislature shall not pass an *ex post facto* law is the same as to declare they shall not do a thing contrary to common sense—that they shall not cause that to be a crime which is no crime." [47] Mere "paper" guarantees were generally considered ineffectual anyway; more substantial safeguards were needed—power alone could check the potential abuses of political power. In the Convention and later, states rights—not individual rights—was the real worry. "What is the government now forming," Luther Martin asked, "over states or persons?"

> As to the latter, their rights cannot be the object of a general government. These are already secured by their guardians, the state governments. The general government is therefore intended only to protect and guard the rights of the states as states. . . . The only necessary check in a general government ought to be a restraint to prevent its absorbing the powers of the state governments. . . .[48]

Ellsworth endorsed these thoughts. "The Natl. Govt. could not descend to the local objects on which this [individual rights] depended. It could only embrace objects of a general nature. He [Ellsworth] turned his eyes therefore for the preservation of his rights to the State Govts." [49]

Rufus King attempted to pacify Ellsworth and others concerned for the rights of the states. King went so far as to suggest a bill of rights for the states to protect them against the effects of unlimited national power:

> Mr. King was for preserving the States in a subordinate degree, and as far as they could be necessary for the purposes stated by Mr. Elsewth. He did not think a full answer had been given to those who apprehended a dangerous encroachment on their jurisdictions. Expedients might be devised as he conceived that would give them all the security the nature of things would admit of. In the establishment of Societies the Constitution was to the Legislature what the laws were to individuals. *As the fundamental rights of individuals are secured by express provisions in the State Constitutions; why may not a like security be provided for the Rights of States in the National Constitution. . . .* He was aware that this will be called a mere *paper security*. . . .[50]

Strong checks were needed to prevent usurpations of legislative power. Gouverneur Morris

> concurred in thinking the public liberty in greatest danger from Legislative usurpations than from any other source. It had been said that the Legislature ought to be relied on as the proper Guardians of liberty. The answer was short and conclusive. Either bad laws will be pushed or not. On the latter supposition no check will be wanted. On the former a strong check will be necessary. And this is the proper supposition. . . .[51]

"Strong" checks did not necessarily mean a bill of rights. They meant built-in, institutional safeguards—tangible mechanisms pitting power against power. "Paper securities" were no match for actual power. Many years later Morris made his meaning quite clear in a letter to Timothy Pickering:

> But, after all, what does it signify, that men should have a written constitution, containing unequivocal provisions and limitations? The legislative lion will not be entangled in the meshes of a logical net. The legislature will always make the power, which it wishes to exercise, *unless it be so organized, as to contain within itself the sufficient check.* Attempts to restrain it from outrage, by other means, will only render it more outrageous. . . .[52]

It is not surprising that George Mason's last-minute efforts on behalf of a bill of rights got short shrift. What is surprising is that men like Mason, strongly dedicated to basic freedoms, waited so long to press their case. It seems that the Antifederalist drive for a bill of rights arose only as they slowly awakened to the "consolidating" implications of the nationalizing provisions adopted with but little disapproval after the nationalists' setbacks of July 16 and 17. It is significant, therefore, that Roger Sherman's reply to Gerry's motion for a committee to prepare a Bill of Rights—that "The State Declarations of Rights are not repealed by this Constitution; and being in force are sufficient"—was met by Mason's retort: "The Laws of the U.S. are to be paramount to State Bills of Rights." [53] By this time the implications of the supremacy clause were clear. Three days later Gerry gave evidence that he, too, was aware of certain provisions that rendered "insecure" the rights of individuals. He could "get over" all other objections but the Convention's failure to protect individual rights from the effects of the necessary-and-proper clause, the unlimited national power to raise money and armies, and the absence of guaranteed jury trials in civil cases. Gerry therefore called for a second Convention.[54]

Slow to see the need for a Bill of Rights, the Antifederalists, once aroused, exploded with fury. The framers had belied their heritage. Having triumphed in the War of Independence, they had stored away, along with their muskets, earlier convictions about natural rights. The Constitution's critics "fancied," Madison wrote Jefferson in Paris, "that the Convention . . . had entered into a conspiracy against the liberties of the people at large, in order to erect an aristocracy for the rich, the well-born, and the men of Education." [55] Madison did not exaggerate these suspicions. When America was in its youth, Patrick Henry commented caustically, "liberty . . . was . . . the primary object." It ranked high both in word and deed. This country had become "a great, mighty, and splendid nation," because liberty was "its direct end and foundation." [56] Patrick Dollard of South Carolina, expressing the sentiments of his constituents, summed up the thrust of much popular opposition to the new Constitution:

> . . . The people of Prince Frederick's Parish, of whom I have the honor to represent are a brave, honest, and industrious people. In the late bloody contest, they bore a conspicuous part, when they fought, bled, and conquered, in defence of their civil rights and privileges, which they expected to transmit untainted to their posterity. They are nearly all, to a man opposed to this new constitution because, they say, they have omitted to insert a bill of rights therein, ascertaining, and fundamentally establishing the unalienable rights of men, without a full, free, and secure enjoyment of which there can be no liberty, and over which it is not necessary that a good government should have the control. They say, that they are by no means against investing congress with ample and sufficient powers; but to make over to them, or any set of men, their birthright, comprised in Magna Carta, which this new constitution absolutely does, they can never agree to. . . .[57]

In Virginia the formidable triumvirate of Henry, Mason, and Richard Henry Lee waged a relentless campaign. Under the proposed Constitution not only had the sovereignty of the states been "relinquished," but also the "rights of conscience, trial by jury, liberty of press, . . . all pretensions to human rights and privileges," were made uncertain.[58] This seemed a strange turn of events. Heretofore, bills of rights had been "a favorite thing" among Americans. "It may be their prejudice," Henry observed, "but the government ought to suit their geniuses, otherwise its operation will be unhappy. A bill of rights, even if its necessity be doubtful, will exclude the possibility of dispute. . . ." [59]

Had the new government been formed on principles "truly federal," Luther Martin explained, "legislating over and acting upon the states only in their collective or political capacity, and not on individuals, there would have been no need of a bill of rights, as far as related to the rights of individuals, but only as to the rights of states." "But," Martin went on, "the proposed constitution being intended and empowered to act not only on states, but also immediately on individuals, it renders a recognition and a stipulation in favour of the rights both of states and of men, not only proper, but . . . absolutely necessary." A Bill of Rights, then, would "serve as a barrier between the general government and the respective states and their citizens." [60]

The combined effect of the supremacy clause and the necessary-and-proper clause seemed especially dangerous to the rights of the states and their citizens. Congress being vested with "the supreme power of legislation, paramount to the constitution and laws of the States," the peril to these rights could hardly be considered imaginary, Antifederalists argued. Infinitude of power, Henry warned, carried with it "an infinitude of means to carry it on . . . and infinitude excludes every idea of subordination." [61] "There is no declaration of rights," Mason observed, "and the laws of the general government being paramount to the laws and constitutions of the several states, the declarations of rights, in the separate states, are no security." [62]

"Is there any act, however atrocious," Henry asked, which Congress could not commit by virtue of the supremacy clause and the "sweeping" necessary-and-proper clause? [63] "It is proper the national laws should be supreme," Richard Henry Lee conceded, "but then the national laws ought to yield to unalienable or fundamental rights—and national laws, made by a few men, should extend only to a few national objects." It was "almost impossible," he continued, "to have a just conception" of national powers, "or of the extent and number of the laws which may be deemed necessary and proper to carry them into effect. . . ." [64]

In view of the supremacy clause and the necessary-and-proper clause, each of which were at various times referred to as "the sweeping clause," "Centinel" (Samuel Bryan) queried, "What security do the *Constitutions* of the several States afford for the *liberty of the press and other invaluable personal rights,* not provided for by the new plan?" [65] Very little security indeed, Richard Henry Lee explained:

> . . . Should the printer say, the freedom of the press was secured by the constitution of the state in which he lived, congress might, and perhaps, with great propriety, answer, that the federal constitution is the only compact existing between them and the people; in this compact the people have named no others, and therefore congress, in exercising the powers assigned them, and in making laws to carry them into execution, are restrained by nothing beside the federal constitution, any more than a state legislature is restrained by a compact between the magistrates and people of a county, city, or town of which the people, in forming the state constitution, have taken no notice.[66]

Robert Yates, writing under the pen name of "Sydney," sought to demonstrate that the new Constitution could obviate nearly every clause of the constitution of New York.[67] The national Constitution was one thing, state constitutions another. It was clear that state bills of rights could not protect individuals—or states—in their relations with the new national government. "Then where is the security?" George Mason asked. "Where is the barrier drawn between the government, and the rights of the citizens, as secured in our own state governments?" [68]

Federalists responded by dismissing lightly the implications of the supremacy and necessary-and-proper clauses. Both were mere tautologies. The supremacy clause meant only that "when congress passes a law consistent with the constitution," said Iredell of North Carolina, "it is to be binding on the people." The national Constitution would, of course, supersede the state constitutions, but "the latter must yield to the former, only in those cases where power is given by it." "If congress under pretence of executing one power, should in fact usurp another," Iredell explained, "they will violate the constitution." The supremacy clause was "merely a general clause" which always raised the question of whether Congress had exceeded its authority. It granted no power itself and made supreme no laws lacking constitutional authority.[69]

The necessary-and-proper clause, likewise, was "only a superfluity." It gave "no supplementary power," Madison declared; it only enabled Congress "to execute the delegated powers."

> If the delegation of their powers be safe, no possible inconvenience can arise from this clause. It is at most but explanatory. For when any power is given, its delegation necessarily involves authority to makes laws to execute it. . . .[70]

Wilson agreed that the necessary-and-proper clause gave Congress no "general legislative power." [71] It meant merely that the powers "already particularly given, shall be effectually carried into execution." [72]

Antifederalists were not satisfied. They realized that the supremacy clause, considered alone, made supreme only those national laws enacted "in pursuance" of the Constitution. But this tautological explanation begged the question; for, as Iredell admitted, the real issue under the supremacy clause would always involve national power. If the Constitution granted Congress indefinite power—circumscribed by no line, undefined, and implied—then all laws Congress made would be "in pursuance" of the Constitution and therefore "the supreme law of the land." The Antifederalist minority in the Pennsylvania convention complained:

> It has been alleged that the words "pursuant to the constitution," are a restriction upon the authority of Congress; but when it is considered that *by other sections* they are invested with every efficient power of government, and which may be exercised to the absolute destruction of the State governments, without any violation of even the forms of the constitution, this seeming restriction, as well as every other restriction in it, appears to us to be nugatory and delusive; and only introduced as a blind upon the real nature of the government. In our opinion, "pursuant to the constitution" will be co-extensive with the *will* and *pleasure* of Congress, which, indeed, will be the only limitation of their powers.[73]

James Galloway of North Carolina recognized "that it is absolutely necessary for every government, and especially for a general government, that its laws should be the supreme law of the land." "I should make no objection to this clause," he allowed, "were the powers granted by the constitution sufficiently defined." [74]

Federalist effort to minimize the significance of "the sweeping clauses" was not convincing. If anything, their rebuttals made even clearer the need for a Bill of Rights to check the undefined power of a national government. Friends of the Constitution, unsuccessful in their attempts to render "the sweeping clauses" mere truisms, tried to meet the challenge by recourse to history. Bills of rights, James Wilson argued, being hangovers from the era of kings, did not fit the American situation. The ratifying conventions were voting on a government of enumerated powers. Any transgression of these bounds would be recognized as *ultra vires*. Under the proposed Constitution the people have all power. After granting some, the rest must remain with the people. Why make exceptions to power not granted? Why declare that certain things shall not be done, which there is no power to do? "In a government possessed of enumerated powers," Wilson declared, "such a measure would be not only unnecessary, but preposterous and dangerous. . . ." [75] "The convention have said nothing to secure the privilege of eating and drinking," 'One of the Four Thousand' observed, "and yet no man supposes that right of nature to be endangered by their silence about it." [76] It seemed to Wilson that "a bill of rights is neither an essential nor a necessary instrument in framing a system of government, since liberty may exist and be as well secured without it." More than that, he maintained, a Bill of Rights would be "impracticable—for who will be bold enough to undertake to enumerate all the rights of the people?"

> —and when the attempt to enumerate them is made, it must be remembered that if the enumeration is not complete, everything not expressly mentioned will be presumed to be purposely omitted. So it must be with a bill of rights, and an omission in stating the powers granted to the government, is not so dangerous as an omission in recapitulating the rights reserved by the people. . . .[77]

"Enumerate all the rights of men!" Wilson exclaimed. "I am sure that no gentleman in the late convention would have attempted such a thing." [78]

Madison shared Wilson's aversion to bills of rights. He considered "a solemn declaration of our essential rights" both "unnecessary and dangerous.—Unnecessary, because it was evident that the general government had no power but what was given it, and that the delegation alone warranted the exercise of power.—Dangerous, because an enumeration which is not complete, is not safe." [79] It was "obviously and self-evidently the case," Madison insisted, "that every thing not granted is reserved." "If an enumeration be made of our rights," he echoed Wilson, "will it not be implied, that every thing omitted, is given to the general government?" [80]

Antifederalists stood firm. To the Federalist argument that any attempt to enumerate rights beyond the reach of government endangered omission of others equally basic, they replied that the risk had already been incurred by the partial listing of rights in Article I, Section 9, and in Article III, Section 2. "No satisfactory reason has yet been offered for the omission of a bill of rights," Whitehill of Pennsylvania charged, "but on the contrary, the honorable members are defeated in the only pretext which they have been able to assign, that everything which is not given is excepted, for we have shown that there are two articles expressly reserved, the writ of habeas corpus and the trial by jury in criminal cases, and we have called upon them in vain to reconcile this reservation with the tenor of their favorite proposition."

> For if there was a danger in the attempt to enumerate the liberties of the people, lest it should prove imperfect and destructive, how happens it that in the instances I have mentioned, that danger has been incurred? Have the people no other rights worth their attention, or is it to be inferred, agreeably to the maxim of our opponents, that every other right is abandoned? Surely, Sir, our language was competent to declare the sentiments of the people and to establish a bar against the intrusion of the general government in other respects as well as these; and when we find some privileges stipulated, the argument of danger is effectually destroyed; and the argument of difficulty which has been drawn from the attempt to enumerate every right, cannot now be urged against the enumeration of more rights than this instrument contains. . . .[81]

Whitehill's compatriot, Smilie, was equally blunt. The presence of a partial bill of rights, he argued, reinforced the Antifederalist case. "It seems that the members of the federal convention were themselves convinced, in some degree, of the expediency and propriety of a bill of rights, for we find them expressly declaring that the writ of habeas corpus and the trial by jury in criminal cases shall not be suspended or infringed. . . . How does this indeed agree with the maxim that whatever is not given is reserved? Does it not rather appear, from the reservation of these two articles, that everything else, which is not specified, is included in the powers delegated to the government?" Whitehill and Smilie had met the Federalists on their own ground. They had used the very premises Wilson and Madison adumbrated against a Bill of Rights to "prove the necessity of a full and explicit declaration of rights. . . ." [82]

Hartley of Pennsylvania attempted to reconcile the apparently contradictory Federalist positions. "Some articles, indeed from their pre-eminence in the scale of political security," he explained, "deserve to be particularly specified, and these have not been omitted in the system before us." [83] Unconvinced, Richard Henry Lee retorted that "the establishing of one right" still implied "the necessity of establishing another and similar one." [84]

"Why is it provided that no bill of attainder shall be passed," Tredwell of New York insisted, "or that no title of nobility shall be granted?" "Some gentlemen say that these, though not necessary, were inserted for greater caution." Tredwell could only wish "that a greater caution had been used to secure to us the freedom of election, a sufficient and responsible representation, the freedom of the press, and the trial by jury both in civil and criminal cases." [85]

The stock Federalist contention that a government of enumerated powers only could not legislate on matters to which, by implication, its powers did not extend, served only to infuriate patriots who had revolted for the expressed purpose of preserving fundamental rights. "We are giving power; they are getting power," Patrick Henry raged; "judge then, on which side the implication will be used."

> When we once put it in their option to assume constructive power, danger will follow—Trial by jury, and liberty of the press, are . . . on this foundation of implication. If they encroach on these rights, and you give your implication for a plea, you are cast; for they will be justified by [that clause] which gives them full power—"To make all laws which shall be necessary and proper to carry their power into execution." Implication is dangerous, because it is unbounded: if it be admitted at all, and no limits be prescribed, it admits of the utmost extension. They say that everything that is not given is retained. The reverse of the proposition is true by implication. They do not carry their implication so far when they speak of the general welfare. No implication when the sweeping clause comes. Implication is only necessary when the existence of privilege is in dispute. *The existence of powers is sufficiently established. If we trust our dearest right to implication, we shall be in a very unhappy situation.*[86]

Nor could states rights be secured by implication. "The constitution grants the power of taxation to congress," Williams of New York argued, "but is silent with regard to the power in the states." "If it is inferred from this," he reasoned, "that it is not taken away from the states, we may . . . with equal justice deduce from the positive establishment of the trial by jury in criminal cases, that it is annihilated in civil." "Ingenious men," Williams warned, "may assign ingenious reasons for opposite constructions of the same clause." "If we adopt this constitution," he concluded, "it is impossible, absolutely impossible, to know what we give up, and what we retain." [87]

Federalists, unsure as to whether the national government would have the necessary power, distrusted express safeguards for the rights of states and individuals lest they sap the energy needed to achieve national objectives. Bills of rights, they countered, were ineffectual; the Constitution's institutional checks provided more effective security. "Gentlemen talk of bills of rights!" James Wilson observed. The people continually clamored that trial by jury was secured in the bill of rights of Pennsylvania, that this right "OUGHT to be kept sacred." But "what is the consequence? There have been more violations of this right in Pennsylvania, since the revolution, than are to be found in England, in the course of a century." [88]

Not all state constitutions contained bills of rights, nor did the Articles of Confederation. Where they existed, as in Pennsylvania, they had proved ineffective. "In Virginia," Madison wrote Jefferson on October 17, 1788, "I have seen the bill of rights violated in every instance where it has been exposed to a popular current." [89] Repeated violations of these parchment barriers had been committed by overbearing legislative majorities in every state. Safeguards must be found elsewhere; the proposed Constitution abounded with them.

In a particularly lucid speech in the Massachusetts ratifying convention, delegate Bowdoin spelled out the Federalist position. A Bill of Rights would seriously weaken the energy of the national government, he contended. Since "all governments are founded on the relinquishment of personal rights in a certain degree, there was a clear impropriety in being very particular about them." "By such a particularity," Bowdoin warned, "the government might be embarrassed, and prevented from doing what the private, as well as the public and general good of the citizens and states might require." Bowdoin admitted that power was liable to abuse, that it "may be employed by congress in oppressing their constituents." "A possibility of abuse, as it may be affirmed of all delegated power whatever, is by itself, no sufficient reason for withholding the delegation." If it were, "no power could be delegated; nor could government of any sort subsist." The possibility of abuse "should make us careful, that in all delegations of importance . . . there should be such checks provided, as would not frustrate the end and intention of delegating the power; but would, as far as it could safely be done, prevent the abuse of it." All such checks were provided in the Constitution, and Bowdoin was convinced that "at least in all flagrant instances," abuse of power would be prevented, "even if Congress should consist wholly of men, who were guided by no other principle than their own interest." [90]

Bowdoin's speech was aimed at dispelling the deep-seated Antifederalist distrust of power, a misgiving so profound that Nathaniel Barrell felt that the power conferred on the new national government was too great even for "such exalted, amiable characters as the great Washington." Barrell queried, "what assurance can we have that such men will always hold the reins of government?" [91] If a Washington could not be trusted, then who could? If no one could, as the Antifederalists insisted, then what good were paper guarantees against the inevitable infirmities of human nature? Implying that no freedom could be secured merely by constitutional affirmation, Bowdoin ran the gamut of institutional checks from separation of powers to popular elections. Absent from his list, however, was a device destined to become intimately linked with the protection of individual rights—judicial review.

Other Federalists supplied this omission, pointing to courts as the guardian of liberty. To Patrick Henry's query, who is to determine the extent of national power, George Nicholas of Virginia retorted: "I say, the same power which in all well regulated communities determines the extent of legislative powers. If they exceed these powers, the judiciary will declare it void." [92] Courts would exercise this authority even without a bill of rights. Edmund Randolph, taking up the cudgels in behalf of the Constitution he had declined to sign, also looked to the federal judiciary for protection. "Can it be believed," he asked, "that the federal judiciary would not be independent enough to prevent such oppressive practices?" [93] On these assumptions the judiciary had been made, as Edmund Pendleton said, "an essential part of the government." Its role was "proper and necessary in all free governments." [94]

Oliver Ellsworth of Connecticut, later Chief Justice, was no less firm. "If the general legislature should at any time overleap their limits," he declared, "the judicial department is a constitutional check. . . . If the United States go beyond their powers, if they make a law which the constitution does not authorize, it is void; and the judicial power, the national judges, who, to secure their impartiality, are to be made independent, will declare it to be void. . . ." [95] Alexander Contee Hanson, a member of the Maryland convention, reinforced Ellsworth's stand. Replying to Antifederalist charges that the new Congress alone would judge the constitutionality of its acts, Hanson emphasized that "every judge in the union, whether of federal or state appointment, . . . will have a right to reject any act, handed to him as a law, which he may conceive repugnant to the constitution." [96] Under the new Constitution, James Wilson declared, "the legislature may be restrained and kept within its prescribed bounds by the interposition of the judicial department." [97]

Perhaps the most forceful support of judicial review came from John Marshall, later Chief Justice, who called the federal judiciary "a great improvement." A tribunal had been established for "*the decision of controversies,* which were before, either not at all, or improperly provided for." The supremacy clause, he admitted, made the laws of the United States paramount, but any fear that "there is no case but what this will extend to" was unwarranted. Congress did not have carte blanche; the government of the United States did not have power to make laws on every conceivable subject. "If they were to make a law not warranted by any of the powers enumerated, it would be considered by the judges as an infringement of the constitution which they are to guard; they would not consider such a law as coming under their jurisdiction. They would declare it void."

"Is it not necessary," Marshall asked, "that the federal courts should have cognizance of cases arising under the constitution, and the laws of the United States?" The future Chief Justice answered this leading question with a series of pointed rhetorical observations. "What is the service or purpose of a judiciary, but to execute the laws in a peaceable, orderly manner, without shedding blood, or creating a contest, or availing themselves of force? If this be the case, where can its jurisdiction be more necessary than here?" "To what quarter will you look for a protection from an infringement on the constitution," Marshall demanded, "if you will not give the power to the judiciary? There is no other body that can afford such a protection." [98] Chief among the guardians of individual rights would be the federal judiciary. It would exercise this authority even in the absence of paper guarantees.

Federalist assurances that individual rights—as well as states rights—would be adequately safeguarded by the multitude of checks, including judicial review, did not allay Antifederalist doubt. So distrustful were they of the corrupting effects of power, that they not only insisted on a Bill of Rights but also urged *more* institutional checks. Melancton Smith continued to lament that "no constitutional checks were provided; such checks as would not leave the exercise of government to the operation of causes, which, in their nature, are variable and uncertain." [99] Bodman of Massachusetts complained about "unlimited" national power and warned the people to be "jealous of their rulers . . . for jealousy was one of the greatest securities of the people in a republic." [100] Grayson of Virginia insisted that power "ought to be granted on a supposition that men will be bad; for it may be eventually so." [101]

"The real rock of political salvation," Patrick Henry declared, "is self-love. . . ." If your rulers "can stand the temptations of human nature, you are safe," he admitted. "If you have a good president, senators, and representatives, there is no danger. But can this be expected from human nature? . . . Without real checks it will not suffice that some of them are good. . . . Where is the rock of your salvation?" It appeared to him that "there is no check in that government." "Till I am convinced that there are actual efficient checks," he concluded, "I will not give my assent to its establishment." [102]

True disciples of Cato, Burgh, and Montesquieu, Antifederalists were hard to please. "Tell me not of checks of paper," Henry cried, sounding more like a Federalist than an advocate of a Bill of Rights, "but tell me of checks founded on self-love." [103]

Even Federalist pledges that the federal judiciary would safeguard individual rights were of no avail. Henry and Grayson felt that the national courts would obviate the state judiciaries, thereby rendering the states impotent to protect individual and states rights. "With respect to the judiciary," Grayson commented, "my grand objection is that it will interfere with the state judiciaries, in the same manner as the exercise of the power of direct taxation, will interfere with the same power in the state governments. . . ." [104] In the same vein, Henry scored the "probable *interference of the federal judiciary with . . . the state judiciaries.*" [105] Henry considered "the Virginia judiciary as one of the best barriers against strides of power; against that power, which . . . has threatened the destruction of liberty." Even this "last barrier" was in jeopardy.

> So small are the barriers against the encroachments and usurpations of congress, that when I see this last barrier, the independence of the judges impaired, I am persuaded I see the prostration of all our rights. In what situation will your judges be in, when they are sworn to preserve the constitution of the state, and of the general government? If there be a concurrent dispute between them, which will prevail? They cannot serve two masters struggling for the same object. The laws of congress being paramount to those of the states and to their constitutions also, whenever they come in competition, the judges must decide in favor of the former. This, instead of relieving or aiding me, deprives me of my only comfort, the independency of the judges. The judiciary are the sole protection against a tyrannical execution of the laws. But if by this system we lose our judiciary, and they cannot help us, we must set down quietly, and be oppressed.[106]

Federal courts as the guardians of basic rights would be handicapped for want of precise criteria against which to judge alleged violation of fundamental liberties. Federalists had opposed a Bill of Rights in part because, as Parsons of New York explained, "no power was given to Congress to infringe on any one of the natural rights of the people by this constitution; and should they attempt it, without constitutional authority, the act would be a nullity, and could not be enforced." [107] Federalists had, of course, assumed that the courts would defend common law rights against legislative usurpation even in the absence of a Bill of Rights. Antifederalists, however, were not convinced. In the first place, they argued, common law rights stood on no higher law foundation; they were inherently subject to legislative alteration. "A legislative assembly," as James Winthrop under the pen name of "Agrippa" declared, "has an inherent right to alter the common law, and to abolish any of its principles, which are not particularly guarded in the constitution. Any system therefore which appoints a legislature, without any reservation of the rights of individuals, surrenders all power in every branch of legislation to the government." [108]

George Mason lodged the same objection against the proposed Constitution. "Nor are the people secured even in the enjoyment of the benefit of the common law, which stands here," he declared, "upon no other foundation than its having been adopted by the respective acts forming the constitutions of the several states." [109] Madison, specifically replying to Mason's criticism, confessed that even the state constitutions did not secure common law rights:

> . . . The Common law is nothing more than the unwritten law, and is left by all the Constitutions equally liable to legislative alterations. I am not sure

that any notice is particularly taken of it in the Constitutions of the States. If there is, nothing more is provided than a general declaration that it shall continue along with other branches of law to be in force till legally changed. . . .[110]

Antifederalists deemed a Bill of Rights necessary as an adjunct to judicial review: common law rights were inherently subject to legislative change; they were left unprotected by some state constitutions; even if incorporated into state Declarations of Rights, these were subject to the supremacy of national law. "The truth is," Smilie of Pennsylvania announced, "that unless some criterion is established by which it could be easily and constitutionally ascertained how far our governors may proceed, and by which it might appear when they transgress their jurisdiction, this idea of altering and abolishing government is a mere sound without substance." [111]

> . . . So loosely, so inaccurately are the powers which are enumerated in this constitution defined, that it will be impossible, without a test of that kind ["a full and explicit declaration of rights"], to ascertain the limits of authority, and to declare when government has degenerated into oppression. In that event the contest will arise between the people and the rulers: "You have exceeded the powers of your office, you have oppressed us," will be the language of the suffering citizen. The answer of the government will be short—"We have not extended our power; you have no test by which you can prove it." Hence, Sir, it will be impracticable to stop the progress of tyranny, for there will be no check but the people, and their exertions must be futile and uncertain; since it will be difficult, indeed, to communicate to them the violation that has been committed, and their proceedings will be neither systematical nor unanimous. . . .[112]

In short, the Federalists had only *partially* succeeded in solving the gaping dilemma John Locke posed toward the end of his *Second Treatise.* When the people's chosen representatives are alleged to violate the trust imposed by the social compact and by "promulgated established laws," who is to judge the transgression? Locke's answer was that in the absence of a "judicature on earth to decide . . . God in heaven is judge"— presumably a Lockean euphemism for force. The Federalists recognized that this yawning hiatus in Locke's system had to be filled. They saw the need for *judges,* but they refused to provide *standards.* Without a Bill of Rights to ascertain and fix the limits of national power in relation to the rights of individuals—and states—the Federalist solvent was but a shallow solution. The prospect that judicial review would provide peaceable means for the redress of infringed rights was more apparent than real. Instead of averting recourse to revolution, the Constitution's failure to convert natural rights into enforceable civil rights through the medium of a Bill of Rights made violent redress the more likely. Thus, rather than containing *"the means of its own preservation,"* [113] the new national government contained the seeds of its own destruction.

Antifederalists would have carried the Federalist solution to the Lockean dilemma one crucial step further. To the mechanism of judicial review, they would have tied a Bill of Rights.

Centering his fire on Madison, Jefferson wrote from Paris: "A bill of rights is what the people are entitled to against every government on earth, general or particular, and what no just government should refuse, or rest on inference." Around this "polar star, and great support of American liberty" [114] fierce battles were fought in New York, Virginia, and Massachusetts. No one queried the sanctity of these rights. There had not been, Hamilton declared, "any diminution of regard for those rights and liberties, in defense of which, the people have fought and suffered." [115] All such reassurances fell on deaf ears. The desirability and necessity of such precautions, not their merit, was the issue. These "dearest possessions" must be written into the Constitution. "That sacred and lovely thing, religion," Patrick Henry observed, "ought not to rest on the ingenuity of logical deduction." [116]

The opposition lost the battle, but not the war. "Without promise of a limiting Bill of Rights," the late Justice Jackson commented in 1943, "it is doubtful if our Constitution could have mustered enough strength to enable its ratification." [117] If the Justice meant that nine states would not have ratified unless a bill of rights were guaranteed, he was perhaps mistaken. Delaware, the first state to consider the Constitution, discussed it four days and ratified unanimously. In Pennsylvania, Robert Whitehill, a western delegate, proposed that there be no ratification without a Bill of Rights, but the convention voted two to one to join the union. The New Jersey convention was in session only seven days and gave unanimous endorsement of an unamended Constitution. The Georgia delegates met on Christmas Day, 1787, and approved unanimously on the second day of the new year. In Connecticut debate lasted less than seven days. On being assured by Lieutenant-Governor Oliver Wolcott that the Constitution was so well guarded that "it seems impossible that the rights either of the States or of the people should be destroyed," the delegates voted 128 to 40 in favor of ratification.[118]

The Constitution first encountered powerful opposition in Massachusetts. For a while it seemed doubtful that enough votes in favor could be mustered. Samuel Adams, whose democratic convictions had highlighted the prerevolutionary years, noted signs of reaction against "the Natural Rights of Man" developing even before the conclusion of that struggle.[119] John Hancock, initially inclined to be negative, finally supplied the formula that won Adams' acquiescence: "I give my assent to the Constitution, in full confidence that the amendments proposed will soon become a part of the system." [120] Recommendatory, not "conditional amendments" was the price exacted. This outcome created "a blemish," Madison admitted, but one "least offensive" in form. The size of the minority, 187 to 168, was "disagreeably large"; but its temper supplied "some atonement." [121]

Meanwhile, Maryland and South Carolina ratified with comfortable margins. New Hampshire became the ninth to ratify by vote of 57 to 47.[122]

The Bay State's procedure had worked so well that Madison now advocated its use wherever the vote promised to be close. "A conditional ratification or a second convention," he wrote Governor Edmund Randolph, "appears to me utterly irreconcilable . . . with the dictates of prudence and safety." Recommendatory alterations alone provided ground for coalition among real Federalists.[123]

The Massachusetts formula caught on. Thereafter the issue was no longer "what the constitution is, but what degree of probability there is that the amendments will hereafter be incorporated. . . ." [124] "My idea is," Virginia delegate Francis Corbin observed, "that we should go hand in hand with Massachusetts; adopt it first, and then propose amendments. . . ."[125] Jefferson, who had earlier urged that ratification be delayed until a bill of rights could be added,[126] now surrendered. "[T]he plan of Massachusetts is far preferable," he agreed, "and will I hope be followed by those who are yet to decide." [127] "It will be more difficult, if we lose this instrument, to recover what is good in it, than to correct what is bad after we shall have adopted it." [128]

Virginia posed the most crucial hurdle. Even if enough states ratified to put the Constitution into effect, no one entertained the slightest hope for its success without New York and Virginia, where the Bill of Rights issue was most hotly and narrowly contested. In Virginia, the Constitution, at first, had evoked great enthusiasm. Then the tide took "a sudden and strong turn in the opposite direction." [129] Nowhere was the opposition so well organized or so well led. Patrick Henry, George Mason, and Richard Henry Lee constituted a formidable trio. It was said that Patrick Henry's purpose was to amend the Constitution and "leave the fate of the measures to depend on all the other States conforming to the will of Virginia," the theory being that "other States cannot do without us. . . ." [130]

George Wythe of Virginia took a decisive step on June 24, 1788, when he admitted the Constitution's imperfections, and "the propriety of some amendments." Wythe then proposed "that whatsoever amendments might be deemed necessary, should be recommended to consideration of the congress which should first assemble under the constitution. . . ." [131] Notwithstanding misgivings as to their efficacy, Madison finally acquiesced. Two days earlier—on June 22—he had written Rufus King that rather than incur the dangers implicit in a temporary adjournment, which he thought the Henry-led Antifederalist forces were seeking, he would support a Bill of Rights. "It has been judged prudent," he wrote,

". . . to maintain so exemplary a fairness on our part, (and even in some points to give way to unreasonable pretensions) as will withhold every pretext for so rash a step." [132] Madison was adamant in his opposition to *prior* amendments or to *any* amendments which would materially alter the structure of the new government.

In the end, the issue which clinched victory in Virginia did not concern "recommendatory" versus "conditional" amendments. It was the one Governor Randolph stated in his final dramatic appeal:

> . . . *I went to the federal Convention,* with the strongest affection for the union; . . . I acted there, in full conformity with this affection: . . . *I refused to subscribe, because I had as I still have objections to the Constitution,* and wished a free inquiry into its merits; and . . . the accession of eight states reduced our *deliberations* to the single question of *union or no union.*[133]

The decision for union stood 89 to 79.

In New York, the Antifederalists, led by Governor Clinton, were strong. Success was by no means assured. During the last days of the convention word came that New Hampshire and Virginia had ratified. It was now certain that the Constitution would be given a trial.

While news of Virginia gladdened the hearts of the Federalists, it served only to harden Antifederalist opposition. Enemies of the new Constitution now proposed conditional ratification—ratification with the right of withdrawal if amendments were not adopted. Alarmed by this move, Hamilton insisted on *recommendatory* amendments only. The Federalists would only "concur in rational recommendations." [134] To stall the Antifederalist drive for prior amendments, Federalists moved for temporary adjournment. Being outvoted, 40-22, they had no recourse but to debate the issue. The situation looked grim. Hamilton, having just received a propitious reply from Madison, repulsed the opposition by apt quotation:

> My opinion is, that a reservation of a right to withdraw, if amendments be not decided on under the form of the constitution within a certain time, is a *conditional* ratification; that it does not make New York a member of the new union, and, consequently, that she could not be received on that plan. The constitution requires an adoption *in toto* and *forever.* It has been so adopted by the other states. An adoption for a limited time would be as defective as an adoption of some of the articles only. In short, any *condition* whatever must vitiate the ratification.[135]

In New York, as in Virginia, the vote, though close (30 to 27), was for union. Eleven states had now ratified; the new system of government would be put in operation.[136] None had joined with anything more than recommendations attached. Justice Jackson's inference that want of a bill of rights weighed heavily in the discussions on ratification is entirely justified.

Jefferson was elated. Previously, a staunch, uncompromising advocate, he now took a more balanced view. Bills of rights were, he agreed, "like all other human blessings alloyed with some inconveniences." Their presence might, under some circumstances, "cramp government." Not all rights could ever be made secure, but it was better to protect some than none. Transcending all other considerations was his conviction that the inconveniences attending omission of a bill of rights would be "permanent, afflicting and irreparable . . . in constant progression from bad to worse." Almost as an afterthought, it seems, he alerted Madison to a crucial oversight: "In the arguments in favor of a declaration of rights, you omit one which has great weight with me, the legal check which it puts into the hands of the judiciary.[137] This is a body which if rendered independent, and kept strictly to their own department merits great confidence for their learning and integrity. . . . [W]hat degree of confidence would be too much for a body composed of such men as Wythe, Blair and Pendleton? On characters like these, the 'civium ardor prava jubentium' would make no impression." [138] Jefferson shared the distrust that has always obsessed Americans, and for which the judiciary is expected to provide safeguards—"passion of the citizens ordaining perverse things."

Under pressure from Jefferson, Madison had capitulated; he now recognized that "political truths declared in that solemn manner" might "acquire by degrees the character of fundamental maxims of free Government." As these became incorporated into national sentiment, the effect might be to "counteract the impulses of interest and passion." [139] He now believed that amendments, "if pursued with a proper moderation and in a proper mode," might serve the "double purpose of satisfying the minds of well meaning opponents, and of providing additional guards in favour of liberty." [140] A Bill of Rights being "anxiously desired by others," it seemed prudent to acquiesce, especially when "the precaution can do no injury." [141] A Bill of Rights had thus become recognized as a sensible expedient "were it only to conciliate the opposition." [142]

Ratification in the key state of New York had been achieved, but only at the price of a Circular letter to other states calling for another convention to provide the amendments demanded.[143] George Mason considered this maneuver the last hope.[144] Some suspected ulterior motives. The Circular letter, Washington warned, was designed "to set everything afloat again." [145]

Madison had earlier speculated that "if a second Convention should be formed, it is as little to be expected that the same spirit of compromise will prevail in it as produced an amicable result to the first." "It will be easy also," he had written Jefferson, "for those who have latent views of disunion, to carry them on under the mask of contending for alterations popular in some but inadmissible in other parts of the U. States." [146]

Everywhere the opposition seized the Circular letter "as the signal for united exertions in pursuit of early amendments." [147] Sending a copy to Jefferson, Madison warned that "mischiefs are apprehended."

> The great danger in the present crisis is that if another Convention should be soon assembled, it would terminate in discord, or in alterations of the federal system which would throw back *essential* powers into the State Legislatures. The delay of a few years will assuage the jealousies which have been artificially created by designing men and will at the same time point out the faults which really call for amendment. At present the public mind is neither sufficiently cool nor sufficiently informed for so delicate an operation.[148]

Less than two weeks later Madison wrote Jefferson again, lamenting North Carolina's failure to ratify the Constitution and "the tendency of the circular letter from the Convention of N. York. . . ." Events there had "somewhat changed the aspect of things" and had "given fresh hopes and exertions to those who opposed the Constitution." [149]

A month later Madison was still pondering the impact of New York's Circular letter. It had "rekindled an ardor among the opponents of the federal Constitution for an *immediate* revision of it by another General Convention." Madison noted ominous signs in Pennsylvania and Virginia of a push for a second convention. While the effect of the Circular letter "on other States is less well known," Madison concluded that "it will be the same every where among those who opposed the Constitution, or contended for a conditional ratification of it." [150]

It turned out that the Circular letter produced much more smoke than fire. While serious efforts for a second convention were made in Pennsylvania, New York, Rhode Island, Virginia, and North Carolina, they were all effectively rebuffed. As Madison had predicted, the drive for a second convention would "certainly be industriously opposed in some parts of the Union, not only by those who wish for no alterations, but by others who would prefer the other mode provided in the Constitution." [151]

By December 8, 1788, Madison seemed set on utilizing that "other mode" to procure unobjectionable "supplemental safeguards to liberty" —if only to placate the Antifederalists. Another letter, describing his strategy and the situation compelling it, went out to Jefferson.[152] Success seemed assured. Writing Jefferson on December 12, 1788, he reported that the results of Pennsylvania's congressional election clinched Federalist domination in the first Congress but did not alter the desirability of securing unobjectionable amendments.

> . . . There will be seven representatives of the federal party, and one a moderate antifederalist [representing Pennsylvania]. I consider this choice as ensuring a majority of friends to the federal Constitution, in both branches of the Congress; as securing the Constitution against the hazardous experiment of a Second Convention; and if prudence should be the character of the

first Congress, as leading to measures which will conciliate the well-meaning of all parties, and put our affairs into an auspicious train.[153]

Three months later, Madison reported to Jefferson that

> the disaffected party in the Senate amounts to two or three members only; and that in the other House it does not exceed a very small minority, some of which will also be restrained by the federalism of the States from which they come. Notwithstanding this character of the Body, I hope and expect that some conciliatory sacrifices will be made, in order to extinguish opposition to the system, or at least break the force of it, by detaching the deluded opponents from their designing leaders. . . .[154]

Federalist acquiescence rendered the task relatively easy—less so, however, than was perhaps anticipated. In the months preceding election of the new Congress, it was rumored that the Federalists had no intention of pressing for amendments. Not only did revision, prior to putting the new system into operation, seem untimely, but friends of the Constitution, including Madison, were concerned lest precipitous change jeopardize the main goal—energetic government. Madison himself was the object of suspicion. In his campaign for a seat in the new Congress, he was charged with abandoning the cause of religious freedom. Now modifying his previous stand as to the wisdom of including a Bill of Rights, he took the position that ratification, without prior attempts at alteration, made amendments safe and proper.

> Under this change of circumstances, it is my sincere opinion that the Constitution ought to be revised, and that the first Congress meeting under it ought to prepare and recommend to the States for ratification, the most satisfactory provision for all essential rights, particularly the rights of Conscience in the fullest latitude, the freedom of press, trials by jury, security against general warrants etc. . . . [so as] to put the judiciary department into such a form as will render vexatious appeals impossible.[155]

As a member of the first Congress, Madison felt "bound in honor and duty" to fulfill this election pledge. Federalist members were inclined to delay "till the more pressing business is dispatched." [156] Having learned that the Antifederalists were eager to take the initiative and possibly promote substantive amendments damaging to national authority, Madison announced that on June 8, 1789, he would place the promised amendments before the House. From the list then submitted came the first ten amendments of the Constitution, including guarantees of freedom of speech, press, religion, petition, and assembly; safeguards against unreasonable search, seizure, and warrants of arrest. Besides the blanket provision that no person be deprived of life, liberty, or property without due process of law, Madison proposed specific protections for accused persons—the right to a speedy and public trial, the right to counsel, the right to be confronted with one's accusers, and to be protected against self-incrimination and against being placed twice in jeopardy for the same offense.

In piloting the proposed amendments through Congress, Madison stressed the very point Jefferson had earlier called to his attention as a glaring omission: "If they [the Bill of Rights] are incorporated into the constitution, independent tribunals of justice will consider themselves in a peculiar manner the guardians of those rights; they will be an impenetrable bulwark against every assumption of power in the legislative or executive; they will be naturally led to resist every encroachment upon rights expressly stipulated for in the constitution by the declaration of rights." [157] "The great object in view," according to the now converted Madison, "is to limit the power of government, by excepting out of the grant of power those cases in which the Government ought not to act, or to act only in a particular mode." [158]

Specific safeguards against government encroachment on individual rights, though of first importance, was not enough. Antifederalists had conjured up the image of the central government as a colossus, destined to swallow up or destroy the defenseless states. To quiet these fears, Madison included among the amendments submitted on June 8 the following: "The powers not delegated by this constitution, nor prohibited by it to the States, are reserved to the States respectively. . . ." [159] In explanation he said:

> I find from looking into the amendments proposed by the State conventions, that several are particularly anxious that it should be declared in the Constitution, that the powers not therein delegated should be reserved to the several States. Perhaps words which may define this more precisely than the whole of the instrument now does, may be considered as superfluous. I admit they may be deemed unnecessary; but there can be no harm in making such a declaration, if gentlemen will allow that the fact is as stated. I am sure I understand it so, and do therefore propose it. . . .[160]

On three occasions it was proposed that the word "expressly" be inserted before "delegated." Madison objected, "because it was impossible to confine a Government to the exercise of express powers; there must necessarily be admitted powers by implication, unless the constitution descended to recount every minutia. He remembered the word 'expressly' had been moved in the convention of Virginia, by the opponents to ratification, and, after full and fair discussion, was given up by them, and the system allowed to retain its present form." [161] Roger Sherman, concurring, observed that "corporate bodies are supposed to possess all powers incident to a corporate capacity, without being absolutely expressed." [162] Congressman Tucker, joined by Gerry, pressed for insertion of the word "expressly," but the proposal was defeated 17 to 32.[163]

Once again men of states rights persuasion were defeated in their attempt to draw a precise line limiting the national government with respect to an area considered free from federal control.

The unavailing struggle to give meaning to the Tenth Amendment underscores the conclusion that for many Antifederalists *states* rights weighed more heavily than their concern for *personal* rights.

Spurring the Antifederalist campaign was the unshakeable conviction that the proposed Constitution would enthrone a consolidated government, thereby rendering *state* protection of individual rights insecure. It seemed not unreasonable, as Spencer and Adams contended, that if state sovereignty in the new system could be adequately safeguarded, this would obviate, in effect, the need for a Bill of Rights. Thus, Adams had maintained that an amendment reserving to the states all power not expressly delegated to the new national government would be "a summary of a bill of rights. . . ." It would remove "a doubt which many have entertained respecting the matter," and would give "assurance that if any law made by the federal government shall be extended beyond the power granted by the proposed constitution, and inconsistent with the constitution of this state, it will be an error, and adjudged by the courts of law to be void. . . ." [164] Spencer, in North Carolina, had admitted, "It might not be so necessary to have a bill of rights in the government of the United States, if such means had not been made use of, as endanger a consolidation of all the states. . . ." [165]

Antifederalist motives are hard to disentangle. Persistent attempts to secure *states* rights seem consistent with their expressed concern for *individual* rights—given the logical connection between state power in the federal system and continued state protection of the rights of their citizens. Subsequent behavior, however, renders any desire to give them the benefit of the doubt at best gratuitous. The conclusion that states rights —regardless of individual rights—was the primary concern seems inescapable. Yates and Lansing, in their letter to Governor Clinton, strongly opposed the new "consolidated system"—however guarded it might be "by declarations of rights, or cautionary provisions. . . ." [166] As the struggle for a Bill of Rights reached its consummation in the first Congress, the word "amendments" came to mean different things to Federalists and Antifederalists. " 'Amendments' to Madison meant a bill of rights. To Clinton and Henry the word 'amendments' also connoted a weakening of the federal system in favor of the states on such all-important questions as direct taxation and the treaty-making power." [167] Madison had agreed to a Bill of Rights to protect *individual* liberties. He firmly opposed any amendments which might sap the energy of the new government.

Antifederalist response to the *kind* of amendments Madison sought— and finally procured—reveal the values they wished most to protect. William Grayson, writing Patrick Henry in June 1789, objected to Madi-

son's proposed amendments as greatly overemphasizing the protection of
personal rights at the expense of states rights. "Some gentlemen here
[in the first Congress] from motives of policy, have it in contemplation
to effect amendments which shall effect personal liberty alone, leaving
the great points of the judiciary, direct taxation, &c, to stand as they are;
. . . after this I presume many of the most sanguine expect to go on
coolly in sapping the independence of the state legislatures. . . ." [168]
Pierce Butler had the same low regard for the Bill of Rights. Instead of
"substantial amendments," Madison had proposed a "few *milk-and-water*
amendments . . . such as liberty of conscience, a free press, and one or
two general things already well secured." "I suppose it was done to keep
his promise with his constituents, to move for alterations," Butler speculated, "but if I am not greatly mistaken, he is not hearty in the cause of
amendments." [169]

As Madison's amendments emerged from the first Congress, the reaction
among Antifereralists was primarily disappointment. To Grayson the
new amendments were "so mutilated and gutted that in fact they are good
for nothing. . . ." [170] Patrick Henry, according to David Stuart, thought
"the single amendment proposed in our Convention [Virginia ratifying
convention], respecting direct taxes, worth all the rest." [171] Not even
Jefferson was entirely satisfied, but his concern had to do with minutia,
not fundamentals.[172]

The most bitter criticism came from Richard Henry Lee. Writing his
brother, Lee lamented the "much mutilated and enfeebled" amendments.
"It is too much the fashion now to look at the rights of the People, as
a Miser inspects a Security, to find a flaw." [173] Expanding on this theme,
Lee told Patrick Henry the next day how much he deplored "the idea
of subsequent amendments," a procedure "little better than putting one-
self to death first, in expectation that the doctor, who wished our destruction, would afterwards restore us to life." Personal rights had been
secured, but the "great points"—such as "the unlimited rights of taxation, and standing armies, remain as they were."

> The most essential danger from the present system arises, in my opinion,
> from its tendency to a consolidated government, instead of a union of Confed-
> erated States. . . . [T]herefore it becomes the friends of liberty to guard
> with perfect vigilance every right that belongs to the states, and to protest
> against every invasion of them, taking care always to procure as many pro-
> testing states as possible; this kind of vigilance will create caution, and
> establish such a mode of conduct as will create a system of precedent that
> will prevent a consolidative effect from taking place by slow but sure degrees.
> A sufficient number of legislatures cannot be got at present to agree in de-
> manding a convention, but I shall be very much mistaken indeed, if ere long
> a great sufficiency will not concur in this measure. . . . A careless reader
> would be apt to suppose that the amendments desired by the states had been

graciously granted, but when the thing done is compared with that desired, nothing can be more unlike. Some valuable rights are indeed declared, but the power to violate them to all intents and purposes remains unchanged.[174]

Lee and Grayson, the two senators from Virginia to the first Congress, summed up their opposition to the new amendments in reports to the Governor of Virginia and to the Speaker of the Virginia House of Representatives. They had hoped to be able to transmit "effectual Amendments" for ratification, "and it is with grief that we now send forward propositions inadequate to the purpose of real and substantial Amendments, and so far short of the wishes of our Country. . . ."[175] "It is impossible for us not to see the necessary tendency to consolidated empire in the natural operation of the Constitution, if no further amended than as now proposed," they wrote the Speaker of the House. "Such Amendments therefore as may secure against the annihilation of the state governments we devoutly wish to see adopted." The letter closed with the hope that an aroused demand by the states for a second convention might achieve that purpose.[176]

Jefferson thought he had divined what lay behind much of the Antifederalist drive. Clinton and Henry, among others, were "moving heaven and earth to have a new Convention to make capital changes," he wrote John Paul Jones in the spring of 1789. "But they will not succeed. There has been just opposition enough to produce probably further safeguards to liberty without touching the energy of the government. . . ."[177] And that is precisely the way it happened.

The campaign for a Bill of Rights had begun as a seemingly partisan move, a strategic maneuver, some believed, to defeat ratification. In the end the goals sought were generally accepted by all. "[S]ecurity for liberty," through a Bill of Rights, was demanded "by the general voice of America."[178] Fundamental maxims of a free society gained no greater moral sanctity by incorporation in our basic law. Yet a significant gain had been made. Rights formerly natural became civil. Individuals could thereafter look to courts for their protection; courts—thanks to the Antifederalists—could look to the Constitution for a standard.

Notes ⚜

1. C. M. Kenyon, "Men of Little Faith: The Anti-Federalists on the Nature of Representation," *William and Mary Quarterly*, 3rd Series, 12 (1955). See, in this connection, Forrest McDonald, "The Anti-Federalists, 1781-1789," *Wisconsin Magazine of History* (Spring, 1963) 46, 206-14. The alignment of delegates was so confused and confusing that the difficulty in arriving at a satisfactory label is understandable. Large-state delegates are sometimes thought of as nationalists, those from small states as sympathetic with states rights. The lineup was not that simple. The delegate

closest to Hamilton, for example, was Read from tiny Delaware. Gerry of Massachusetts, on the other hand, was an Antifederalist. Nor were delegates of whatever
persuasion always simon pure. In the Convention, Mason, though a strong states
rights man, endorsed the provision for ratification by the people rather than by
state legislatures. Edmund Randolph symbolizes the confusion—a sponsor of the
nationalist plan in Philadelphia, a nonsigner of the Convention's handiwork, and
a supporter of ratification in Virginia.

2. Jonathan Elliot, ed., *The Debates in the Several State Conventions on the Adoption
   of the Federal Constitution* (Washington, D.C., 1836), II, 372ff. Cited hereafter as
   Elliot.
3. *Ibid.*, II, 372-77.
4. Paul Leicester Ford, *Essays on the Constitution of the United States* (Brooklyn,
   N.Y., 1892), p. 392. Cited hereafter as Ford, *Essays.*
5. Elliot, III, 72.
6. *Ibid.*, p. 54.
7. Elliot, II, 144.
8. Elliot, IV, 53.
9. *Ibid.*, p. 54.
10. John Bach McMaster and Frederick D. Stone, eds., *Pennsylvania and the Federal
    Constitution, 1787-1788.* Published by The Historical Society of Pennsylvania (1888),
    pp. 230-31. Hereafter referred to as McMaster and Stone.
11. *Ibid.*, p. 249.   12. *Ibid.*, p. 235.
13. *Ibid.*, pp. 300-301.   14. *Ibid.*, pp. 301-2.
15. *Ibid.*, p. 316.   16. *Ibid.*, p. 317.
17. *Ibid.*, p. 318.   18. *Ibid.*, p. 321.
19. *Ibid.*, p. 341.
20. H. A. Cushing, ed., *The Writings of Samuel Adams* (New York: Putnam's, 1908), IV,
    324.
21. Elliot, III, 29.
22. Paul Leicester Ford, ed., *Pamphlets on the Constitution of the United States*
    (Brooklyn, N.Y., 1888), p. 280. Hereafter referred to as Ford, *Pamphlets.*
23. Elliot, III, 82.
24. McMaster and Stone, p. 302. See also pp. 322 and 389ff., where Wilson, pressing
    Antifederalists for a definition, gives a similar answer.
25. *Ibid.*, p. 322.
26. Elliot, II, 334-36.
27. Elliot, III, 114. See also *The Federalist*, No. 39.
28. Elliot, III, 405.   29. *Ibid.*, pp. 179-80.
30. McMaster and Stone, p. 282.   31. *Ibid.*, p. 267; emphasis added.
32. Elliot, II, 82-83.   33. *Ibid.*, p. 315.
34. *Ibid.*, p. 321.   35. *Ibid.*, pp. 316-21.
36. *Ibid.*, p. 301.   37. McMaster and Stone, p. 297.
38. *Ibid.*, pp. 343-44.   39. *Ibid.*, p. 394.
40. General Thompson, Massachusetts, in Elliot, II, 99-100.
41. Max Farrand, ed., *The Records of the Federal Convention* (New Haven, Conn:
    Yale University Press, 1911), II, 587. Cited hereafter as Farrand.
42. "Madison to Jefferson," Oct. 24, 1787. Gaillard Hunt, ed., *The Writings of James
    Madison* (New York: Putnam's, 1904), V, 34.
43. Elliot, II, 408-9.
44. Madison to Washington, Oct. 18, 1787, in Farrand, III, 130.
45. Elliot, II, 409.
46. All quotations in this paragraph from Farrand, II, 375-76; emphasis added.
47. *Ibid.*, pp. 378-79.
48. Farrand, I, 453, June 28, from Yates.
49. *Ibid.*, p. 492, June 30.

50. *Ibid.*, pp. 492-93, June 30; emphasis added except for "paper security."
51. Farrand, II, 76.
52. Gouverneur Morris to Timothy Pickering, in Congress, Morrisania, December 22, 1814; cited in Elliot, I, 549; emphasis added.
53. Farrand, II, 588, Sept. 12.
54. *Ibid.*, p. 633, Sept. 15.
55. Madison to Jefferson, Feb. 19, 1788, in Hunt, *Madison*, V, 102.
56. Elliot, III, 80.
57. Elliot, IV, 321.
58. Henry, in Elliot, III, 72.
59. *Ibid.*, p. 413.
60. Farrand, III, 290.
61. Elliot, III, 369.
62. Elliot, I, 533.
63. Elliot, III, 403.
64. Ford, *Pamphlets*, p. 312.
65. McMaster and Stone, p. 580.
66. Ford, *Pamphlets*, pp. 316-17.
67. Ford, *Essays*, pp. 297-314.
68. Elliot, III, 260.
69. Elliot, IV, 184-85. For similar Federalist views, see McKean, Penna., McMaster and Stone, p. 277, and Wilson, *ibid.*, p. 354; see also Johnston, N.C., in Elliot, IV, 191-92.
70. Elliot, III, 405.
71. McMaster and Stone, p. 308.
72. *Ibid.*, p. 330.
73. *Ibid.*, p. 467; emphasis added to "by other sections."
74. Elliot, IV, 194.
75. Elliot, IV, 409.
76. McMaster and Stone, p. 116.
77. *Ibid.*, pp. 253-54.
78. *Ibid.*, p. 314.
79. Elliot, III, 565.
80. *Ibid.*, p. 560.
81. McMaster and Stone, pp. 286-87.
82. *Ibid.*, p. 255.
83. *Ibid.*, p. 291.
84. Ford, *Pamphlets*, p. 314.
85. Elliot, II, 373.
86. Elliot, III, 161-62; emphasis added.
87. Elliot, II, 322.
88. McMaster and Stone, pp. 353-54.
89. Hunt, *Madison*, V, 272.
90. Elliot, II, 103-5.
91. *Ibid.*, p. 166.
92. Elliot, III, 409.
93. *Ibid.*, p. 431.
94. *Ibid.*, pp. 472-73.
95. Elliot, II, 198.
96. Ford, *Pamphlets*, p. 234.
97. McMaster and Stone, p. 304.
98. Elliot, III, 501-3 *passim*.
99. Elliot, II, 255; see also pp. 300-301.
100. *Ibid.*, pp. 82-83.
101. Elliot, III, 511.
102. *Ibid.*, pp. 174-75.
103. *Ibid.*, p. 174.
104. *Ibid.*, p. 511.
105. *Ibid.*, p. 523.
106. *Ibid.*, p. 491.
107. Elliot, II, 167.
108. Ford, *Essays*, p. 95.
109. Elliot, I, 533.
110. Madison to Washington, Oct. 18, 1787, in Farrand, III, 130.
111. McMaster and Stone, pp. 250-51.
112. *Ibid.*, p. 255.
113. *The Federalist*, No. 59, p. 302.
114. James Monroe's characterization of the projected Bill of Rights in Elliot, III (1836), 219.
115. Elliot, II (1836), 254.
116. Elliot, III (1836), 303.
117. *West Virginia Board of Education* v. *Barnette*, 319 U.S. 624 (1943), 636-37.
118. George Bancroft, *History of the Formation of the Constitution of the United States of America* (New York: Appleton, 1889), II, 257.
119. Samuel Adams to Richard Henry Lee, Dec. 3, 1787, in H. A. Cushing, ed., *The Writings of Samuel Adams* (New York: Putnam's 1908), IV, 325.
120. Elliot, II (1836), 179.
121. James Madison to George Washington, Feb. 15, 1788, in Hunt, *Madison*, V, 100.
122. *Ibid.*

123. James Madison to Governor Randolph, April 10, 1788, in *ibid.*, p. 119.
124. Moses Ames in Massachusetts, in Elliot, II (1836), 161.
125. Elliot, III (1836), 131.
126. "Were I in America, I would advocate it warmly till nine should have adopted, and then as warmly take the other side to convince the remaining four that they ought not to come into it till the declaration of rights is annexed to it. By this means we should secure all the good of it, and procure so respectable an opposition as would induce the accepting states to offer a bill of rights." To W. Smith, Feb. 2, 1788, in *The Papers of Thomas Jefferson*, Julian P. Boyd, ed., XII, 558. Cited hereafter as Boyd.
127. To Edward Carrington, May 27, 1788, in Boyd, XIII, 208.
128. To William Carmichael, June 3, 1788, in Boyd, XII, 232.
129. James Madison to Thomas Jefferson, Feb. 19, 1788, in Hunt, *Madison*, V, 103.
130. Edward Carrington to James Madison, Jan. 18, 1788, in *Documentary History of the Constitution of the United States* (Washington, D.C.: Department of State, 1905), IV, 447.
131. Elliot, III (1836), 531, 532.
132. Madison to Rufus King, June 22, 1788, in King, *Life and Correspondence of Rufus King*, I, 337.
133. Elliot, III (1836), 587.
134. Hamilton to Madison, July 8, 1788, in *Documentary History of the Constitution*, IV, 768.
135. Bancroft, II, 346.
136. Order, dates, and votes on ratification:

Delaware	December 7, 1787;	yeas, 30 (unanimous).
Pennsylvania . .	December 12, 1787;	yeas, 46; nays, 23.
New Jersey . . .	December 18, 1787;	yeas, 38 (unanimous).
Georgia . . .	January 2, 1788;	yeas, 26 (unanimous).
Connecticut . . .	January 9, 1788;	yeas, 128; nays, 40.
Massachusetts . .	February 6, 1788;	yeas, 187; nays, 168.
Maryland . . .	April 28, 1788;	yeas, 63; nays 11.
South Carolina . .	May 23, 1788;	yeas, 149; nays, 73.
New Hampshire .	June 21, 1788;	yeas, 57; nays, 47.
Virginia	June 26, 1788;	yeas, 89; nays, 79.
New York . . .	July 26, 1788;	yeas, 30; nays, 27.
North Carolina .	November 21, 1789;	yeas, 194; nays, 77.
Rhode Island . .	May 29, 1790;	yeas, 34; nays, 32.

137. As early as the spring of 1787, Jefferson in his *Notes on Virginia* had implied the connection between judicial review and a Bill of Rights as a remedy "to render unnecessary an appeal to the people, or in other words a rebellion, on every infraction of their rights. . . ." Quoted in Mason, *Free Government in the Making*, p. 169.
138. Thomas Jefferson to James Madison, March 15, 1789. Boyd XIV 659-61 *passim*.
139. Hunt, *Madison*, V, 273.
140. James Madison to Mr. Eve, Jan. 2, 1789. *Ibid.*, p. 320.
141. James Madison to Thomas Jefferson, Oct. 17, 1788. *Ibid.*, pp. 271-73 *passim*.
142. Thomas Jefferson to Admiral Paul Jones, March 23, 1789. Boyd XIV 688.
143. See Edward P. Smith, "The Movement towards a Second Constitutional Convention in 1788," in J. Franklin Jameson, *Essays in the Constitutional History of the United States in the Formative Period, 1775-1789* (Boston: Houghton, Mifflin, 1889), pp. 46-115.
144. To John Mason, Sept. 2, 1788, in Rutland, p. 181.
145. To Benjamin Lincoln, Aug. 28, 1788, in Fitzpatrick, ed., *Writings of Washington*, XXX, 63.

146. To Jefferson, April 22, 1788, in Boyd, XIII, 98-99.
147. Madison to Washington, Aug. 24, 1788, in *Documentary History of the Constitution*, V, 29.
148. To Jefferson, Aug. 10, 1788, in Boyd, XIII, 497-98.
149. See Document 5, p. 171.
150. *Ibid.*
151. *Ibid.*
152. *Ibid.*
153. Madison to Jefferson, Dec. 12, 1788, in Boyd, XIV, 352.
154. Madison to Jefferson, March 29, 1789, in Boyd, XV, 6-7.
155. James Madison to Mr. Eve, Jan. 2, 1789, in Hunt, *Madison*, V, 320.
156. *Annals of Congress*, I, First Cong., First sess., June 8, 1789 (Washington, D.C., 1834), 445.
157. *Ibid.*, I, 457. See also pp. 454-55.
158. *Ibid.*, p. 453.
159. *Ibid.*
160. See Document 5, p. 180.
161. *Annals of Congress*, I, 790.
162. *Ibid.*
163. *Ibid.*, p. 797.
164. Elliot, II, 142.
165. Elliot, IV, 150.
166. Farrand, III, 246.
167. Robert Allen Rutland, *The Birth of the Bill of Rights, 1776-1791* (Chapel Hill, N.C.: University of North Carolina Press, 1955), pp. 94-95.
168. Grayson to Henry, June 12, 1789, in William Wirt Henry, *Patrick Henry—Life, Correspondence and Speeches* (New York: Charles Scribner's Sons, 1891), III, 391.
169. Pierce Butler to James Iredell, Aug. 11, 1789, in Griffith J. McRee, *Life and Correspondence of James Iredell* (New York: D. Appleton and Company, 1857), II, 265.
170. Grayson to Henry, Sept. 29, 1789, in Henry, *Patrick Henry*, III, 406.
171. David Stuart to George Washington, Sept. 12, 1789, in *Documentary History of the Constitution*, V, 205.
172. Jefferson to Madison, Aug. 28, 1789, in Boyd, XV, 367-68.
173. R. H. Lee to Francis Lightfoot Lee, Sept. 13, 1789, in James Curtis Ballagh, ed., *The Letters of Richard Henry Lee* (New York: The Macmillan Company, 1914), II, 500.
174. Lee to Patrick Henry, Sept. 14, 1789, in *ibid.*, II, 501-3.
175. R. H. Lee and William Grayson to the Governor of Virginia, Sept. 28, 1789, in *Documentary History of the Constitution*, V, 216.
176. Lee and Grayson to the Speaker of the House of Representatives in Virginia, Sept. 28, 1789, in *ibid.*, V, 217-18.
177. Jefferson to John Paul Jones, March 23, 1789, in Boyd, XIV, 689.
178. *Ibid.*, p. 688.

Leonard Levy seems inclined to think of the Bill of Rights as an historical accident, a sham battle, an unwanted victory. He writes: ". . . Indeed the history of the framing and ratification of the First Amendment and the other nine scarcely manifests a passion on the part of anyone concerned with the process. Considering its immediate background, our precious Bill of Rights was in the main the chance result of certain Federalists having been reluctantly forced to capitalize for their own cause the propaganda that had been originated in vain by the Anti-Federalists for ulterior purposes. Thus the party that had first opposed a Bill of Rights inadvertently wound up with the responsibility of its framing and ratification, while the party that had at first professedly wanted it discovered too late that its framing and ratification were not only embarrassing but inexpedient." Leonard Levy, *Legacy of Suppression* (Cambridge, Mass.: Harvard University Press, 1960), p. 233.

From a variety of motives, Antifederalists advocated a Bill of Rights as early as the final days of the Philadelphia Convention. In the state-ratifying conventions, passion was not, as we have seen, in short supply. From Paris, Jefferson's exertions were both passionate and persistent. His influence on Madison—the prime mover in the first Congress—was incalculable. Federalists and Antifederalists did, in fact, switch positions. Madison himself switched. This not unusual political phenomenon does not dwarf the significance of the achievement.

Documents 🌿

LEADING SPOKESMEN

1 · Robert Yates and John Lansing · *Letter to Governor Clinton of New York* · 1787

Robert Yates and John Lansing of New York left the Convention on July 10, convinced that their very presence among delegates bent on ignoring the Articles of Confederation violated their instructions. Their letter to Governor Clinton of New York states reasons for quitting the Convention.

It is with the sincerest concern we observe, that, in the prosecution of the important objects of our mission, we have been reduced to the disagreeable alternative, of either exceeding the powers delegated to us, and giving assent to measures which we conceive destructive to the political happiness of the citizens of the United States, or opposing our opinions to that of a body of respectable men, to whom those citizens had given the most unequivocal proofs of confidence.—Thus circumstanced, under these impressions, to have hesitated, would have been to be culpable; we, therefore, gave the principles of the constitution, which has received the sanction of a majority of the convention, our decided and unreserved dissent; but we must candidly confess, that we should have been equally opposed to any system however modified, which had in object the consolidation of the United States into one government.

We beg leave, briefly, to state some cogent reasons which, among others, influenced us to decide against a consolidation of the state. These are reducible into two heads:

1st. The limited and well defined powers under which we acted, and which could not, on any possible construction, embrace an idea of such magnitude, as to assent to a general constitution, in subversion of that of the state.

2d. A conviction of the impracticability of establishing a general government, pervading every part of the United States, and extending essential benefits to all.

Our powers were explicit, and confined to the sole and express pur-

Elliot, I, 516-18.

pose of revising the articles of confederation, and reporting such alterations and provisions therein, as should render the federal constitution
adequate to the exigencies of government, and the preservation of the
union.

From these expressions, we were led to believe, that a system of consolidated government could not in the remotest degree, have been in
contemplation of the legislature of this state, for that so important a
trust, as the adopting measures which tended to deprive the state government of its most essential rights of sovereignty, and to place it in a de-
pendant situation, could not have been confided by implication; and the
circumstances, that the acts of the convention were to receive a state
approbation in the last resort, forcibly corroborated the opinion, that
our powers could not involve the subversion of a constitution, which
being immediately derived from the people, could only be abolished by
their express consent and not by a legislature, possessing authority vested
in them for its preservation. Nor could we suppose, that if it had been
the intention of the legislature, to abrogate the existing confederation,
they would, in such pointed terms, have directed the attention of their
delegates to the revision and amendment of it, in total exclusion of every
other idea.

Reasoning in this manner, we were of opinion, that the leading feature
of every amendment, ought to be the preservation of the individual
states, in their uncontrolled constitutional rights, and that in reserving
these, a mode might have been devised of granting to the confederacy,
the moneys arising from a general system of revenue; the power of regulating commerce, and enforcing the observance of foreign treaties and
other necessary matters of less moment.

Exclusive of our objections originating from the want of power, we
entertained an opinion, that a general government, however guarded by
declarations of rights, or cautionary provisions, must unavoidably, in a
short time, be productive of the destruction of the civil liberty of such
citizens who could be effectually coerced by it; by reason of the extensive
territory of the United States, the dispersed situation of its inhabitants
and the insuperable difficulty of controlling or counteracting the views
of a set of men (however unconstitutional and oppressive their acts might
be) possessed of all the powers of government; and who from their re-
moteness from their constituents and necessary permanency of office,
could not be supposed to be uniformly actuated by an attention to their
welfare and happiness; that however wise and energetic the principles
of the general government might be, the extremities of the United States
could not be kept in due submission and obedience to its laws, at the
distance of many hundred miles from the seat of government; that if the
general legislature was composed of so numerous a body of men, as to
represent the interests of all the inhabitants of the United States, in the
usual and true ideas of representation, the expense of supporting it

would become intolerably burthensome and that if a few only were vested with a power of legislation, the interests of a great majority of the inhabitants of the United States, must necessarily be unknown; or if known, even in the first stages of the operations of the new government, unattended to.

These reasons were, in our opinion, conclusive against any system of consolidated government. . . .

We were not present at the completion of the new constitution; but before we left the convention, its principles were so well established, as to convince us, that no alteration was to be expected to conform it to our ideas of expediency and safety. . . .

2 • Robert Yates • *"Letters of Brutus"* • 1788

"You have given us a good Constitution," a friend told Gouverneur Morris soon after the Convention adjourned. "That depends," Morris answered soberly, "on how it is construed." Prior to the Constitution's adoption, no one, Federalist or Antifederalist, so accurately forecast the judicial construction of the Constitution as did Robert Yates in the "Letters of Brutus." Yates took judicial review for granted. The Supreme Court, he predicted, could be expected to extend national power, including its own, to unconscionable limits, and "abolish entirely the State governments." Later, Antifederalists John Taylor and Hugh Legaré interpreted the constitutional jurisprudence of Chief Justice John Marshall as a complete vindication of Yates' words.*

To allay the fears aroused by Yates' ominous forecast, Hamilton wrote essays 78 and 81 of The Federalist. *Said he: "Some perplexity respecting the rights of courts to pronounce legislative acts void, because, contrary to the Constitution, has arisen from an imagination that the doctrine [judicial review] would imply a superiority of the judiciary to the legislative power." In combatting this proposition, Hamilton fused reason and magic, concluding: "Nor does this conclusion [that the Constitution ought to be preferred to a statute] by any means suppose a superiority of the judicial to the legislative power. It only supposes that the power of the people is superior to both [court and legislature]; and that the will of the legislature, declared in statutes, stands in opposition to that of the people declared in the Constitution, the judges ought to be governed by the latter rather than by the former."*

BRUTUS, No. XI • January 31, 1788

. . . Much has been said and written upon the subject of this new system on both sides, but I have not met with any writer, who has discussed the judicial powers with any degree of accuracy. And yet it is obvious, that

Published in the *New York Journal and Weekly Register*. Reprinted in full in E. S. Corwin, *Court over Constitution* (Princeton, N.J.: Princeton University Press, 1938), Appendix, pp. 231-62.

we can form but very imperfect ideas of the manner in which this government will work, or the effect it will have in changing the internal police and mode of distributing justice at present subsisting in the respective states, without a thorough investigation of the powers of the judiciary and of the manner in which they will operate. This government is a complete system, not only for making, but for executing laws. And the courts of law, which will be constituted by it, are not only to decide upon the constitution and the laws made in pursuance of it, but by officers subordinate to them to execute all their decisions. The real effect of this system of government, will therefore be brought home to the feelings of the people, through the medium of the judicial power. It is, moreover, of great importance, to examine with care the nature and extent of the judicial power, because those who are to be vested with it, are to be placed in a situation altogether unprecedented in a free country. They are to be rendered totally independent, both of the people and the legislature, both with respect to their offices and salaries. No errors they may commit can be corrected by any power above them, if any such power there be, nor can they be removed from office for making ever so many erroneous adjudications.

The only causes for which they can be displaced, is, conviction of treason, bribery, and high crimes and misdemeanors.

This part of the plan is so modelled, as to authorize the courts, not only to carry into execution the powers expressly given, but where these are wanting or ambiguously expressed, to supply what is wanting by their own decisions. . . .

They [the courts] will give the sense of every article of the constitution, that may from time to time come before them. And in their decisions they will not confine themselves to any fixed or established rules, but will determine, according to what appears to them, the reason and spirit of the constitution. The opinions of the supreme court, whatever they may be, will have the force of law; because there is no power provided in the constitution, that can correct their errors, or controul their adjudications. From this court there is no appeal. And I conceive the legislature themselves, cannot set aside a judgment of this court, because they are authorized by the constitution to decide in the last resort. The legislature must be controuled by the constitution, and not the constitution by them. They have therefore no more right to set aside any judgment pronounced upon the construction of the constitution, than they have to take from the president, the chief command of the army and navy, and commit it to some other person. The reason is plain; the judicial and executive derive their authority from the same source, that the legislature do theirs; and therefore in all cases, where the constitution does not make the one responsible to, or controulable by the other, they are altogether independent of each other.

The judicial power will operate to effect, in the most certain, but yet silent and imperceptible manner, what is evidently the tendency of the constitution:—I mean, an entire subversion of the legislative, executive and judicial powers of the individual states. Every adjudication of the supreme court, on any question that may arise upon the nature and extent of the general government, will affect the limits of the state jurisdiction. In proportion as the former enlarge the exercise of their powers, will that of the latter be restricted.

That the judicial power of the United States, will lean strongly in favour of the general government, and will give such an explanation to the constitution, as will favour an extension of its jurisdiction, is very evident from a variety of considerations:

1st. The constitution itself strongly countenances such a mode of construction. Most of the articles in this system, which convey powers of any considerable importance, are conceived in general and indefinite terms, which are either equivocal, ambiguous, or which require long definitions to unfold the extent of their meaning. The two most important powers committed to any government, those of raising money, and of raising and keeping up troops, have already been considered, and shewn to be unlimited by anything but the discretion of the legislature. The clause which vests the power to pass all laws which are proper and necessary, to carry the powers given into execution, it has been shewn, leaves the legislature at liberty, to do every thing, which in their judgment is best. It is said, I know, that this clause confers no power on the legislature, which they would not have had without it—though I believe this is not the fact, yet, admitting it to be, it implies that the constitution is not to receive an explanation strictly, according to its letter; but more power is implied than is expressed. And this clause, if it is to be considered, as explanatory of the extent of the powers given, rather than giving a new power, is to be understood as declaring, that in construing any of the articles conveying power, the spirit, intent and design of the clause, should be attended to, as well as the words in their common acceptation.

This constitution gives sufficient colour for adopting an equitable construction, if we consider the great end and design it professedly has in view—this appears from its preamble to be, "to form a more perfect union, establish justice, insure domestic tranquility, provide for the common defence, promote the general welfare, and secure the blessings of liberty to ourselves and posterity." The design of this system is here expressed, and it is proper to give such a meaning to the various parts, as will best promote the accomplishment of the end; this idea suggests itself naturally upon reading the preamble, and will countenance the court in giving the several articles such a sense, as will the most effectually promote the ends the constitution had in view—how this manner of explaining the constitution will operate in practice, shall be the subject of future enquiry.

2d. Not only will the constitution justify the courts in inclining to this mode of explaining it, but they will be interested in using this latitude of interpretation. Every body of men invested with office are tenacious of power; they feel interested, and hence it has become a kind of maxim, to hand down their offices, with all its rights and privileges, unimpaired to their successors; the same principle will influence them to extend their power, and increase their rights; this of itself will operate strongly upon the courts to give such a meaning to the constitution in all cases where it can possibly be done, as will enlarge the sphere of their own authority. Every extension of the power of the general legislature, as well as of the judicial powers, will increase the powers of the courts; and the dignity and importance of the judges, will be in proportion to the extent and magnitude of the powers they exercise. I add, it is highly probable that emolument of the judges will be increased, with the increase of the business they will have to transact and its importance. From these considerations the judges will be interested to extend the powers of the courts, and to construe the constitution as much as possible, in such a way as to favour it; and that they will do it, appears probable.

3d. Because they will have a [precedent] to plead, to justify them in it. It is well known, that the courts in England, have by their own authority, extended their jurisdiction far beyond the limits set them in their original institution, and by the laws of the land. . . .

When the courts will have a [precedent] before them of a court which extended its jurisdiction in opposition to an act of the legislature, is it not to be expected that they will extend theirs, especially when there is nothing in the constitution expressly against it? and they are authorized to construe its meaning, and are not under any controul?

This power in the judicial, will enable them to mould the government, into almost any shape they please. . . .

BRUTUS, No. XII • February 14, 1788

. . . To discover the spirit of the constitution, it is of the first importance to attend to the principal ends and designs it has in view. These are expressed in the preamble. . . . If the end of the government is to be learned from these words, which are clearly designed to declare it, it is obvious it has in view every object which is embraced by any government. The preservation of internal peace—the due administration of justice—and to provide for the defence of the community, seems to include all the objects of government; but if they do not, they are certainly comprehended in the words, "to provide for the general welfare." If it be further considered, that this constitution, if it is ratified, will not be a compact entered into by states, in their corporate capacities, but an agreement of the people of the United States, as one great body politic, no doubt can remain, but that the great end of the constitution, if it is to be collected from the preamble, in which its end is declared, is to constitute a government which is to extend to every case for which any government is instituted, whether external or internal. The courts, therefore, will establish this as a principle in expounding the constitution, and will give every part of it such an explanation, as will give latitude to every department under it, to take cognizance of every matter, not only that affects the general and national concerns of the union, but also of such as relate to the administration of private justice, and to regulating the internal and local affairs of the different parts.

Such a rule of exposition is not only consistent with the general spirit of the preamble, but it will stand confirmed by considering more minutely the different clauses of it.

The first object declared to be in view is, "To form a perfect union." It is to be observed, it is not an union of states or bodies corporate; had this been the case the existence of the state governments, might have been secured. But it is a union of the people of the United States considered as one body, who are to ratify this constitution, if it is adopted. Now to make a union of this kind perfect, it is necessary to abolish all inferior governments, and to give the general one compleat legislative, executive and judicial powers to every purpose. The courts there will establish it as a rule in explaining the constitution. To give it such a construction as will best tend to perfect the union or take from the state governments every power of either making or executing laws. The second object is "to establish justice." This must include not only the idea of instituting the rule of justice, or of making laws which shall be the measure or rule of right, but also of providing for the application of this rule or of administering justice under it. And under this the courts will in their decisions extend the power of the government to all cases they possibly can, or otherwise they will be restricted in doing what appears to be the intent of the constitution they should do, to wit, pass laws and provide for the execution of them, for the general distribution of justice between man and man. Another end declared is "to insure domestic tranquility." This comprehends a provision against all private breaches of the peace, as well as against all public commotions or general insurrections; and to attain the object of this clause fully, the government must exercise the power of passing laws on these subjects, as well as of appointing magistrates with authority to execute them. And the courts will adopt these ideas in their expositions. I might proceed to the other clause, in the preamble, and it would appear by a consideration of all of them separately, as it does by taking them together, that if the spirit of this system is to be known from its declared end and design in the preamble, its spirit is to subvert and abolish all the powers of the state government, and to embrace every object to which any government extends.

As it sets out in the preamble with this declared intention, so it proceeds in the different parts with the same idea. Any person, who will peruse the 8th section with attention, in which most of the powers are enumerated, will perceive that they either expressly or by implication extend to almost every thing about which any legislative power can be employed. But if this equitable mode of construction is applied to this part of the constitution; nothing can stand before it.

This will certainly give the first clause in that article a construction which I confess I think the most natural and grammatical one, to authorize the Congress to do any thing which in their judgment will tend to provide for the general welfare, and this amounts to the same thing as general and unlimited powers of legislation in all cases.

BRUTUS, No. XV · March 20, 1788

I said in my last number, that the supreme court under this constitution would be exalted above all other powers in the government, and subject to no control. The business of this paper will be to illustrate this, and to shew the danger that will result from it. I question whether the world ever saw, in any period of it, a court of justice invested with such immense powers, and yet placed in a situation so little responsible. . . .

The framers of this constitution appear to have followed that of the British, in rendering the judges independent, by granting them their offices during good behavior, without following the constitution of England, in instituting a tribunal in which their errors may be corrected; and without adverting to this, that the judicial under this system have a power which is above the legislative, and which indeed transcends any power before given to a judicial by any free government under heaven.

I do not object to the judges holding their commissions during good behaviour. I suppose it a proper provision provided they were made properly responsible. But I say, this system has followed the English government in this, while it has departed from almost every other principle of their jurisprudence, under the idea, of rendering the judges independent; which, in the British constitution, means no more than that they hold their places during good behaviour, and have fixed salaries, they have made the judges *independent,* in the fullest sense of the word. There is no power above them, to controul any of their decisions. There is no authority that can remove them, and they cannot be controuled by the laws of the legislature. In short, they are independent of the people, of the legislature, and of every power under heaven. Men placed in this situation will generally soon feel themselves independent of heaven itself. . . .

The supreme court then have a right, independent of the legislature, to give a construction of the constitution and every part of it, and there is no power provided in this system to correct their construction or do it away. If, therefore, the legislature pass any laws, inconsistent with the sense the judges put upon the constitution, they will declare it void; and therefore in this respect their power is superior to that of the legislature. . . .

I have, in the course of my observation on this constitution, affirmed and endeavored to shew, that it was calculated to abolish entirely the state governments, and to melt down the states into one entire government, for every purpose as well internal and local, as external and national. In this opinion the opposers of the system have generally agreed—and this has been uniformly denied by its advocates in public. Some individuals indeed, among them, will confess, that it has this tendency, and scruple not to say, it is what they wish; and I will venture to predict, without the spirit of prophecy, that if it is adoption without amendments, or some such precautions as will ensure amendments immediately after its adoption, that the same gentlemen who have employed their talents and abilities with such success to influence the public mind to adopt this plan, will employ the same to persuade the people, that it will be for their good to abolish the state governments as useless and burdensome.

Perhaps nothing could have been better conceived to facilitate the abolition of the state government than the constitution of the judicial. They will be able to extend the limits of the general government gradually, and by insensible degrees, and to accommodate themselves to the temper of the people. . . .

Had the construction of the constitution been left with the legislature, they would have explained it at their peril; if they exceed their powers, or sought to find, in the spirit of the constitution, more than was expressed in the letter, the people from whom they derived their power could remove them, and do themselves right; and indeed I can see no other remedy that the people can have against their rulers for encroachments of this nature. A constitution is a compact of a people with their rulers; if the rulers break the compact, the people have a right and ought to remove them and do themselves justice; but in order to enable them to do this with the greater facility, those whom the people chuse at stated periods, should have the power in the last resort to determine the sense of the compact; if they determine contrary to the understanding of the people, an appeal will lie to the people at the period when the rulers are to be elected, and they will have it in their power to remedy the evil; but when this power is lodged in the hands of men independent of the people, and of their representatives, and who are not, constitutionally, accountable for their opinions, no way is left to controul them but *with a high hand and an outstretched arm.*

3 • Luther Martin • *"Genuine Information"* • 1787

Luther Martin, later known as "the bulldog of Federalism," was the leading Antifederalist in Maryland. This is a portion of his "Genuine In-

Jonathan Elliot, ed., *The Debates in the Several State Conventions on the Adoption of the Federal Constitution* (Washington, D.C.: 1836), I, pp. 430, 436-37.

*formation . . . Relative to the Proceedings of the General Convention,"
delivered to the Legislature of the State of Maryland.*

By the principles of the American revolution arbitrary power may,
and ought to be resisted even by arms if necessary. The time may come
when it shall be the duty of a state, in order to preserve itself from the
oppression of the general government, to have recourse to the sword. In
which case the proposed form of government declares, that the state and
every one of its citizens who act under its authority, are guilty of a direct
act of treason; reducing by this provision the different states to this alternative, that they must tamely and passively yield to despotism, or
their citizens must oppose it at the hazard of the halter if unsuccessful,
and reducing the citizens of the state which shall take arms, to a situation in which they must be exposed to punishment, let them act as they
will, since if they obey the authority of their state government, they will
be *guilty of treason against the United States,* if they join the general
government they will be guilty of treason against their own state. . . .

I was of opinion, that the states considered as states, in their political
capacity, are the members of a federal government; that the states in
their political capacity, or as sovereignties, are entitled, and *only entitled*
originally to agree upon the form of, and submit themselves to, a federal
government, and afterwards by mutual consent to dissolve or alter it.
That every thing which relates to the formation, the dissolution or the
alteration of a federal government over states equally free, sovereign
and independent, is the peculiar province of the state in their *sovereign*
or *political* capacity, in the same manner as what relates to forming alliances or treaties of peace, amity or commerce, and that the people at
large in their individual capacity, have no more right to interfere in the
one case than in the other: That according to these principles we originally acted in forming our confederation; it was the states as states, by
their representatives in Congress, that formed the articles of confederation; it was the states as states, by their legislatures, who ratified those
articles, and it was there established and provided, that the states as
states, that is, by their legislatures, should agree to any alterations that
should hereafter be proposed in the federal government, before they
should be binding, and any alterations agreed to any manner cannot re-
lease the states from the obligation they are under to each other by virtue
of the original articles of confederation. The people of the different
states never made any objection to the manner the articles of confederation were formed or ratified, or to the mode by which alterations were to
be made in that government, with the rights of their respective states they
wished not to interfere. Nor do I believe the people in their individual
capacity, would ever have expected or desired to have appealed to on the
present occasion, in violation of the rights of their respective states, if the
favorers of the proposed constitution, imagining they had a better chance

of forcing it to be adopted by a hasty appeal to the people at large, who could not be so good judges of the dangerous consequence, had not insisted upon this mode. Nor do these positions in the least interfere with the principle, that all power originates from the people, because when once the people have *exercised their power,* in establishing and forming themselves into a *state government,* it never devolves back to them, nor have they a right to resume or again to exercise that power until such events take place as will amount to a dissolution of their state government. And it is an established principle that a dissolution or alteration of a federal government doth not dissolve the state governments which compose it. It was also my opinion, that upon principles of sound policy, the agreement or disagreement to the proposed system, ought to have been by the state legislatures, in which case, let the event have been what it would, there would have been but little prospect of the public peace being disturbed thereby. Whereas, the attempt to force down this system, although Congress and the respective state legislatures should disapprove, by appealing to the people, and to procure its establishment in a manner totally unconstitutional, has a tendency to set the state governments and their subjects at variance with each other—to lessen the obligations of government—*to weaken the bands of society*—to introduce *anarchy* and *confusion*—and to light the torch of discord and civil war throughout this continent. All these considerations weighed with me most forcibly against giving my assent to the mode by which it is resolved by this system is to be ratified, and were urged by me in opposition to the measure.

4 • Luther Martin • *"Letters"* • March 21, 1788

. . . With respect to a bill of rights, had the government been formed upon principles truly federal, as I wished it, legislating over and acting upon the states only in their collective or political capacity, and not on individuals, there would have been no need of a bill of rights, as far as related to the rights of individuals, but only as to the rights of states. But the proposed constitution being intended and empowered to act not only on states, but also immediately on individuals, it renders a recognition and a stipulation in favour of the rights both of states and of men, not only proper, but in my opinion absolutely necessary. I endeavoured to obtain a restraint on the powers of the general government, as to standing armies, but it was rejected. It was my wish that the general government should not have the power of suspending the privilege of the writ of habeas corpus, as it appears to me altogether unnecessary, and that the power given to it may and will be used as a dangerous engine of oppression, but I could not succeed. . . . The more the system advanced the more was I impressed with the necessity of not merely attempting to

Paul Leicester Ford, ed., *Essays on the Constitution of the United States, 1787-1788* (Brooklyn, N.Y., 1892), pp. 364-68.

secure a few rights, but of digesting and forming a complete bill of rights, including those of states and of individuals, which should be assented to, and prefixed to the Constitution, to serve as a barrier between the general government and the respective states and their citizens; because the more the system advanced the more clearly it appeared to me that the framers of it did not consider that either states or men had any rights at all, or that they meant to secure the enjoyment of any to either the one or the other accordingly, I devoted a part of my time to the actually preparing and draughting such a bill of rights, and had it in readiness before I left the Convention, to have laid it before a committee. I conversed with several members on the subject; they agreed with me on the propriety of the measure, but at the same time expressed their sentiments that it would be impossible to procure its adoption if attempted. . . .

. . . And from the best judgment I could form while in Convention, I then was, and yet remained, decidedly of the opinion that ambition and interest had so far blinded the understanding of some of the principal framers of the Constitution, that while they were labouring to erect a fabric by which they themselves might be exalted and benefited, they were rendered insensible to the sacrifice of the freedom and happiness of the states and their citizens, which must, inevitably be the consequence. I most sacredly believe their object is the total abolition and destruction of all state governments, and the erection on their ruins of one great and extensive empire, calculated to aggrandize and elevate its rulers and chief officers far above the common herd of mankind, to enrich them with wealth, and to encircle them with honours and glory, and which according to my judgment on the maturest reflection, must inevitably be attended with the most humiliating and abject slavery of their fellow citizens, by the sweat of whose brows, and by the toil of whose bodies, it can only be effected.

. . . I must frankly acknowledge, however it may operate as a proof of my dullness and stupidity, that the "ignorance in the science of government" under which I laboured at first was not removed by more than two months close application under those august and enlightened masters of the science with which the Convention abounded, nor was I able to discover during that time, either by my own researches, or by any light borrowed from those luminaries, anything in the history of mankind or in the sentiments of those who have favoured the world with their ideas on government, to warrant or countenance the motley mixture of a system proposed: a system which is an innovation in government of the most extraordinary kind; a system neither wholly federal, nor wholly national— but a strange hotch-potch of both—just so much federal in appearance as to give its advocates in some measure, an opportunity of passing it as such upon the unsuspecting multitude, before they had time and opportunity to examine it, and yet so predominantly national as to put it in the power of its movers, whenever the machine shall be set agoing, to strike out

every part that has the appearance of being federal, and to render it
wholly and entirely a national government. . . .

5 · Elbridge Gerry · *Letter to the Presiding Officers of the Massachusetts Legislature* · 1787

*Elbridge Gerry of Massachusetts had the dubious distinction of being the
only Northern delegate to refuse to sign the Constitution. Two other
delegates who remained in Philadelphia—George Mason and Edmund
Randolph of Virginia—joined Gerry in declining to sign. Gerry's reasons
are stated in the letter addressed to the President of the Senate and the
Speaker of the House of Representatives of Massachusetts.*

My principal objections to the plan, are, that there is no adequate
provision for a representation of the people—that they have no security
for the right of election—that some of the powers of the legislature are
ambiguous, and, others indefinite and dangerous—that the executive is
blended with, and will have an undue influence over, the legislature—
that the judicial department will be oppressive—that treaties of the highest importance may be formed by the president with the advice of two-
thirds of a quorum of the senate—and that the system is without the
security of a bill of rights. These are objections which are not local, but
apply equally to all the states.

As the convention was called for "the sole and express purpose of revising the articles of confederation, and reporting to Congress, and the
several legislatures, such alterations and provisions as shall render the
federal constitution adequate to the exigencies of government, and the
preservation of the union," I did not conceive that these powers extend to
the formation of the plan proposed: but the convention being of a different opinion, I acquiesced in it, being fully convinced that to preserve the
union, an efficient government was indispensably necessary; and that it
would be difficult to make proper amendments to the articles of confederation.

The constitution proposed, has few, if any federal features; but is rather
a system of national government. Nevertheless, in many respects, I think
it has great merit, and, by proper amendments, may be adapted to "the
exigencies of government, and preservation of liberty."

The question on this plan involves others of the highest importance:
1st. Whether there shall be a dissolution of the federal government? 2dly.
Whether the several state governments shall be so altered, as in effect to
be dissolved? 3dly. Whether, in lieu of the federal and state governments,
the national constitution now proposed, shall be substituted without

amendment? Never, perhaps, were a people called on to decide a question of greater magnitude. Should the citizens of America adopt the plan as it now stands, their liberties may be lost: or should they reject it altogether, anarchy may ensue. It is evident, therefore, that they should not be precipitate in their decisions; that the subject should be well understood, lest they should refuse to support the government, after having hastily accepted it. . . .

It may be urged by some, that an implicit confidence should be placed in the convention; but, however respectable the members may be, who signed the constitution, it must be admitted, that a free people are the proper guardians of their rights and liberties—that the greatest men may err—and that their errors are sometimes of the greatest magnitude.

Others may suppose, that the constitution may be safely adopted, because therein provision is made to amend it. But cannot this object be better attained before a ratification than after it? And should a free people adopt a form of government, under conviction that it wants amendment?

And some may conceive, that if the plan is not accepted by the people, they will not unite in another: but surely while they have the power to amend, they are not under the necessity of rejecting it. . . .

6 • Richard Henry Lee • *Letters from the Federal Farmer to the Republican* • 1787

Richard Henry Lee of Virginia was appointed a delegate to the Philadelphia Convention, but refused to serve. His Letters from the Federal Farmer to the Republican *were among the most popular and widely circulated of the Antifederalist literature. Contrasting Lee's exposition with the "temper and argument" of* The Federalist, *V. L. Parrington declares that "the calmness and fair-mindedness of the work persuade one that it ill-deserves the name partisan."*

LETTER I   October 8, 1787

. . . My uniform federal attachments, and the interest I have in the protection of property, and a steady execution of the laws, will convince you, that, if I am under any bias at all, it is in favor of any general system which shall promise those advantages. The instability of our laws increases my wishes for firm and steady government; but then, I can consent to no government, which, in my opinion, is not calculated equally to preserve the rights of all orders of men in the community. . . . I am not

Ford, *Pamphlets,* pp. 277-324, *passim.* (Also in the Spectrum Classics in History series, S-CH-5.)

disposed to unreasonably contend about forms. I know our situation is critical, and it behooves us to make the best of it. A federal government of some sort is necessary. We have suffered the present to languish; and whether the confederation was capable or not originally of answering any valuable purposes, it is now but of little importance. . . . A constitution is now presented which we may reject, or which we may accept with or without amendments, and to which point we ought to direct our exertions is the question. To determine this question with propriety, we must attentively examine the system itself, and the probable consequences of either step. . . .

The first principal question that occurs is, Whether, considering our situation, we ought to precipitate the adoption of the proposed constitution? If we remain cool and temperate, we are in no immediate danger of any commotions; we are in a state of perfect peace, and in no danger of invasions; the state governments are in the full exercise of their powers; and our governments answer all present exigencies, except the regulation of trade, securing credit, in some cases, and providing for the interest, in some instances, of the public debts; and whether we adopt a change three or nine months hence, can make but little odds with the private circumstances of individuals; their happiness and prosperity, after all, depend principally upon their own exertions. We are hardly recovered from a long and distressing war: The farmers, fishmen, etc. have not fully repaired the waste made by it. Industry and frugality are again assuming their proper station. Private debts are lessened, and public debts incurred by the war have been, by various ways, diminished; and the public lands have now become a productive source for diminishing them much more. I know uneasy men, who with very much to precipitate, do not admit all these facts; but they are facts well known to all men who are thoroughly informed in the affairs of this country. It must, however, be admitted, that our federal system is defective, and that some of the state governments are not well administered; but, then, we impute to the defects in our governments many evils and embarrassments which are most clearly the result of the late war. . . .

It is natural for men, who wish to hasten the adoption of a measure, to tell us, now is the crisis—now is the critical moment which must be seized or all will be lost; and to shut the door against free enquiry, whenever conscious the thing presented has defects in it, which time and investigation will probably discover. This has been the custom of tyrants, and their dependents in all ages. If it is true, what has been so often said, that the people of this country cannot change their condition for the worse, I presume it still behooves them to endeavour deliberately to change it for the better. . . .

Our object has been all along, to reform our federal system, and to strengthen our governments—to establish peace, order and justice in the community— but a new object now presents. The plan of government now proposed is evidently calculated totally to change, in time, our condition as a people. Instead of being thirteen republics, under a federal head, it is clearly designed to make us one consolidated government. . . . This consolidation of the states has been the object of several men in this country for some time past. Whether such a change can ever be effected, in any manner; whether it can be effected without convulsions and civil wars; whether such a change will not totally destroy the liberties of this country—time only can determine.

To have a just idea of the government before us, and to show that a consolidated one is the object in view, it is necessary not only to examine the plan, but also its history, and the politics of its particular friends.

The confederation was formed when great confidence was placed in the voluntary exertions of individuals, and of the respective states; and the framers of it, to guard against usurpation, so limited, and checked the powers, that, in many respects, they are inadequate to the exigencies of the union. We find, therefore, members of congress urging alterations in the federal system almost as soon as it was adopted. . . . We expected too much from the return of peace, and of course we have been disappointed. Our governments have been new and unsettled; and several legislatures, by making tender, suspension, and paper money laws, have given just cause of uneasiness to creditors. By these and other causes, several orders of men in the community have been prepared, by degrees, for a change of government; and this very abuse of power in the legislatures, which in some cases has been charged upon the democratic part of the community, has furnished aristocratical men with those very weapons, and those very means, with which, in great measure, they are rapidly effecting their favourite object. And should an oppressive government be the consequence of the proposed change, posterity may reproach not only a few overbearing, unprincipled men, but those parties in the states which have misused their powers.

The conduct of several legislatures, touching paper money, and tender laws, has prepared many honest men for changes in government, which otherwise they would not have thought of—when by the evils, on the one hand, and by the secret instigations of artful men, on the other, the minds of men were become sufficiently uneasy, a bold step was taken, which is usually followed by a revolution, or a civil war. . . .

The first interesting question, therefore suggested, is, how far the states can be consolidated into one entire government on free principles. In considering this question extensive objects are to be taken into view, and important changes in the forms of government to be carefully attended to in all their consequences. The happiness of the people at large must be the great object with every honest statesman, and he will direct every movement to this point. If we are so situated as a people, as not to be able to enjoy equal happiness and advantages under one government, the consolidation of the states cannot be admitted. . . .

LETTER II   October 9, 1787

. . . There are certain unalienable and fundamental rights, which in forming the social compact, ought to be explicitly ascertained and fixed —a free and enlightened people, in forming this compact, will not resign all their rights to those who govern, and they will fix limits to their legislators and rulers, which will soon be plainly seen by those who are governed, as well as by those who govern: and the latter will know they cannot be passed unperceived by the former, and without giving a general alarm—These rights should be made the basis of every constitution; and if a people be so situated, or have such different opinions that they cannot agree in ascertaining and fixing them, it is a very strong argument against their attempting to form one entire society, to live under one system of laws only. . . .

LETTER III   October 10, 1787

. . . I am fully convinced that we must organize the national government on different principles, and make the parts of it more efficient, and secure in it more effectually the different interests in the community. . . . It is not my object to multiply objections, or to contend about inconsiderable powers or amendments. I wish the system adopted with a few alterations; but those, in my mind, are essential ones. . . .

It is necessary . . . to examine the extent, and the probable operations of some of those extensive powers proposed to be vested in this government. These powers, legislative, executive, and judicial, respect internal as well as external objects. Those respecting external objects, as all foreign concerns, commerce, imposts, all causes arising on the seas, peace and war, and Indian affairs can be lodged no where else, with any propriety, but in this government. Many powers that respect internal objects ought clearly to be lodged in it; as those to regulate trade between the states, weights and measures, the coin or current monies, post-offices, naturalization, etc. These powers may be exercised without essentially effecting the internal police of the respective states: But powers to lay and collect internal taxes, to form the militia, to make bankrupt laws, and to decide on appeals, questions arising on the internal laws of the respective states, are of a very serious nature, and carry with them almost all other powers. These taken in connection with the others, and powers to raise armies and build navies, proposed to be lodged in this government, appear to me to comprehend all the essential powers in this community, and those which will be left to the states will be of no great importance. . . .

LETTER IV   October 12, 1787

. . . Third, there appears to me to be not only a premature deposit of some important powers in the general government—but many of those deposited there are undefined, and may be used to good or bad purposes as honest or designing men shall prevail. . . .

4th. There are certain rights which we have always held sacred in the United States, and recognized in all our constitutions, and which, by the adoption of the new constitution in its present form, will be left unsecured. By article 6, the proposed constitution, and the laws of the United States, which shall be made in pursuance thereof; and all treaties made, or which shall be made under the authority of the United States, shall be the supreme law of the land; and the judges in every state shall be bound thereby; anything in the constitution or laws of any state to the contrary notwithstanding.

It is to be observed that when the people shall adopt the proposed constitution it will be their last and supreme act; it will be adopted not by the people of New Hampshire, Massachusetts, &c., but by the people of the United States; and wherever this constitution, or any part of it, shall be incompatible with the ancient customs, rights, the laws or the constitutions heretofore established in the United States, it will entirely abolish them and do them away: And not only this, but the laws of the United States which shall be made in pursuance of the federal constitution will be also supreme laws, and wherever they shall be incompatible with those customs, rights, laws or constitutions heretofore established, they will also entirely abolish them and do them away.

By the article before recited, treaties also made under the authority of the United States, shall be the supreme law: It is not said that these treaties shall be made in pursuance of the constitution—nor are there any constitutional bounds set to those who shall make them: The president and two-thirds of the senate will be empowered to make treaties indefinitely, and when these treaties shall be made, they will also abolish all laws and state constitutions incompatible with them. This power in the president and senate is absolute, and the judges will be bound to allow full force to whatever rule, article or thing the president and senate shall establish by treaty, whether it be practicable to set any bounds to those who make treaties, I am not able to say; if not, it proves that this power ought to be more safely lodged.

The federal constitution, the laws of congress made in pursuance of the constitution, and all treaties must have full force and effect in all parts of the United States; and all other laws, rights and constitutions which stand in their way must yield: It is proper the national laws should be supreme, and superior to state or district laws; but then the national laws ought to yield to unalienable or fundamental rights—and national laws, made by a few men, should extend only to a few national objects. This will not be the case with the laws of congress: To have any proper idea of their extent, we must carefully examine the legislative, executive and judicial powers proposed to be lodged in the general government, and consider them in connection with a general clause in art. 1, sect. 8

in these words (after enumerating a number of powers) "To make all laws which shall be necessary and proper for carrying into execution the foregoing powers, and all other powers vested by this constitution in the government of the United States, or in any department or officer thereof." —The powers of this government as has been observed, extend to internal as well as external objects, and to those objects to which all others are subordinate; it is almost impossible to have a just conception of their powers, or of the extent and number of the laws which may be deemed necessary and proper to carry them into effect, till we shall come to exercise those powers and make the laws. In making laws to carry those powers into effect, it is to be expected, that a wise and prudent congress will pay respect to the opinions of a free people, and bottom their laws on those principles which have been considered as essential and fundamental in the British, and in our government: But a congress of a different character will not be bound by the constitution to pay respect to those principles.

It is said that when people make a constitution, and delegate powers, that all powers are not delegated by them to those who govern, is reserved in the people; and that the people, in the present case, have reserved in themselves, and in their state governments, every right and power not expressly given by the federal constitution to those who shall administer the national government. It is said, on the other hand, that the people, when they make a constitution, yield all power not expressly reserved to themselves. The truth is, in either case, it is mere matter of opinion, and men usually take either side of the argument, as will best answer their purposes: But the general presumption being, that men who govern, will in doubtful cases, construe laws and constitutions most favourably for increasing their own powers; all wise and prudent people, in forming constitutions, have drawn the line, and carefully described the powers parted with and the powers reserved. By the state constitutions, certain rights have been reserved in the people; or rather, they have been recognized and established in such a manner, that state legislatures are bound to respect them, and to make no laws infringing upon them. The state legislatures are obliged to take notice of the bills of rights of their respective states. The bills of rights, and the state constitutions, are fundamental compacts only between those who govern, and the people of the same state.

In the year 1788 the people of the United States made a federal constitution, which is a fundamental compact between them and their federal rulers; these rulers, in the nature of things, cannot be bound to take notice of any other compact. It would be absurd for them, in making laws, to look over thirteen, fifteen, or twenty state constitutions, to see what rights are established as fundamental, and must not be infringed upon, in making laws in the society. It is true, they would be bound to do it if the people, in their federal compact, should refer to the state constitutions, recognize all parts not inconsistent with the federal constitution, and direct their federal rulers to take notice of them accordingly; but this is not the case, as the plan stands proposed at present; and it is absurd, to suppose so unnatural an idea is intended or implied. I think my opinion is not only founded in reason, but I think it is supported by the report of the convention itself. If there are a number of rights established by the state constitutions, and which will remain sacred, and the general government is bound to take notice of them—it must take notice of one as well as another; and if unnecessary to recognize or establish one by the federal constitution, it would be unnecessary to recognize or establish another by it. If the federal constitution is to be construed so far in connection with the state constitution, as to leave the trial by jury in civil causes, for instance, secured; on the same principles it would have left the trial by jury in criminal causes, the benefits of the writ of habeas corpus, &c. secured; they all stand on the same footing; they are the common rights of Americans, and have been recognized by the state constitutions: But the convention found it necessary to recognize or reestablish the benefits of that writ, and the jury trial in criminal cases. As to *expost facto* laws, the convention has done the same in one case, and gone further in another, It is a part of the compact between the people of each state and their rulers, that no *expost facto* laws shall be made. But the convention, by Art. 1, Sect. 10, have put a sanction upon this part even of the state compacts. In fact, the 9th and 10th Sections in Art. 1, in the proposed constitution, are no more nor less, than a partial bill of rights; they establish certain principles as part of the compact upon which the federal legislators and officers can never infringe. It is here wisely stipulated, that the federal legislature shall never pass a bill of attainder, or *expost facto* law; that no tax shall be laid on articles exported, &c. The establishing of one right implies the necessity of establishing another and similar one.

On the whole, the position appears to me to be undeniable, that this bill of rights ought to be carried farther, and some other principles established, as a part of this fundamental compact between the people of the United States and their federal rulers.

It is true, we are not disposed to differ much, at present, about religion; but when we are making a constitution, it is to be hoped, for ages and millions yet unborn, why not establish the free exercise of religion, as a part of the national compact. There are other essential rights, which we have justly understood to be the rights of freemen; as freedom from hasty and unreasonable search warrants, warrants not founded on oath, and not issued with due caution, for searching and seizing men's papers, property, and persons. The trials by jury in civil causes, it is said, varies so much in the several states, that no words could be found for the uniform establishment of it. If so, the federal legislation will not be able to establish it by any general laws. I confess I am of opinion it may be established, but not in that beneficial manner in which we may enjoy it, for the reasons beforementioned. When I speak of the jury trial of the vicinage, or the trial of the fact in the neighborhood, I do not lay so much stress upon the circumstance of our being tried by our neighbors: in this enlightened country men may be probably impartially tried by those who do not live very near them: but the trial of facts in the neighbourhood is of great importance in other respects. Nothing can be more essential than the cross examining witnesses, and generally before the triers of the facts in question. The common people can establish facts with much more ease with oral than written evidence; when trials of facts are removed to a distance from the homes of the parties and witnesses, oral evidence becomes intolerably expensive, and the parties must depend on written evidence, which to the common people is expensive and almost useless; it must be frequently taken ex parte, and but very seldom leads to the proper discovery of truth.

The trial by jury is very important in another point of view. It is essential in every free country, that common people should have a part and share of influence, in the judicial as well as in the legislative department. To hold open to them the offices of senators, judges, and offices to fill which an expensive education is required, cannot answer any valuable purposes for them; they are not in a situation to be brought forward and to fill those offices; these, and most other offices of any considerable importance, will be occupied by the few. The few, the well born, &c. as Mr. Adams calls them, in judicial decisions as well as in legislation, are generally disposed, and very naturally too, to favour those of their own description. . . .

I confess I do not see in what cases the congress can, with any pretence of right, make a law to suppress the freedom of the press; though I am not clear, that congress is restrained from laying any duties whatever on printing, and from laying duties particularly heavy on certain pieces printed, and perhaps congress may require large bonds for the payment of these duties. Should the printer say, the freedom of the press was secured by the constitution of the state in which he lived, congress might, and perhaps, with great propriety, answer, that the federal constitution is the only compact existing between them and the people; in this compact the people have named no others, and therefore congress, in exercising the powers assigned them, and in making laws to carry them into execution, are restrained by nothing beside the federal constitution, any more than a state legislature is restrained by a compact between the magistrates and people of a county, city, or town of which the people, in forming the state constitution, have taken no notice.

It is not my object to enumerate rights of inconsiderable importance; but there are others, no doubt, which ought to be established as a fundamental part of the national system. . . .

It may also be worthy our examination, how far the provision for amending this plan, when it shall be adopted, is of any importance. No measures can be taken towards amendments, unless two-thirds of the congress, or two-thirds of the legislature of the several states shall agree. While power is in the hands of the people, or democratic part of the community, more especially as the present, it is easy, according to the general course of human affairs, for the few influential men in the community, to obtain conventions, alterations in government, and to persuade the common people that they may change for the better, and to get from them a part of the power: But when power is once transferred from the many to the few, all changes become extremely difficult; the government, in this case, being beneficial to the few, they will be exceedingly artful and adroit in preventing any measures which may lead to a change; and nothing will produce it, but great exertions and severe struggles on the part of the common people. Every man of reflection must see, that the change now proposed, is a transfer of power from the many to the few, and the probability is, the artful and ever active aristocracy, will prevent all peaceful measures for changes, unless when they shall discover some favorable moment to increase their own influence. . . .

7 • George Mason • *Objections to the Constitution* • October 1787 • *Refuted by* James Iredell

George Mason of Virginia, a nonsigner, explained his reasons in a series of objections. They did not go unanswered. James Iredell, a member of the North Carolina ratifying convention and later Associate Justice of the Supreme Court of the United States, attempted to meet Mason's objections point by point.

I. OBJECTION.

"There is no declaration of rights, and the laws of the general government being paramount to the laws and constitutions of the several States, the declarations of rights in the separate States are no security. Nor are the people secured even in the enjoyment of the benefit of the common law, which stands here upon no other foundation than its having been adopted by the respective acts forming the Constitutions of the several States."

ANSWER.

1. As to the want of a declaration of rights. The introduction of these in England, from which the idea was originally taken, was in conse-

Mason: Elliot, I, 533-35.
Iredell: Ford, *Pamphlets*, pp. 335-70.

quence of usurpations of the Crown, contrary, as was conceived, to the principles of their government. But there no original constitution is to be found, and the only meaning of a declaration of rights in that country is, that in certain particulars specified, the Crown had no authority to act. Could this have been necessary had there been a constitution in being by which it could have been clearly discerned whether the Crown had such authority or not? Had the people, by a solemn instrument, delegated particular powers to the Crown at the formation of their government, surely the Crown, which in that case could claim under that instrument only, could not have contended for more power than was conveyed by it. So it is in regard to the new Constitution here: the future government which may be formed under that authority certainly cannot act beyond the warrant of that authority. . . .

2. As to the common law, it is difficult to know what is meant by that part of the objection. So far as the people are now entitled to the benefit of the common law, they certainly will have a right to enjoy it under the new Constitution until altered by the general legislature, which even in this point has some cardinal limits assigned to it. . . . The principles of the common law, as they now apply, must surely always hereafter apply, except in those particulars in which express authority is given by this constitution; in no other particulars can the Congress have authority to change it. . . .

IV. OBJECTION.

"The judiciary of the United States is so constructed and extended, as to absorb and destroy the judiciaries of the several States; thereby rendering law as tedious, intricate and expensive and justice as unattainable by a great part of the community, as in England; and enabling the rich to oppress and ruin the poor."

ANSWER.

. . . How is this the case? Are not the State judiciaries left uncontrolled as to the affairs of that *State* only? In this, as in all other cases, where there is a wise distribution, power is commensurate to its object. With the mere internal concerns of a State, Congress are to have nothing to do: In no case but where the Union is in some measure concerned, are the federal courts to have any jurisdiction. The State Judiciary will be a satellite waiting upon its proper planet: That of the Union, like the sun, cherishing and preserving a whole planetary system.

In regard to a possible ill construction of this authority, we must depend upon our future legislature in this case as well as others, in respect to which it is impracticable to define every thing, that it will be provided for so as to occasion as little expense and distress to individuals as can be. *In parting with the coercive authority over the States as States, there must be a coercion allowed as to individuals. The former power no man of common sense can any longer seriously contend for; the latter is the only alternative. . . .*

VIII. OBJECTION.

"Under their own construction of the general clause at the end of the enumerated powers, the Congress may grant monopolies in trade and commerce, constitute new crimes, inflict unusual and severe punishment, and extend their power as far as they shall think proper; so that the State Legislatures have no security for the powers now presumed to remain to them: or the people for their rights. There is no declaration of any kind for preserving the liberty of the press, the trial by jury in civil causes, nor against the danger of standing armies in time of peace."

ANSWER.

The general clause at the end of the enumerated power is as follows:
"To make all laws which shall be necessary and proper for carrying into execution the *foregoing powers, and all other powers vested by this Constitution in the United States, or in any department or office thereof.*"
Those powers would be useless, except acts of legislation could be exercised upon them. It was not possible for the Convention, nor is it for any human body, to foresee and provide for all contingent cases that may arise. Such cases must therefore be left to be provided for by the general Legislature as they shall happen to come into existence. If Congress, under pretence of exercising the power delegated to them, should in fact, by the exercise of any other power, usurp upon the rights of the different Legislatures, or of any private citizens, the people will be exactly in the same situation as if there had been an express provision against such power in particular, and yet they had presumed to exercise it. It would be an act of tyranny, against which no parchment stipulations can guard; and the Convention surely can be only answerable for the propriety of the powers given, not for the future virtues of all with whom those powers may be intrusted. It does not therefore appear to me that there is any weight in this objection more than in others. . . .

THE DEBATES

PENNSYLVANIA

1 • James Wilson • *State House Speech in Philadelphia* • October 10, 1787

For clarity of argument, the debate in Pennsylvania was unsurpassed. Three Antifederalists—Robert Whitehill, John Smilie, and William

John Bach McMaster and Frederick D. Stone, eds., *Pennsylvania and the Federal Constitution, 1787-1788,* The Historical Society of Pennsylvania (1888), pp. 143-78, *passim.*

Findley, all delegates from western counties—tried in vain both to match the force of James Wilson's argument and to stem the tide of federalism. Wilson's State House Speech, delivered before the ratifying convention met, ranks as a classic defense of the proposed Constitution. An unblushing aspirant, Wilson was named an Associate Justice of the first Supreme Court appointed under the new Constitution.

It will be proper . . . before I enter into the refutation of the charges that are alleged, to mark the leading discrimination between the State constitutions and the constitution of the United States. When the people established the powers of legislation under their separate governments, they invested their representatives with every right and authority which they did not in explicit terms reserve; and therefore upon every question respecting the jurisdiction of the House of Assembly, if the frame of government is silent, the jurisdiction is efficient and complete. But in delegating federal powers, another criterion was necessarily introduced, and the congressional power is to be collected, not from tacit implication, but from the positive grant expressed in the instrument of the union. Hence, it is evident, that in the former case everything which is not reserved is given; but in the latter the reverse of the proposition prevails, and everything which is not given is reserved.

This distinction being recognized, will furnish an answer to those who think the omission of a bill of rights a defect in the proposed constitution; for it would have been superfluous and absurd to have stipulated with a federal body of our own creation, that we should enjoy those privileges of which we are not divested, either by the intention or the act that has brought the body into existence. For instance, the liberty of the press, which has been a copious source of declamation and opposition—what control can proceed from the Federal government to shackle or destroy that sacred palladium of national freedom? If, indeed, a power similar to that which has been granted for the regulation of commerce had been granted to regulate literary publications, it would have been as necessary to stipulate that the liberty of the press should be preserved inviolate, as that the impost should be general in its operation. . . . In truth, then, the proposed system possesses no influence whatever upon the press, and it would have been merely nugatory to have introduced a formal declaration upon the subject—nay, that very declaration might have been construed to imply that some degree of power was given, since we undertook to define its extent.

Another objection that has been fabricated against the new constitution, is expressed in this disingenious form—"The trial by jury is abolished in civil cases." . . . Let it be remembered . . . that the business of the Federal Convention was not local, but general—not limited to the views and establishments of a single State, but co-extensive with the continent, and comprehending the views and establishments of thirteen independent sovereignties. When, therefore, this subject was in discussion, we were involved in difficulties which pressed on all sides, and no precedent could be discovered to direct our course. The cases open to a trial by jury differed in the different States. It was therefore impracticable, on that ground, to have made a general rule. The want of uniformity would have rendered any reference to the practice of the States idle and useless; and it could not with any propriety be said that, "The trial by jury shall be as heretofore," since there has never existed any federal system of jurisprudence, to which the declaration could relate. Besides, it is not in all cases that the trial by jury is adopted in civil questions; for depending in courts of admiralty, such as relate to maritime captures, and such as are agitated in courts of equity, do not require the intervention of that tribunal. How, then was the line of discrimination to be drawn? The Convention found the task too difficult for them, and they left the business as it stands, in the fullest confidence that no danger could possibly ensue, since the proceedings of the Supreme Court are to be regulated by the Congress, which is a faithful representation of the people; and the oppression of government is effectually barred, by declaring that in all criminal cases the trial by jury shall be preserved.

This constitution, it has been further urged, is of a pernicious tendency, because it tolerates a standing army in the time of peace. This has always been a topic of popular declamation; and yet I do not know a nation in the world which has not found it necessary and useful to maintain the appearance of strength in a season of the most profound tranquility. Nor is it a novelty with us; for under the present articles of confederation, Congress certainly possesses this reprobated power, and the exercise of that power is proved at this moment by her cantonments along the banks of the Ohio. But what would be our national situation were it otherwise? Every principle of policy must be subverted, and the government must declare war, before they are prepared to carry on. Whatever may be the provocation, however important the object in view, and however necessary dispatch and secrecy may be, still the declaration must precede the preparation, and the enemy will be informed of your intention, not only before you are equipped for an attack, but even before you are fortified for a defence. The consequence is too obvious to require any further delineation, and no man who regards the dignity and safety of his country can deny the necessity of a military force, under the control and with the restrictions which the new constitution provides. . . .

The next accusation I shall consider is that which represents the federal constitution, as not only calculated, but designedly framed, to reduce the State governments to mere corporations, and eventually to annihilate them. Those who have employed the term corporation upon this occasion are not perhaps aware of its extent. In common parlance, indeed, it is generally applied to petty associations for the ease and convenience of a few individuals; but in its enlarged sense, it will comprehend the government of Pennsylvania, the existing union of the States, and even this projected system is nothing more than a formal act of incorporation. But upon what pretence can it be alleged that it was designed to annihilate the State governments? For I will undertake to prove that upon their existence depends the existence of the Federal plan. For this purpose, permit me to call your attention to the manner in which the President, Senate and House of Representatives are proposed to be appointed. The President is to be chosen by electors, nominated in such manner as the legislature of each State may direct; so that if there is no legislature there can be no electors, and consequently the office of President cannot be supplied.

The Senate is to be composed of two Senators from each State, chosen by the Legislature; and, therefore, if there is no Legislature, there can be no Senate. The House of Representatives is to be composed of members chosen every second year by the people of the several States, and the electors in each State shall have the qualifications requisite for electors of the most numerous branch of the State Legislature; unless, therefore, there is a State Legislature, that qualification cannot be ascertained, and the popular branch of the federal constitution must be extinct. From this view, then, it is evidently absurd to suppose that the annihilation of the separate governments will result from their union; or, that having that intention, the authors of the new system would have bound their connection with such indissoluble ties. Let me here advert to an arrangement highly advantageous, for you will perceive, without prejudice to the powers of the Legislature in the election of Senators, the people at large will acquire an additional privilege in returning members to the House of Representatives; whereas, by the present confederation, it is the Legislature alone that appoints the delegates to Congress.

The power of direct taxation has likewise been treated as an improper delegation to the federal government; but when we consider it as the duty of that body to provide for the national safety, to support the dignity of the union, and to discharge the debts contracted upon the collected faith of the States for their common benefit, it must be acknowledged that those upon whom such important obligations are imposed, ought in justice and in policy to possess every means requisite for a faithful performance of their trust. But why should we be alarmed with visionary evils? I will venture to predict that the great revenue of the United States must, and always will, be raised by impost, for, being at once less obnoxious and more productive, the interest of the government will be best promoted by the accommodation of the people. Still, however, the objects of direct taxation should be within reach in all cases of emergency; and there is no more reason to apprehend oppression in the mode of collecting a revenue from this resource, than in the form of an impost, which, by universal assent, is left to the authority of the federal government. In either case, the force of civil institutions will be adequate to the purpose; and the dread of military violence, which has been assiduously disseminated, must eventually prove the mere effusion of a wild imagination or a factious spirit. But the salutary consequences that must flow from thus enabling the government to receive and support the credit of the union, will afford another answer to the objections upon this ground. . . .

. . . I will confess . . . that I am not a blind admirer of this plan of government, and that there are some parts of it which, if my wish had prevailed, would certainly have been altered. . . . If there are errors, it should be remembered that the seeds of reformation are sown in the work itself, and the concurrence of two-thirds of the Congress may at any time introduce alterations and amendments. Regarding it, then, in every point of view, with a candid and disinterested mind, I am bold to assert that it is the best form of government which has ever been offered to the world.

2 · Excerpts from the Ratifying Convention · 1787

Debate between Whitehill and Smilie, on the one hand, and Wilson, on the other, highlighted the Pennsylvania ratifying convention.

Mr. Wilson. . . . In delivering my sentiments on a former day, I had occasion to show that the supreme power of government was the inalienable and inherent right of the people, and the system before us opens with a practical declaration of that principle. Here, Sir, it is expressly announced: "We, the people of the United States, do ordain, constitute, and establish." . . . This single sentence in the preamble is tantamount to a volume, and contains the essence of all the bills of rights that have been or can be devised; for it establishes at once, that in the great article of government, the people have a right to do what they please. It is with pride, Mr. President, I remark the difference between the terms of this constitution, and the British declaration of rights, or even their boasted Magna Charta. For, Sir, from what source does Magna Charta derive the liberties of the people? The very words of that celebrated instrument declare them to be the gift or grant of the king; and under the influence of that doctrine, no wonder the people should then and at subsequent periods wish to obtain some evidence of their formal liberties by the concessions of petitions and bills of right. But here, Sir, the fee simple of freedom and government is declared to be in the people, and it is an inheritance with which they will not part.

Mr. Smilie. . . . I shall proceed to make a few remarks upon those words in the preamble of this plan, which he [Wilson] has considered of so super-excellent a quality. Compare them, Sir, with the language used in

McMaster and Stone, *op. cit.*, pp. 249-51, 254-63, 267-71.

forming the state constitution, and however superior they may be to the terms of the great charter of England; still, in common candor, they must yield to the more sterling expressions employed in this act. Let these speak for themselves:

"That all men are born equally free and independent, and have certain natural, inherent and unalienable rights, among which are the enjoying and defending life and liberty, acquiring and possessing and protecting property, and pursuing and obtaining happiness and safety.

"That the people of this state have the sole, exclusive and inherent right of governing and regulating the internal police of the same.

"That all power being originally inherent in, and consequently derived from the people; therefore all officers of government, whether legislative or executive, are their trustees and servants, and at all times accountable to them.

"That government is, or ought to be, instituted for the common benefit, protection and security of the people, nation or community; and not for the particular emolument or advantage of any single man, family, or set of men, who are a part only of that community. And that the community hath an indubitable, unalienable, and indefeasible right to reform, alter or abolish government in such manner as shall be by that community judged most conducive to the public weal." . . . True, sir, the supreme authority naturally rests in the people, but does it follow, that therefore a declaration of rights would be superfluous? Because the people have a right to alter and abolish government, can it therefore be inferred that every step taken to secure that right would be superfluous and nugatory? The truth is, that unless some criterion is established by which it could be easily and constitutionally ascertained how far our governors may proceed, and by which it might appear when they transgress their jurisdiction, this idea of altering and abolishing government is a mere sound without substance. Let us recur to the memorable declaration of the 4th of July, 1776. Here it is said:

"When in the course of human events, it becomes necessary for one people to dissolve the political bands which have connected them with another, and to assume among the powers of the earth the separate and equal station to which the laws of nature's God entitle them, a decent respect to the opinions of mankind requires that they should declare the causes which impel them to the separation.

"We hold these truths to be self-evident; that all men are created equal; that they are endowed by their Creator with certain unalienable rights; that among these are life, liberty, and the pursuit of happiness. That to secure these rights, governments are instituted among men, deriving their just powers from the consent of the governed; that when any form of government becomes destructive of these ends, it is the right of the people to alter or to abolish it, and to institute a new government, laying its foundation on such principles, and organizing its powers in such form, as to them shall seem most likely to effect their safety and happiness."

Now, Sir, if in the proposed plan, the gentleman can show any similar security for the civil rights of the people, I shall certainly be relieved from a weight of objection to its adoption, and I sincerely hope, that as he has gone so far, he will proceed to communicate some of the reasons (and undoubtedly they must have been powerful ones) which induced the late federal convention to omit a bill of rights, so essential in the opinion of many citizens to a perfect form of government. . . .

The arguments which have been urged, Mr. President, have not, in my opinion, satisfactorily shown that a bill of rights would have been an improper, nay, that it is not a necessary appendage to the proposed system. . . . It seems, . . . that the members of the federal convention were themselves convinced, in some degree, of the expediency and propriety of a bill of rights, for we find them expressly declaring that the writ of habeas corpus and the trial by jury in criminal cases shall not be suspended or infringed. How does this indeed agree with the maxim that whatever is not given is reserved? Does it not rather appear from the reservation of these two articles that everything else, which is not specified, is included in the powers delegated to the government? This, Sir, must prove the necessity of a full and explicit declaration of rights; and when we further consider the extensive, the undefined powers vested in the administrators of this system, when we consider the system itself as a great political compact between the governors and the governed, a plain, strong, and accurate criterion by which the people might at once determine when, and in what instance their rights were violated, is a preliminary, without which, this plan ought not to be adopted. So loosely, so inaccurately are the powers which are enumerated in this constitution defined, that it will be impossible, without a test of that kind, to ascertain the limits of authority, and to declare when government has degenerated into oppression. In that event the contest will arise between the people and the rulers: "You have exceeded the powers of your office, you have oppressed us," will be the language of the suffering citizen. The answer of the government will be short—"We have not exceeded our power; you have no test by which you can prove it." Hence, Sir, it will be impracticable to stop the progress of tyranny, for there will be no check but the people, and their exertions must be futile and uncertain; since it will be difficult, indeed, to communicate to them the violation that has been committed, and their proceedings will be neither systematical nor unanimous. It is said, however, that the difficulty of framing a bill of rights was insurmountable; but, Mr. President, I cannot agree in this opinion. Our experience, and the numerous precedents before us, would have furnished a very sufficient guide. At present there is no security even for the rights of conscience, and under the sweeping force of the sixth article [Supremacy Clause], every principle of a bill of rights, every stipulation for the most sacred and invaluable privileges of man, are left at the mercy of government.

Mr. Whitehill. I differ, Sir, from the honorable member from the city [Wilson] as to the impropriety or necessity of a bill of rights. If, indeed, the constitution itself so well defined the powers of the government that no mistake could arise, and we were well assured that our governors would always act right, then we might be satisfied without an explicit reservation of those rights with which the people ought not, and mean not to part. But, Sir, we know that it is the nature of power to seek its own augmentation, and thus the loss of liberty is the necessary consequence of a loose or extravagant delegation of authority. National freedom has been, and will be the sacrifice of ambition and power, and it is our duty to employ the present opportunity in stipulating such restrictions as are best calculated to protect us from oppression and slavery. Let us then, Mr. President, if other countries cannot supply an adequate example, let us proceed upon our own principles, and with the great end of government in view, the happiness of the people, it will be strange if we err. Government, we have been told, Sir, is yet in its infancy: we ought not therefore to submit to the shackles of foreign schools and opinions. In entering into the social compact, men ought not to leave their rulers at large, but erect a permanent land-mark by which they may learn the extent of their authority, and the people be able to discover the first encroachments on their liberties. But let us attend to the language of the system before us. "We the people of the United States," is a sentence that evidently shows the old foundation of the union is destroyed, the principle of confederation excluded, and a new and unwieldy system of consolidated empire is set up, upon the ruins of the present compact between the states. Can this be denied? No, Sir: It is artfully indeed, but it is incontrovertibly designed to abolish the independence and sovereignty of the states individually, an event which cannot be the wish of any good citizen of America, and therefore it ought to be prevented, by rejecting the plan which is calculated to produce it. What right indeed have we in the manner here proposed to violate the existing confederation? It is declared, that the agreement of nine states shall be sufficient to carry the new system into operation, and consequently to abrogate the old one. Then, Mr President, four of the present confederated states may not be comprehended in the compact: shall we, Sir, force these dissenting states into the measure? The consequences of that attempt are evidently such as no man can either justify or approve. But reverse the idea—would not these states have a fair pretext to charge the rest with an unconstitutional and unwarrantable abandonment of the nature and obligation of the union of 1776? And having shown sufficient reason why they could not accede to the proposed government, would they not still be entitled to demand a performance of the original compact between the states? Sir, these questions must introduce a painful anticipation of the confusion, contest, and a civil war, which, under such circumstances, the adoption of the offered system must produce. It will be proper, perhaps, to review the origin of this business. It was certainly, Mr. President, acknowledged on all hands, that an additional share of power for federal purposes ought to be delegated to Congress; and with a view to enquire how far it was necessary to strengthen and enlarge the jurisdiction of that body, the late convention was appointed under the authority, and by legislative acts of the several states. But how, Sir, did the convention act upon this occasion? Did they pursue the authority which was given to them? . . .

. . . [I]t appears that no other power was given to the delegates from this state (and I believe the power given by the other states was of the same nature and extent) than to increase in a certain degree the strength and energy of Congress; but it never was in the contemplation of any man that they were authorized to dissolve the present union, to abrogate the state sovereignties, and to establish one comprehensive government, novel in its structure, and in its probable operation oppressive and despotic. Can it then be said that the late convention did not assume powers to which they had no legal title? On the contrary, Sir, it is clear that they set aside the laws under which they were appointed, and under which alone they could derive any legitimate authority, they arrogantly exercised any powers that they found convenient to their object, and in the end they have overthrown that government which they were called upon to amend, in order to introduce one of their own fabrication.

True it is, Mr. President, that if the people intended to engage in one comprehensive system of continental government, the power to frame that system must have been conferred by them; for the legislatures of the states are sworn to preserve the independence of their respective constitutions, and therefore they could not, consistently with their most sacred obligations, authorize an act which sacrificed the individual to the aggregate sovereignty of the states. But it appears from the origin and nature of the commission under which the late convention assembled, that a more perfect confederation was the only object submitted to their wisdom, and not, as it is attempted by this plan, the total destruction of the government of Pennsylvania, and of every other state. So far, Sir, the interference of the legislatures was proper and efficient; but the moment the convention went beyond that object, they ceased to act under any legitimate authority, for the assemblies could give them none, and it cannot be pretended that they were called together by the people; for, till the preamble was produced, it never was understood that the people at large had been consulted upon the occasion, or that otherwise than through their representatives in the several states, they had given a sanction to the proceedings of that body. If, indeed, the federal convention, finding that the old system was incapable of repair, had represented the incurable defects to Congress, and advised that the original and inherent power of the people might be called into exercise for the institution of a new government, then, Sir, the subject would have come fairly into view, and we should have known upon what principles we proceeded. At present we find a convention appointed by one authority, but acting under the arbitrary assumption of another; and instead of transacting the business which was assigned to them, behold! they have produced a work of supererogation, after a mysterious labor of three months. Let us, however, Sir, attend for a moment to the constitution. And here we shall find, in a single line, sufficient matter for weeks of debate, and which it will puzzle any one member to investigate and define. But, besides the powers enumerated, we find in this constitution an authority is given to make all laws that are necessary to carry it effectually into operation, and what laws are necessary is a consideration left for Congress to decide. In constituting the representative body, the interposition of the Congress is likewise made conclusive; for, with the power of regulating the place and manner of elections, it is easy to perceive that the returns will always be so managed as to answer their purpose. It is strange to mark, however, what a sudden and striking revolution has taken place in the political sentiments of America; for, Sir, in the opening of our struggle with Great Britain, it was often insisted that annual parliaments were necessary to secure the liberties of the people, and yet it is here proposed to establish a house of representatives which shall continue for two, a senate for six, and a president for four years! What is there in this plan indeed, which can even assure us that the several departments shall continue no longer in office? Do we not know that an English parliament elected for three years, by a vote of their own body, extended their existence to seven, and with this example, Congress possessing a competent share of power may easily be tempted to exercise it. The advantages of annual elections are not at this day to be taught, and when every other security was withheld, I should still have thought there was some safety in the government, had this been left. The seats of Congress being held for so short a period, and by a tenure so precarious as popular elections, there could be no inducement to invade the liberties of the people, nor time enough to accomplish the schemes of ambition and tyranny. But when the period is protracted, an object is presented worthy of contention, and the duration of the office affords an opportunity for perpetuating the influence by which it was originally obtained. Another power designed to be vested in the new government, is the superlative power of taxation, which may be carried to an inconceivable excess, swallowing up every object of taxation, and consequently plundering the several states of every means to support their governments, and to administer their laws. Then, Sir, can it longer be doubted that this is a system of consolidation? That government which possesses all the powers of raising and maintaining armies, of regulating and commanding the militia, and of laying imposts and taxes of every kind, must be supreme, and will (whether in twenty or in one year, it signifies little to the event) naturally absorb every subordinate jurisdiction. It is in vain, Sir, to flatter ourselves that the forms of popular elections will be the means of self-preservation, and that the officers of the proposed government will uniformly act for the happiness of the people—for why should we run a risk which we may easily avoid? The giving such extensive and undefined power is a radical wrong that cannot be justified by any subsequent merit in the exercise; for in framing a new system, it is our duty rather to indulge a jealousy of the human character, than an expectation of unprecedented perfection. . . . A bill of rights, Mr. President, it has been said, would not only be unnecessary, but it would be dangerous, and for this special reason, that because it is not practicable to enumerate all the rights of the people, therefore it would be hazardous to secure such of the rights as we can enumerate! Truly, Sir, I will agree that a bill of rights may be a dangerous instrument, but it is to the views and projects of the aspiring ruler, and not the liberties of the citizen. Grant but this explicit criterion, and our governors will not venture to encroach; refuse it, and the people cannot venture to complain. From the formal language of magna charta we are next taught to consider a declaration of rights as superfluous; but, Sir, will the situation and conduct of Great Britain furnish a case parallel to that of America? It surely will not be contended that we are about to receive our liberties as a grant or concession from any power upon earth; so that if we learn anything from the English charter, it is this: that the people having negligently lost or submissively resigned their rights into the hands of the crown, they were glad to recover them upon any terms; their anxiety to secure the grant by the strongest evidence will be an argument to prove, at least, the expediency of the measure, and the result of the whole is a lesson instructing us to do by an easy precaution, what will hereafter be an arduous and perhaps insurmountable task. . . . Will it still be said, that the state governments would be adequate to the task of correcting the usurpations of Congress? Let us not, however, give the weight of proof to the boldness of assertion; for, if the opposition is to succeed by force, we find both the purse and the sword are almost exclusively transferred to the general government; and if it is to succeed by legislative remonstrance, we shall find that expedient rendered nugatory by the law of Congress, which is to be the supreme law of the land. Thus, Mr. President, must the powers and sovereignty of the several states be eventually destroyed. . . . Upon the whole, therefore, I wish it to be seriously considered, whether we have a right to leave the liberties of the people to such future constructions and expositions as may possibly be made upon this system. . . . I am not anxious, Mr. President, about forms—it is the substance which I wish to obtain; and therefore I acknowledge, if our liberties are secured by the frame of government itself, the supplementary instrument of a declaration of rights may well be dispensed with. . . . The question at present, Sir, is, however, of a preliminary kind—does the plan now in discussion propose a consolidation of the states? and will a consolidated government be most likely to promote the interests and happiness of America? If it is satisfactorily demonstrated, that in its principles or in its operation, the dissolution of the state sovereignties is not a necessary consequence, I shall then be willing to accompany the gentlemen on the other side in weighing more particularly its merits and demerits. But my judgment, according to the information I now possess, leads me to anticipate the annihilation of the several state governments—an event never expected by the people, and which would, I fervently believe, destroy the civil liberties of America.

Mr. Smilie. I am happy, Mr. President, to find the argument placed upon the proper ground, and that the honorable member from the city has so fully spoken on the question, whether this system proposes a consolidation or a confederation of the states, as that is, in my humble opinion, the source of the greatest objection, which can be made to its adoption. I agree likewise with him, Sir, that it is, or ought to be, the object of all governments, to fix upon the intermediate point between tyranny and licentiousness; and therefore, it will be one of the great objects of our enquiry, to ascertain how far the proposed system deviates from that point of political happiness. . . . I think however, Mr. President, it has been clearly argued, that the proposed system does not directly abolish, the governments of the several States, because its organization, and, for some time, perhaps, its operations, naturally pre-suppose their existence. But, Sir, it is not said, nor is thought, that the words of this instrument expressly announce that the sovereignty of the several States, their independency, jurisdiction, and power, are at once absorbed and annihilated by the general government. To this position and to this alone, the arguments of the honorable gentlemen can effectually apply, and there they must undoubtedly hold as long as the forms of State Government remain, at least, till a change takes place in the federal constitution. It is, however, upon other principles that the final destruction of the individual governments is asserted to be a necessary consequence of their association under this general form,—for, Sir, it is the silent but certain operation of the powers, and not the cautious, but artful tenor of the expressions contained in this system, that can excite terror, or generate oppression.

Hence, Sir, we may trace that passage which has been pronounced by the honorable delegate to the late convention with exultation and applause; but when it is declared that "We the people of the United States do ordain and establish this constitution," is not the very foundation a proof of a consolidated government, by the manifest subversion of the principle that constitutes a union of States, which are sovereign and independent, except in the specific objects of confederation? These words have a plain and positive meaning, which could not be misunderstood by those who employed them; and therefore, Sir, it is fair and reasonable to infer, that it was in contemplation of the framers of this system, to absorb and abolish the efficient sovereignty and independent powers of the several States, in order to invigorate and aggrandize the general government. The plan before us, then, explicitly proposes the formation of a new constitution upon the original authority of the people, and not an association of States upon the authority of their respective governments. On that ground, we perceive that it contains all the necessary parts of a complete system of government, the executive, legislative and judicial establishments; and when two separate governments are at the same time in operation, over the same people, it will be difficult indeed to provide for each the means of safety and defence against the other; but if those means are not provided, it will be easily foreseen, that the stronger must eventually subdue and annihilate the weaker institution. Let us then examine the force and influence of the new system, and enquire whether the small remnant of power left to the States can be adequate even to the trifling charge of its own preservation. Here, Sir, we find the right of making laws for every purpose is invested in the future governors of America, and in this is included the uncontrolled jurisdiction over the purses of the people. The power of raising money is indeed the soul, the vital prop of legislation, without which legislation itself cannot for a moment exist. It will, however, be remarked that the power of taxation, though extended to the general government, is not taken from the States individually. Yes, Sir!—but it will be remembered that the national government may take from the people just what they please, and if anything should afterwards remain, then indeed the exigencies of the State governments may be supplied from the scanty gleanings of the harvest. Permit me now, Sir, to call your attention to the powers enumerated in the 8th section of the first article, and particularly to that clause which authorizes the proposed Congress, "to lay and collect taxes, duties, imposts and excises, to pay the debts and provide for the common defence and general welfare of the United States." With such powers, Mr. President, what cannot the future governors accomplish? It will be said, perhaps, that the treasure, thus accumulated, is raised and appropriated for the general welfare and the common defence of the States; but may not this pretext be easily perverted to other purposes, since those very men who raise and appropriate the taxes, are the only judges of what shall be deemed the general welfare and common defence of the national government? If then, Mr. President, they have unlimited power to drain the wealth of the people in every channel of taxation, whether by imposts on our commercial intercourse with foreign nations, or by direct levies on the people, I repeat it, that this system must be too formidable for any single State, or even for a combination of the States, should an attempt be made to break and de-

stroy the yoke of domination and tyranny which it will hereafter set up.
. . . To assemble a military force would be impracticable; for the general
government, foreseeing the attempt would anticipate the means, by the
exercise of its indefinite control over the purses of the people; and, in
order to act upon the consciences as well as the persons of men, we find
it is expressly stipulated, that every officer of the State government shall
be sworn to support the constitution of the United States. Hence likewise,
Sir, I conclude that in every point of rivalship, in every contention for
power on the one hand and for freedom on the other, the event must
be favorable to the views and pretensions of a government gifted with
so decisive a pre-eminence. . . . For, Sir, the attachment of citizens to
their government and its laws is founded upon the benefits which they
derive from them, and it will last no longer than the duration of the
power to confer those benefits. When, therefore, the people of the respective States shall find their governments grown torpid, and divested of the
means to promote their welfare and interests, they will not, Sir, vainly
idolize a shadow, nor disburse their hard earned wealth without the prospect of a compensation. The constitution of the States having become
weak and useless to every beneficial purpose, will be suffered to dwindle
and decay, and thus if the governors of the Union are not too impatient
for the accomplishment of unrivalled and absolute dominion, the destruction of State jurisdiction will be produced by its own insignifi-
cance. . . .

3 · *Dissent of the Antifederalist Minority* · December 18, 1787

Following the Pennsylvania convention's approval of the new Constitu-
tion, the Antifederalist minority submitted a list summarizing their
objections. Here is perhaps the most complete single statement of the
Antifederalist position.

. . . We dissent, first, because it is the opinion of the most celebrated
writers on government, and confirmed by uniform experience, that a very
extensive territory cannot be governed on the principles of freedom, otherwise than by a confederation of republics, possessing all the powers of
internal government, but united in the management of their general and
foreign concerns. . . .

We dissent, secondly, because the powers vested in Congress by this
constitution, must necessarily annihilate and absorb the legislative, executive, and judicial powers of the several States, and produce from their
ruins one consolidated government, which from the nature of things will
be *an iron handed despotism,* as nothing short of the supremacy of despotic sway could connect and govern these United States under one government.

McMaster and Stone, *op. cit.,* pp. 464-83.

As the truth of this position is of such decisive importance, it ought to be fully investigated, and if it is founded to be clearly ascertained; for, should it be demonstrated that the powers vested by this constitution in Congress will have such an effect as necessarily to produce one consolidated government, the question then will be reduced to this short issue, viz.: whether satiated with the blessings of liberty, whether repenting of the folly of so recently asserting their unalienable rights against foreign despots at the expense of so much blood and treasure, and such painful and arduous struggles, the people of America are now willing to resign every privilege of freemen, and submit to the dominion of an absolute government that will embrace all America in one chain of despotism; or whether they will, with virtuous indignation, spurn at the shackles prepared for them, and confirm their liberties by a conduct becoming freemen.

That the new government will not be a confederacy of States, as it ought, but one consolidated government, founded upon the destruction of the several governments of the States, we shall now show.

The powers of Congress under the new constitution are complete and unlimited over the *purse* and the *sword,* and are perfectly independent of and supreme over the State governments, whose intervention in these great points is entirely destroyed. By virtue of their power of taxation, Congress may command the whole or any part of the property of the people. They may impose what imposts upon commerce, they may impose what land taxes, poll taxes, excises, duties on all written instruments and duties on every other article, that they may judge proper; in short, every species of taxation, whether of an external or internal nature, is comprised in section the eighth of article the first, viz.:

"The Congress shall have power to lay and collect taxes, duties, imposts, and excises, to pay the debts, and provide for the common defence and general welfare of the United States."

As there is no one article of taxation reserved to the State governments, the Congress may monopolize every source of revenue, and thus indirectly demolish the State governments, for without funds they could not exist; the taxes, duties and excises imposed by Congress may be so high as to render it impracticable to levy farther sums on the same articles; but whether this should be the case or not, if the State governments should presume to impose taxes, duties or excises on the same articles with Congress, the latter may abrogate and repeal the laws whereby they are imposed, upon the allegation that they interfere with the due collection of their taxes, duties or excises, by virtue of the following clause, part of section eighth, article first, viz.:

"To make all laws which shall be necessary and proper for carrying into execution the foregoing powers, and all other powers vested by this constitution in the government of the United States, or in any department or officer thereof."

The Congress might gloss over this conduct by construing every purpose for which the State legislatures now lay taxes, to be for the *"general welfare,"* and therefore as of their jurisdiction.

And the supremacy of the laws of the United States is established by article sixth, viz.: "That this constitution and the laws of the United States which shall be made in pursuance thereof, and *all treaties* made, or which shall be made under the authority of the United States, shall be the *supreme law* of the *land;* and *the judges in every State shall be bound thereby; anything in the constitution or laws of any State to the contrary notwithstanding."* It has been alleged that the words "pursuant to the constitution," are a restriction upon the authority of Congress; but when it is considered that by other sections they are invested with every efficient power of government, and which may be exercised to the absolute destruction of the State governments, without any violation of even the forms of the constitution, this seeming restriction, as well as every other restriction in it, appears to us to be nugatory and delusive; and only introduced as a blind upon the real nature of the government. In our opinion, "pursuant to the constitution" will be co-extensive with the *will* and *pleasure* of Congress, which, indeed, will be the only limitation of their powers.

We apprehend that two co-ordinate sovereignties would be a solecism in politics; that, therefore, as there is no line of distinction drawn between the general and State governments, as the sphere of their jurisdiction is undefined, it would be contrary to the nature of things that both should exist together—one or the other would necessarily triumph in the fulness of dominion. However, the contest could not be of long continuance, as the State governments are divested of every means of defence, and will be obliged by "the supreme law of the land" *to yield at discretion.*

It has been objected to this total destruction of the State governments that the existence of their legislatures is made essential to the organization of Congress; that they must assemble for the appointment of the senators and President-general of the United States. True, the State legislatures may be continued for some years, as boards of appointment merely, after they are divested of every other function; but the framers of the constitution, foreseeing that the people will soon become disgusted with this solemn mockery of a government without power and usefulness, have made a provision for relieving them from the imposition in section fourth of article first, viz.: "The times, places and manner of holding elections for senators and representatives shall be prescribed in each State by the legislature thereof; *but the Congress may at any time by law make or alter such regulations, except as to the place of choosing senators."*

As Congress have the control over the time of the appointment of the President-general, of the senators and of the representatives of the United States, they may prolong their existence in office for life by postponing the time of their election and appointment from period to period under various pretences, such as an apprehension of invasion, the factious disposition of the people, or any other plausible pretence that the occasion may suggest; and having thus obtained life-estates in the government, they may fill up the vacancies themselves by their control over the mode of appointment; with this exception in regard to the senators that as the place of appointment for them must, by the constitution, be in the particular State, they may depute some body in the respective States, to fill up the vacancies in the senate, occasioned by death, until they can venture to assume it themselves. . . .

The new Constitution, consistently with the plan of consolidation, contains no reservation of the rights and privileges of the State governments, which was made in the confederation of the year 1778, by article the 2d, viz.: "That each State retains its sovereignty, freedom and independence, and every power, jurisdiction and right which is not by this confederation expressly delegated to the United States in Congress assembled."

The legislative power vested in Congress by the foregoing recited sections, is so unlimited in its nature, may be so comprehensive and boundless in its exercise, that this alone would be amply sufficient to annihilate the State governments, and swallow them up in the grand vortex of general empire.

The judicial powers vested in Congress are also so various and extensive, that by legal ingenuity they may be extended to every case, and thus absorb the State judiciaries; and when we consider the decisive influence that a general judiciary would have over the civil polity of the several States, we do not hesitate to pronounce that this power, unaided by the legislative, would effect a consolidation of the States under one government. . . .

In short, consolidation pervades the whole constitution. It begins with an annunciation that such was the intention. The main pillars of the fabric correspond with it, and the concluding paragraph is a confirmation of it. The preamble begins with the words, "We the people of the United States," which is the style of a compact between individuals entering into a state of society, and not that of a confederation of States. . . .

We dissent, thirdly, because if it were practicable to govern so extensive a territory as these United States include, on the plan of a consolidated government, consistent with the principles of liberty and the happiness of the people, yet the construction of this Constitution is not calculated to attain the object; for independent of the nature of the case, it would of itself necessarily produce a despotism, and that not by the usual gradations, but with the celerity that has hitherto only attended revolutions effected by the sword.

To establish the truth of this position, a cursory investigation of the principles and form of this constitution will suffice.

The first consideration that this review suggests, is the omission of a

BILL OF RIGHTS ascertaining and fundamentally establishing those unalienable and personal rights of men, without the full, free and secure enjoyment of which there can be no liberty, and over which it is not necessary for a good government to have the control—the principal of which are the rights of conscience, personal liberty by the clear and unequivocal establishment of the writ of *habeas corpus,* jury trial in criminal and civil cases, by an impartial jury of the vicinage or county, with the common law proceedings for the safety of the accused in criminal prosecutions; and the liberty of the press, that scourge of tyrants, and the grand bulwark of every other liberty and privilege. The stipulations heretofore made in favor of them in the State constitutions, are entirely superseded by this Constitution.

The legislature of a free country should be so formed as to have a competent knowledge of its constituents, and enjoy their confidence. To produce these essential requisites, the representation ought to be fair, equal and sufficiently numerous to possess the same interests, feelings, opinions and views which the people themselves would possess, were they all assembled; and so numerous as to prevent bribery and undue influence, and so responsible to the people, by frequent and fair elections, as to prevent their neglecting or sacrificing the views and interests of their constituents to their own pursuits.

We will now bring the legislature under this Constitution to the test of the foregoing principles, which will demonstrate that it is deficient in every essential quality of a just and safe representation.

The House of Representatives is to consist of sixty-five members; that is one for about every 50,000 inhabitants, to be chosen every two years. Thirty-three members will form a quorum for doing business, and seventeen of these, being the majority, determine the sense of the house.

The Senate, the other constituent branch of the legislature, consists of twenty-six members, being *two* from each State, appointed by their legislatures every six years; fourteen senators make a quorum—the majority of whom, eight, determines the sense of that body, except in judging on impeachments, or in making treaties, or in expelling a member, when two-thirds of the senators present must concur.

The president is to have the control over the enacting of laws, so far as to make the concurrence of two-thirds of the representatives and senators present necessary, if he should object to the laws. . . .

The representation is moreover inadequate and unsafe, because of the long terms for which it is appointed, and the mode of its appointment, by which Congress may not only control the choice of the people, but may so manage as to divest the people of this fundamental right, and become self-elected. . . .

The next consideration that the constitution presents, is the undue and dangerous mixture of the powers of government; the same body possessing legislative, executive and judicial powers. The Senate is a constituent branch of the legislature, it has judicial power in judging on impeachments, and in this case unites in some measure the characters of judge and party, as all the principal officers are appointed by the president-general, with the concurrence of the Senate, and therefore they derive their offices in part from the Senate. This may bias the judgments of the senators, and tend to screen great delinquents from punishment. And the Senate has, moreover, various and great executive powers, viz., in concurrence with the president-general, they form treaties with foreign nations, that may control and abrogate the constitutions and laws of the several States. Indeed, there is no power, privilege or liberty of the State governments, or of the people, but what may be affected by virtue of this power. For all treaties, made by them, are to be the "supreme law of the land; anything in the constitution or laws of any State, to the contrary notwithstanding. . . ."

We have before considered internal taxation as it would effect the destruction of the State governments, and produce one consolidated government. We will now consider that subject as it affects the personal concerns of the people.

The power of direct taxation applies to every individual, as Congress, under this government, is expressly vested with the authority of laying a capitation or poll tax upon every person to any amount. This is a tax that, however oppressive in its nature, and unequal in its operation, is certain as to its produce and simple in its collection; it cannot be evaded like the objects of imposts or excise, and will be paid, because all that a man hath will he give for his head. This tax is so congenial to the nature of despotism, that it has ever been a favorite under such governments. Some of those who were in the late general convention from this State, have labored to introduce a poll tax among us.

The power of direct taxation will further apply to every individual, as Congress may tax land, cattle, trades, occupations, etc., to any amount, and every object of internal taxation is of that nature that however oppressive, the people will have but this alternative, either to pay the tax or let their property be taken, for all resistance will be vain. The standing army and select militia would enforce the collection.

For the moderate exercise of this power, there is no control left in the State governments, whose intervention is destroyed. No relief, or redress of grievances, can be extended as heretofore by them. There is not even a declaration of RIGHTS to which the people may appeal for the vindication of their wrongs in the court of justice. They must therefore, implicitly obey the most arbitrary laws, as the most of them will be pursuant to the principles and form of the constitution, and that strongest of all checks upon the conduct of administration, *responsibility to the people,* will not exist in this government. The permanency of the appointments of senators and representatives, and the control the congress have over their election, will place them independent of the sentiments and resentment of the people, and the administration having a greater interest in the government than in the community, there will be no consideration to restrain them from oppression and tyranny. In the government of this State, under the old confederation, the members of the legislature are taken from among the people, and their interests and welfare are so inseparably connected with those of their constituents, that they can derive no advantage from oppressive laws and taxes; for they would suffer in common with their fellow-citizens, would participate in the burthens they impose on the community, as they must return to the common level, after a short period; and notwithstanding every exertion of influence, every means of corruption, a necessary rotation excludes them from permanency in the legislature. . . .

A standing army in the hands of a government placed so independent of the people, may be made a fatal instrument to overturn the public liberties; it may be employed to enforce the collection of the most oppressive taxes, and to carry into execution the most arbitrary measures. An ambitious man who may have the army at his devotion, may step up into the throne, and seize upon absolute power.

The absolute unqualified command that Congress have over the militia may be made instrumental to the destruction of all liberty, both public and private; whether of a personal, civil or religious nature.

First, the personal liberty of every man, probably from sixteen to sixty years of age, may be destroyed by the power Congress have in organizing and governing of the militia. As militia they may be subjected to fines to any amount, levied in a military manner; they may be subjected to corporal punishments of the most disgraceful and humiliating kind; and to death itself, by the sentence of a court martial. To this our young men will be more immediately subjected, as a select militia, composed of them, will best answer the purposes of government.

Secondly, the rights of conscience may be violated, as there is no exemption of those persons who are conscientiously scrupulous of bearing arms. These compose a respectable proportion of the community in the State. This is the more remarkable, because even when the distresses of the late war, and the evident disaffection of many citizens of that description, inflamed our passions, and when every person who was obliged to risk his own life, must have been exasperated against such as on any account kept back from the common danger, yet even then, when outrage and violence might have been expected, the rights of conscience were held sacred.

At this momentous crisis, the framers of our State Constitution made the most express and decided declaration and stipulations in favor of the rights of conscience; but now, when no necessity exists, those dearest rights of men are left insecure.

Thirdly, the absolute command of Congress over the militia may be destructive of public liberty; for under the guidance of an arbitrary government, they may be made the unwilling instruments of tyranny. The militia of Pennsylvania may be marched to New England or Virginia to quell an insurrection occasioned by the most galling oppression, and aided by the standing army, they will no doubt be successful in subduing their liberty and independency; but in so doing, although the magnanimity of their minds will be extinguished, yet the meaner passions of resentment and revenge will be increased, and these in turn will be the ready and obedient instruments of despotism to enslave the others; and that with an irritated vengeance. Thus may the militia be made the instruments of crushing the last efforts of expiring liberty, of riveting the chains of despotism on their fellow-citizens, and on one another. This power can be exercised not only without violating the Constitution, but in strict conformity with it; it is calculated for this express purpose, and will doubtless be executed accordingly. . . .

We have not noticed the smaller, nor many of the considerable blemishes, but have confined our objections to the great and essential defects, the main pillars of the constitution; which we have shown to be inconsistent with the liberty and happiness of the people, as its establishment will annihilate the State governments, and produce one consolidated government that will eventually and speedily issue in the supremacy of despotism. . . .

VIRGINIA

4 · Excerpts from the Ratifying Convention · 1788

Excerpts from Virginia reveal the richness of the debate as well as some of the eloquence of leading Antifederalists—George Mason, James Monroe, Patrick Henry, and William Grayson. The converted Edmund Randolph and George Nicholas reflect the Federalist position.

Mr. George Mason. Mr. Chairman, whether the constitution be good or bad, the present clause clearly discovers, that it is a national government, and no longer a confederation. I mean that clause which gives the first hint of the general government laying direct taxes. The assumption of this power of laying direct taxes, does of itself, entirely change the confederation of the states into one consolidated government. This power being at discretion, unconfined, and without any kind of control, must carry every thing before it. The very idea of converting what was formerly a confederation, to a consolidated government, is totally subversive of every principle which has hitherto governed us. This power is calculated to annihilate totally the state governments. Will the people of this great community submit to be individually taxed by two different and distinct powers? Will they suffer themselves to be doubly harrassed? These two concurrent powers cannot exist long together; the one will destroy the

Elliot, III, 59-63, 218-20, 408, 410-16, 424-33.

other: the general government being paramount to, and in every respect more powerful than the state governments, the latter must give way to the former. Is it to be supposed that one national government will suit so extensive a country, embracing so many climates, and containing inhabitants, so very different in manners, habits, and customs? It is ascertained by history, that there never was a government, over a very extensive country, without destroying the liberties of the people: history also, supported by the opinions of the best writers, shews us, that monarchy may suit a large territory, and despotic, governments ever so extensive a country: but that popular governments can only exist in small territories. Is there a single example, on the face of the earth, to support a contrary opinion? Where is there one exception to this general rule? Was there ever an instance of a general national government extending over so extensive a country, abounding in such a variety of climates, &c. where the people retained their liberty? I solemnly declare, that no man is a greater friend to a firm union of the American states than I am: but, sir, if this great end can be obtained without hazarding the rights of the people, why should we recur to such dangerous principles? Requisitions have been often refused, sometimes from an impossibility of complying with them; often from that great variety of circumstances which retard the collection of monies, and perhaps, sometimes from a wilful design of procrastinating. But why shall we give up to the national government this power, so dangerous in its nature, and for which its members will not have sufficient information? Is it not well known, that what would be a proper tax in one state, would be grievous in another. . . .

The mode of levying taxes is of the utmost consequence, and yet here it is to be determined by those who have neither knowledge of our situation, nor a common interest with us, nor a fellow feeling for us: . . . if we trust the national government with an effectual way of raising the necessary sums, it is sufficient: every thing we do further is trusting the happiness and rights of the people: why then should we give up this dangerous power of individual taxation? Why leave the manner of laying taxes to those, who in the nature of things, cannot be acquainted with the situation of those on whom they are to impose them, when it can be done by those who are well acquainted with it? . . . I candidly acknowledge the inefficacy of the confederation, but requisitions have been made, which were impossible to be complied with: requisitions for more gold and silver than were in the United States. If we give the general government the power of demanding their quotas of the states, with an alternative of laying direct taxes, in case of noncompliance, then the mischief would be avoided; and the certainty of this conditional power would, in all human probability, prevent the application, and the sums necessary for the union would be then laid by the states, by those who know how it can best be raised, by those who have a fellow feeling for us. . . .[M]y principal objection is, that the confederation is converted to one general consolidated government, which, from my best judgment of it (and which perhaps will be shewn in the course of this discussion, to be really well founded) is one of the worst curses that can possibly befal a nation. Does any man suppose, that one general national government can exist in so extensive a country as this? I hope that a government may be framed which may suit us, by drawing a line between the general and state governments, and prevent that dangerous clashing of interest and power, which must, as it now stands, terminate in the destruction of one or the other. When we come to the judiciary, we shall be more convinced, that this government will terminate in the annihilation of the state governments: the question then will be, whether a consolidated government can preserve the freedom, and secure the rights of the people.

If such amendments be introduced as shall exclude danger, I shall most gladly put my hand to it. When such amendments, as shall, from the best information, secure the great essential rights of the people, shall be agreed to by gentlemen, I shall most heartily make the greatest concessions, and concur in any reasonable measure to obtain the desirable end of conciliation and unanimity. An indispensable amendment in this case, is, that congress shall not exercise the power of raising direct taxes till the states shall have refused to comply with the requisitions of congress. On this condition it may be granted, but I see no reason to grant it unconditionally; as the states can raise the taxes with more ease and lay them on the inhabitants with more propriety, than it is possible for the general government to do. If congress hath this power without control, the taxes will be laid by those who have no fellow-feeling or acquaintance with the people. This is my objection to the article now under consideration. It is a very great and important one. I therefore, beg gentlemen to consider it. Should this power be restrained, I shall withdraw my objections to this part of the constitution: but as it stands, it is an objection so strong in my mind, that its amendment is with me, a *sine qua non*, of its adoption. I wish for such amendments and such only, as are necessary to secure the dearest rights of the people.

Mr. James Monroe. . . . It [the national government] will also be strongly supported by the last clause in the eighth section of the first article, which vests it with the power of making all laws necessary to carry its powers into effect. The correspondent judicial powers will be an additional aid. There is yet another circumstance, which will throw the balance in the scale of the general government. A disposition in its favor, has shewn itself in all parts of the continent and will certainly become more and more predominant. Is it not to be presumed, that if a contest between the state legislatures and the general governments should arise, the latter would preponderate? The confederation has been deservedly reprobated, for its inadequacy to promote the public welfare. But this change is, in my opinion, very dangerous. It contemplates objects with which a federal government ought never to interfere. The concurrent interfering power, of laying taxes on the people, will occasion a perpetual conflict between the general and individual governments; which, for the reasons I have already mentioned, must terminate to the disadvantage, if not in the annihilation of the latter. Can it be presumed, that the people of America can patiently bear such a double oppression? Is it not to be presumed, that they will endeavor to get rid of one of the oppressors? I fear, sir, that it will ultimately end in the establishment of a monarchical government. The people, in order to be delivered from one species of tyranny, may submit to another. I am strongly impressed with the necessity of having a firm national government; but I am decidedly against giving it the power of direct taxation; because I think it endangers our liberties. My attachment to the union and an energetic government, is such, that I would consent to give the general government every power contained in that plan, except that of taxation.

As it will operate on all states and individuals, powers given it generally should be qualified. It may be attributed to the prejudice of my education, but I am a decided and warm friend to a bill of rights—the polar star, and great support of American liberty; and I am clearly of opinion, that the general powers conceded by that plan such as the impost, &c. should be guarded and checked by a bill of rights.

Permit me to examine the reasoning that admits, that all powers not given up are reserved. Apply this. If you give to the United States the power of direct taxation—in making all laws necessary to give it operation . . . suppose they should be of opinion that the right of the trial by jury was not one of the requisites to carry it into effect; there is no check on this constitution to prevent the formal abolition of it. There is a general power given to them, to make all laws that will enable them to carry their powers into effect. There are no limits pointed out. They are not restrained or controlled from making any law, however oppressive in its operation, which they may think necessary to carry their powers into effect. By this general unqualified power, they may infringe not only the trial by jury, but the liberty of the press, and every right that is not expressly secured or excepted, from that general power. I conceive that such general powers are very dangerous. Our great unalienable rights ought to be secured from being destroyed by such unlimited powers, either by a bill of rights, or by an express provision in the body of the constitution. It is immaterial in which of these two modes rights are secured. . . .

. . . There is a distinction between this government, and ancient and modern ones. The division of power in ancient governments, or in any government at present in the world, was founded on different principles from those of this government. What was the object of the distribution of power in Rome? It will not be controverted, that there was a composition or mixture of aristocracy, democracy, and monarchy, each of which had a repellent quality, which enabled it to preserve itself from being destroyed by the other two—so that the balance was continually maintained. . . .

What is the object of the division of power in America? Why is the government divided into different branches? For a more faithful and regular administration. Where is there a check? We have more to apprehend from the union of these branches, than from the subversion of any; and this union will destroy the rights of the people. There is nothing to prevent this coalition. But the contest which will probably subsist between the general government and the individual governments, will tend to produce it. There is a division of sovereignty between the national and state governments. How far then will they coalesce together? Is it not to be supposed that there will be a conflict between them? If so, will not the members of the former combine together? Where then will be the check to prevent encroachments on the rights of the people? There is not a third essentially distinct branch to preserve a just equilibrium, or to prevent such encroachments. In developing this plan of government, we ought to attend to the necessity of having checks. I can see no real checks in it.

Mr. George Mason. Mr. Chairman, gentlemen say there is no new power given by this clause [necessary-and-proper clause]. Is there any thing in this constitution which secures to the states the powers which are said to be retained? Will powers remain to the states which are not expressly guarded and reserved? . . . Among the enumerated powers, congress are to lay and collect taxes, duties, imposts and excises, and to pay the debts, and to provide for the general welfare, and common defence; and by that clause (so often called the sweeping clause) they are to make all laws necessary to execute those laws. Now suppose oppressions should arise under this government, and any writer should dare to stand forth and expose to the community at large, the abuses of those powers, could not congress, under the idea of providing for the general welfare, and under their own construction, say, that this was destroying the general peace, encouraging sedition, and poisoning the minds of the people? And could they not, in order to provide against this, lay a dangerous restriction on the press? . . . That congress should have power to provide for the general welfare of the union, I grant. But I wish a clause in the constitution with respect to all powers which are not granted, that they are retained by the states. Otherwise the power of providing for the general welfare may be perverted to its destruction.

. . . There was a clause in the confederation reserving to the states respectively, every power, jurisdiction, and right, not expressly delegated to the United States. This clause has never been complained of, but approved by all. Why not then have a similar clause in this constitution, in which it is the more indispensably necessary than in the confederation, because of the great augmentation of power vested in the former? In my humble apprehension, unless there be some such clear and finite expression, this clause now under consideration will go to any thing our rulers may think proper. Unless there be some express declaration, that every thing not given is retained, it will be carried to any power congress may please. . . .

   Mr. Henry. Mr. Chairman, the necessity of a bill of rights appears to me to be greater in this government, than ever it was in any government, before. . . . Let us consider the sentiments which have been entertained by the people of America on this subject. At the revolution it must be admitted, that it was their sense to put down those great rights which ought in all countries to be held inviolable and sacred. Virginia did so, we all remember. She made a compact to reserve, expressly, certain rights.

   When fortified with full, adequate and abundant representation, was she satisfied with that representation? No. She most cautiously and guardedly reserved and secured those invaluable, inestimable rights and privileges, which no people, inspired with the least glow of the patriotic liberty, ever did inspire or ever can, abandon. She is called upon now to abandon them, and dissolve that compact which secured them to her. She is called upon to accede to another compact which most infallibly supersedes and annihilates her present one. . . . If you intend to reserve your unalienable rights, you must have the most express stipulation. For if implication be allowed, you are ousted of those rights. If the people do not think it necessary to reserve them they will be supposed to be given up. How were the congressional rights defined when the people of America united by a confederacy to defend their liberties and rights against the tyrannical attempts of Great Britain? The states were not then contented with implied reservation. . . . It was expressly declared in our confederation that every right was retained by the states respectively, which was not given up to the government of the United States. But there is no such thing here. You therefore, by a natural and unavoidable implication, give up your rights to the general government. . . . You have disposed of them to congress, without a bill of rights—without check, limitation, or control. And still you have checks and guards—still you keep barriers—pointed where? Pointed against your weakened, prostrated, enervated state government! You have a bill of rights to defend you against the state government, which is bereaved of all power; and yet you have none against congress, though in full and exclusive possession of all power! . . . What barriers have you to oppose to this most strong energetic government? To that government, you have nothing to oppose. All your defence is given up. This is a real actual defect.

   . . . By this constitution, some of the best barriers of human rights are thrown away. Is there not an additional reason to have a bill of rights? By the ancient common law, the trial of all facts is decided by a jury of impartial men from the immediate vicinage. This paper speaks of different juries from the common law, in criminal cases; and in civil controversies excludes trial by jury altogether. There is therefore more occasion for the supplementary check of a bill of rights now, than then. Congress from their general powers may fully go into business of human legislation. They may legislate in criminal cases from treason to the lowest offence, petty larceny. They may define crimes and prescribe punishments. In the definition of crimes, I trust they will be directed by what wise representatives ought to be governed by. But when we come to punishments, no latitude ought to be left, nor dependence put on the virtue of representatives. What says our bill of rights? "That excessive bail ought not to be required, nor excessive fines imposed, nor cruel and unusual punishments inflicted." Are you not therefore now calling on those gentlemen who are to compose congress, to prescribe trials and define punishments without this control? Will they find sentiments there similar to this bill of rights? You let them loose—you do more—you depart from the genius of your country. That paper tells you, that the trial of crimes shall be by jury, and held in the state where the crime shall have been committed. Under this extensive provision, they may proceed in a manner extremely dangerous to liberty—persons accused may be carried from one extremity of the state to another, and be tried, not by an impartial jury of the vicinage, acquainted with his character, and the circumstances of the fact, but by a jury unacquainted with both, and who may be biassed against him. Is not this sufficient to alarm men? . . .

A bill of rights may be summed up in a few words. What do they tell us? That our rights are reserved. Why not say so? Is it because it will consume too much paper? Gentlemen's reasoning against a bill of rights, do not satisfy me. . . . A bill of rights is a favorite thing with the Virginians, and the people of the other states likewise. It may be their prejudice, but the government ought to suit their geniuses, otherwise its operation will be unhappy. A bill of rights, even if its necessity be doubtful, will exclude the possibility of dispute; and with great submission, I think the best way is to have no dispute. . . .

Mr. Grayson thought it questionable, whether rights not given up were reserved. A majority of the states, he observed, had expressly reserved certain important rights by bills of rights, and that in the confederation there was a clause, declaring expressly, that every power and right not given up, was retained by the states. It was the general sense of America, that such a clause was necessary; otherwise why did they introduce a clause which was totally unnecessary? It had been insisted, he said, in many parts of America, that a bill of rights, was only necessary between a prince and people, and not in such a government as this, which was a compact between the people themselves. This did not satisfy his mind, for so extensive was the power of legislation, in his estimation, that he doubted, whether when it was once given up, *any thing* was retained. He further remarked, that there were some negative clauses in the constitution, which refuted the doctrine contended for by the other side: for instance, the second clause of the ninth section, of the first article, provided, that "the privilege of the writ of *habeas corpus* shall not be suspended, unless when in cases of rebellion or invasion, the public safety may require it."—And by the last clause of the same section "no title of nobility shall be granted by the United States." Now if these restrictions had not been here inserted he asked, whether congress would not most clearly have had a right to suspend that great and valuable right, and to grant titles of nobility? When, in addition to these considerations, he saw they had an indefinite power to provide for the general welfare, he thought there were great reasons to apprehend great dangers. He thought therefore, that there ought to be a bill of rights.

Mr. George Nicholas, in answer to the two gentlemen last up, observed, that though there was a declaration of rights in the government of Virginia, it was no conclusive reason that there should be one in this constitution. For, if it was unnecessary in the former, its omission in the latter could be no defect. They ought therefore to prove, that it was essentially necessary to be inserted in the constitution of Virginia: that there were five or six states in the union, which had no bill of rights, separately and distinctly as such. But they annexed the substance of a bill of rights of their respective constitutions. These states, he further observed, were as free as this state, and their liberties as secure as ours. If so, gentlemen's arguments from the precedent were not good. In Virginia, all powers were given to the government without any exception. It was different in the general government, to which certain special powers were delegated for certain purposes. He asked, which was the more safe? Was it safer to grant general powers, than certain limited powers? This much as to the theory, continued he. What is the practice of this invaluable government? Have your citizens been bound by it? They have not, Sir. You have violated that maxim, "that no man shall be condemned without a fair trial." That man who was killed, not *secundum artem,* was deprived of his life, without the benefit of law, and in express violation of this declaration of rights, which they confide in so much. But, Sir, this bill of rights was no security. It is but a paper check. It has been violated in many other instances. Therefore from theory and practice, it may be concluded, that this government with special powers, without any express exceptions, is better than a government with general powers, and special exceptions. But the practice of England is against us. The rights there reserved to the people, are to limit and check the king's prerogative. It is easier to enumerate the exceptions to his prerogative, than to mention all the cases to which it extends. Besides, these reservations being only formed in acts of the legislature, may be altered by the representatives of the people, when they think proper. No comparison can be made of this, with the other governments he mentioned. There is no stipulation between the king and people. The former is possessed of absolute unlimited authority. . . . A bill of rights is only an acknowledgment of the pre-existing claim to rights in the people. They belong to us, as much as if they had been inserted in the constitution. But it is said, that if it be doubtful, the possibility of dispute ought to be precluded. Admitting it was proper for the convention to have inserted a bill of rights, it is not proper here to propose it, as the condition of our accession to the union. Would you reject this government for its omission, dissolve the union, and bring miseries on yourselves and posterity? I hope the gentleman does not oppose it on this ground solely. Is there another reason? He said, that it is not only the general wish of this state, but all the states, to have a bill of rights. If it be so, where is the difficulty of having this done by way of subsequent amendments? We shall find the other states willing to accord with their own favorite wish. The gentleman last up says, that the power of legislation includes every thing a general power of legislation does. But this is a special power of legislation. Therefore it does not contain that plenitude of power which he imagines. They cannot legislate in any case but those particularly enumerated. No gentleman, who is a friend to the government, ought to withhold his assent from it for this reason. . . .

Mr. Henry. . . . There are express restrictions which are in the shape of a bill of rights, but they bear the name of the ninth section [of article 1]. The design of the negative expressions in this section, is to prescribe limits beyond which the powers of congress shall not go. These are the sole bounds intended by the American government. Whereabouts do we stand with respect to a bill of rights? Examine it and compare it to the idea manifested by the Virginian bill of rights, or that of the other states. The restraints in this congressional bill of rights, are so feeble and few, that it would have been infinitely better, to have said nothing about it. The fair implication is, that they can do every thing they are not forbidden to do. What will be the result if congress, in the course of their legislation, should do a thing not restrained by this ninth section? It will fall as an incidental power to congress, not being prohibited expressly in the constitution. The first prohibition is, that the privilege of the writ of *habeas corpus* shall not be suspended, but when in case of rebellion, or invasion, the public safety may require it. It results clearly, that if it had not said so, they could suspend it in all cases whatsoever. It reverses the position of the friends of this constitution, that every thing is retained which is not given up. For instead of this, every thing is given up, which is not expressly reserved. It does not speak affirmatively, and say that it shall be suspended in those cases. But that it shall not be suspended but in certain cases; going on a supposition that every thing which is not negatived, shall remain with congress. If the power remains with the people, how can congress supply the want of an affirmative grant? They cannot do it by implication, which destroys their doctrine. The Virginia bill of rights interdicts the relinquishment of the sword and purse without control. That bill of rights secures the great and principal rights of mankind. But this bill of rights extends to but very few cases, and is destructive of the doctrine advanced by the friends of that paper. . . . You are told, that your rights are secured in this new government. They are guarded in no other part, but this ninth section. The few restrictions in that section are your own safeguards. They may control your actions, and your every words, without being repugnant to that paper. The existence of your dearest privileges will depend on the consent of congress, for they are not within the restrictions of the ninth section. . . .

Gov. Randolph. Mr. Chairman, the general review which the gentleman has taken of the ninth section is . . . inconsistent. . . . I declared some days ago that I would give my suffrage for this constitution, not because I considered it without blemish, but because the critical situation of our country demanded it. I invite those who think with me to vote for the constitution. But where things occur in it, which I disapprove of, I shall be candid in exposing my objections.

Permit me to return to that clause, which is called by gentlemen the sweeping clause. I observed yesterday, that I conceived the construction which had been put on this clause by the advocates of the constitution was too narrow; and that the construction put upon it by the other party, was extravagant. The immediate explanation appears to me most rational. The former contend, that it gives no supplementary power, but only enables them to make laws to execute the delegated powers, or in other words, that it only involves the powers incidental to those expressly delegated. By incidental powers they mean those which are necessary for the principal thing. That the incident is inseparable from the principal, is a maxim in the construction of laws. A constitution differs from a law. For a law only embraces one thing—but a constitution embraces a number of things, and is to have a more liberal construction. . . . The European constitutions sometimes consist in detached statutes or ordinances.—Sometimes they are on record, and sometimes they depend on immemorial tradition. The American constitutions are singular, and their construction ought to be liberal. On this principle what should be said of the clause under consideration. If incidental powers be those only which are necessary for the principal thing, the clause would be superfluous. . . .

The gentleman supposes, that complete and unlimited legislation is vested in the congress of the United States. This supposition is founded on false reasoning. What is the present situation of this state? She has possession of all rights of sovereignty, except those given to the confederation. She must delegate powers to the confederate government. It is necessary for her public happiness. Her weakness compels her to confederate with the twelve other governments. She trusts certain powers to the general government in order to support, protect, and defend the union. Now is there not a demonstrable difference between the principle of the state government, and the general government? There is not a word said in the state government of the powers given to it, because they are general. But in the general constitution, its powers are enumerated. Is it not then fairly deducible, that it has no power but what is expressly given it? For if its powers were to be general, an enumeration would be needless. . . .

But the rhetoric of the gentleman has highly colored the dangers of giving the general government an indefinite power of providing for the general welfare. I contend that no such power is given. They have power "to lay and collect taxes, duties, imposts and excises, to pay the debts, and provide for the common defence, and general welfare of the United States." Is this an independent, separate, substantive power, to provide for the general welfare of the United States? No, Sir. They can lay and collect taxes, &c. For what? To pay the debts and provide for the general welfare. Were not this the case, the following part of the clause would be absurd. It would have been treason against common language. Take it altogether, and let me ask if the plain interpretation be not this: a power to lay and collect taxes, &c. in order to provide for the general welfare, and pay debts.

On the subject of a bill of rights, the want of which has been complained of, I will observe that it has been sanctified by such reverend authority, that I feel some difficulty in going against it. I shall not, however, be deterred from giving my opinion on this occasion, let the consequence be what it may. At the beginning of the war we had no certain bill of rights; for our charter cannot be considered as a bill of rights. It is nothing more than an investiture in the hands of the Virginia citizens, of those rights which belonged to the British subjects. When the British thought proper to infringe our rights, was it not necessary to mention in our constitution, those rights which ought to be paramount to the power of the legislature? Why is the bill of rights distinct from the constitution? I consider bills of rights in this view, that the government should use them when there is a departure from its fundamental principles, in order to restore them.

This is the true sense of a bill of rights. If it be consistent with the constitution, or contains additional rights, why not put it in the constitution? If it be repugnant to the constitution, here will be a perpetual scene of warfare between them. The honorable gentleman has praised the bill of rights of Virginia, and called it his guardian angel, and vilified this constitution for not having it. Give me leave to make a distinction between the representatives of the people of a particular country, who are appointed as the ordinary legislature, having no limitation to their powers, and another body arising from a compact and certain delineated powers. Were a bill of rights necessary in the former, it would not [be] in the latter; for the best security that can be in the latter, is the express enumeration of its powers. But let me ask the gentleman where his favorite rights are violated? They are not violated by the tenth section, which contains restrictions on the states. Are they violated by the enumerated powers? . . . Is there not provision made in this constitution for the trial by jury in criminal cases? Does not the third article provide, that the trial of all crimes shall be by jury, and held where the said crimes shall have been committed? Does it not follow, that the cause and nature of the accusation must be produced, because otherwise they cannot proceed on the cause? . . .

As to the exclusion of excessive bail and fines, and cruel and unusual punishments, this would follow of itself without a bill of right. . . . Before these cruel punishments can be inflicted, laws must be passed, and judges must judge contrary to justice. This would excite universal discontent, and detestation of the members of the government. They might involve their friends in the calamities resulting from it, and could be removed from office. I never desire a greater security than this which I believe to be absolutely sufficient. . . .

Then, Sir, the freedom of the press is said to be insecure. God forbid that I should give my voice against the freedom of the press. But I ask (and with confidence that it cannot be answered), where is the page where it is restrained? If there had been any regulation about it, leaving it insecure, then there might have been reason for clamors. But this is not the case. If it be, I again ask for the particular clause which gives liberty to destroy the freedom of the press?

He has added religion to the objects endangered in his conception. Is there any power given over it? Let it be pointed out. Will he not be contented with the answer that has been frequently given to that objection? The variety of sects which abounds in the United States is the best security for the freedom of religion. No part of the constitution, even if strictly construed, will justify a conclusion, that the general government can take away, or impair the freedom of religion.

The gentleman asks, with triumph, shall we be deprived of these valuable rights? Had there been an exception, or an express infringement of those rights, he might object. But I conceive every fair reasoner will agree, that there is no just cause to suspect that they will be violated. . . .

I said when I opened my observations, that I thought the friends of the constitution were mistaken, when they supposed the powers granted by the last clause of the eighth section [necessary-and-proper] to be merely incidental; and that its enemies were equally mistaken when they put such an extravagant construction upon it.

My objection is, that the clause is ambiguous, and that that ambiguity may injure the states. My fear is, that it will by gradual accessions gather to a dangerous length. This is my apprehension, and I disdain to disown it. I will praise it where it deserves it, and censure it where it appears defective. But, sir, are we to reject it, because it is ambiguous in some particular instances? I cast my eyes to the actual situation of America; I see the dreadful tempest, to which the present calm is a prelude, if disunion takes place. I see the anarchy which must happen, if no energetic government be established. In this situation, I would take the constitution, were it more objectionable than it is. For if anarchy and confusion follow disunion, an enterprising man may enter into the American throne. I conceive there is no danger. The representatives are chosen by and from among the people. They will have a fellow-feeling for the farmers and planters. The twenty-six senators, representatives of the states, will not be those desperadoes and horrid adventurers which they are represented to be. The state legislatures, I trust, will not forget the duty they owe to their country so far, as to choose such men to manage their federal interests. I trust that the members of congress themselves will explain the ambiguous parts: and if not, the states can combine in order to insist on amending the ambiguities. I would depend on the present actual feeling of the people of America, to introduce any amendment which may be necessary. I repeat it again, though I do not reverence the constitution, that its adoption is necessary to avoid the storm which is hanging over America, and that no greater curse can befal her, than the dissolution of the political connection between the states. Whether we shall propose previous or subsequent amendments, is now the only dispute.—It is supererogation to repeat again the arguments in support of each. But I ask gentlemen, whether, as eight states have adopted it, it be not safer to adopt it, and rely on the probability of obtaining amendments, than by a rejection to hazard a breach of the union? . . .

NORTH CAROLINA

5 · *Excerpts from the Ratifying Convention* · 1788

In North Carolina, Antifederalists Spencer, Bloodworth, and Lenoir matched wits with Federalists Galloway, Iredell, and Maclaine.

Mr. Spencer. . . . It appears to me that the state governments are not sufficiently secured, and that they may be swallowed up by the great mass of powers given to congress. If that be the case, such power should

Elliot, IV, 76-78, 162, 169-75, 184-87, 194-98, 203-7.

not be given; for from all the notions which we have concerning our happiness and well-being, the state governments are the basis of our happiness security and prosperity. A large extent of country ought to be divided into such a number of states, as that the people may conveniently carry on their own government. This will render the government perfectly agreeable to the genius and wishes of the people. If the United States were to consist of ten times as many states they might all have a degree of harmony. Nothing would be wanting but some cement for their connection. On the contrary, if all the United States were to be swallowed up by the great mass of powers given to congress, the parts that are more distant in this great empire would be governed with less and less energy. It would not suit the genius of the people to assist in the government. Nothing would support government in such a case as that but military coercion. Armies would be necessary in different parts of the United States. The expence which they would cost, and the burdens which . . . would . . . be laid upon the people, would be ruinous. I know of no way that is likely to produce the happiness of the people, but to preserve, as far as possible, the existence of the several states, so that they shall not be swallowed up.

It has been said, that the existence of the state governments is essential to that of the general government, because they choose the senators. By this clause it is evident, that it is in the power of congress to make any alterations, except as to the place of choosing senators. They may alter the time from six to twenty years, or to any time; for they have an unlimited control over the time of elections. They have also an absolute control over the election of the representatives. It deprives the people of the very mode of choosing them. It seems nearly to throw the whole power of election into the hands of congress. It strikes at the mode, time and place of choosing representatives. It puts all but the place of electing senators, into the hands of congress. This supersedes the necessity of continuing the state legislatures. This is such an article as I can give no sanction to, because it strikes at the foundation of the government on which depends the happiness of the states, and the general government. It is with reluctance I make the objection. I have the highest veneration for the characters of the framers of this constitution. I mean to make objections only which are necessary to be made. I would not take up time unnecessarily. As to this matter, it strikes at the foundation of every thing. . . .

Mr. Iredell. . . . I apprehend, that the honorable gentlemen is mistaken as to the extent of the operation of this clause [article 1, section 4, par. 1]. He supposes, that the control of the general government over elections looks forward to a consolidation of the states; and that the general word, *time,* may extend to twenty, or any number of years. In my humble opinion, this clause does by no means warrant such a construction. We ought to compare other parts with it. Does not the constitution say, that representatives shall be chosen every second year? The right of choosing them, therefore, reverts to the people every second year. . . . The very existence of the general government depends on that of the state governments. The state legislatures are to choose the senators. Without a senate there can be no congress. The state legislature are also to direct the manner of choosing the president. Unless, therefore, there are state legislatures to direct that manner, no president can be chosen. The same observation may be made as to the house of representatives, since, as they are to be chosen by the electors of the most numerous branch of each state legislature. If there are no state legislatures, there are no persons to choose the house of representatives. Thus it is evident, that the very existence of the general government depends on that of the state legislatures, and of course, that their continuance cannot be endangered by it. . . .

Mr. Spencer. . . . The states do not act in their political capacities, but the government is proposed for individuals. The very caption of the constitution shews that this is the case. The expression, "We the people of the United States," shews that this government is intended for individuals; there ought therefore to be a bill of rights. I am ready to acknowledge that the congress ought to have the power of executing its laws. Heretofore, because all the laws of the confederation were binding on the states in their political capacities, courts had nothing to do with them; but now the thing is entirely different. The laws of congress will be binding on individuals, and those things which concern individuals will be brought properly before the courts. . . . I still think that a bill of rights is necessary. This necessity arises from the nature of human societies. When individuals enter into society, they give up some rights to secure the rest. There are certain human rights that ought not to be given up, and which ought in some manner to be secured. With respect to these great essential rights, no latitude ought to be left. They are the most inestimable gifts of the great creator, and therefore ought not to be destroyed, but ought to be secured. They ought to be secured to individuals in consideration of the other rights which they give up to support society. . . .

Mr. Maclaine. Mr. Chairman, I beg leave to make a few observations. One of the gentleman's objections to the constitution now under consideration is, that it is not the act of the states but of the people; but that it ought to be the act of the states, and he instances the delegation of power by the states to the confederation, at the commencement of the war as a proof of this position. I hope, sir, that all power is in the people, and not in the state governments. If he will not deny the authority of the people to delegate power to agents, and to devise such a government as a majority of them thinks will promote their happiness, he will withdraw his objection. The people, sir, are the only proper authority to form a government. They, sir, have formed their state governments, and can alter them at pleasure. Their transcendent power is competent to form this or any other government which they think promotive to their happiness. But the gentleman contends that there ought to be a bill of rights, or something of that kind—something declaring expressly, that all power not expressly given to the constitution, ought to be retained by the states, and he produces the confederation as an authority for its necessity. When the confederation was made, we were by no means so well acquainted with the principles of government as we are now. We were then jealous of the power of our rulers, and had an idea of the British government when we entertained that jealousy. There is no people on earth so well acquainted with the nature of government as the people of America generally are. We know now, that it is agreed upon by most writers, and men of judgment and reflection, that all power is in the people and immediately derived from them. The gentleman surely must know, that if there be certain rights which never can, nor ought to be given up, these rights cannot be said to be given away, merely because we have omitted to say that we have not given them up. Can any security arise from declaring that we have a right to what belongs to us? Where is the necessity of such a declaration? If we have this inherent, this unalienable, this indefeasible title to those rights, if they are not given up, are they not retained? If congress should make a law beyond the powers and the spirit of the constitution, should we not say to congress, "You have no authority to make this law. There are limits beyond which you cannot go. You cannot exceed the power prescribed by the constitution. You are amenable to us for your conduct. This act is unconstitutional. We will disregard it, and punish you for the attempt."

But the gentleman seems to be most tenacious of the judicial power of the states. The honorable gentleman must know, that the doctrine of reservation of power not relinquished, clearly demonstrates that the judicial power of the states is not impaired. . . .

The federal court has jurisdiction only in some instances. There are many instances in which no court but the state courts can have any jurisdiction whatsoever, except where parties claim land under the grant of different states, or the subject of dispute arises under the constitution itself. The state courts have exclusive jurisdiction over every other possible controversy that can arise between the inhabitants of their own states; nor can the federal courts intermeddle with such disputes either originally or by appeal. There is a number of other instances where, though jurisdiction is given to the federal courts, it is not taken away from the state courts. If a man in South Carolina owes me money, I can bring suit in the courts of that state, as well as in any inferior federal court. I think gentlemen cannot but see the propriety of leaving to the general government the regulation of the inferior federal tribunals. This is a power which our own state legislature has. We may trust congress as well as them.

Mr. *Spencer* answered, that the gentleman last up had misunderstood him. . . . I do not mean to contend, that the laws of the general government should not operate upon individuals. I before observed that this was necessary, as laws could not be put in execution against states, without the agency of the sword, which instead of answering the ends of government would destroy it. I endeavored to show, that as the government was not to operate against states, but against individuals, the rights of individuals ought to be properly secured. In order to constitute this security, it appears to me there ought to be such a clause in the constitution as there was in the confederation, expressly declaring, that every power, jurisdiction and right, which are not given up by it, remain in the states. Such a clause would render a bill of rights unnecessary. But as there is no such clause, I contend, that there should be a bill of rights, ascertaining and securing the great rights of the states and people. . . .

Mr Chairman, the gentleman . . . insists, that what is not given up in the constitution, is retained. He must recollect I said yesterday, that we could not guard with too much care, those essential rights and liberties which ought never to be given up. There is no express negative—no fence against their being trampled upon. They might exceed the proper boundary, without being taken notice of. When there is no rule but a vague doctrine, they might make great strides and get possession of so much power, that a general insurrection of the people would be necessary to bring an alteration about. But if a boundary were set up, when the boundary is passed, the people would take notice of it immediately. . . .

Mr. *Iredell.* This clause [article VI, par. 2] is supposed to give too much power, when in fact it only provides for the execution of those powers which are already given in the foregoing articles. What does it say? That "this constitution, and the laws of the United States which shall be made in pursuance thereof, and all treaties made or which shall be made under the authority of the United States, shall be the supreme law of the land; and the judges in every state shall be bound thereby, any thing in the constitution or laws of any state to the contrary notwithstanding." What is the meaning of this, but that as we have given power we will support the execution of it? We should act like children to give power and deny the legality of executing it. It is saying no more than that when we adopt the government we will maintain and obey it: in the same manner as if the constitution of this state had said, that when a law is passed in conformity to it, we must obey that law. Would this be objected to? Then when the congress passes a law consistent with the constitution, it is to be binding on the people. If congress under pretence of executing one power, should in fact usurp another they will violate the constitution. . . .

Mr. Chairman, every power delegated to congress, is to be executed by laws made for that purpose. It is necessary to particularise the powers intended to be given in the constitution, as having no existence before, but after having enumerated what we give up, it follows of course, that whatever is done by virtue of that authority, is legal without any new authority or power. The question then under this clause, will always be whether congress has exceeded its authority. If it has not exceeded it we must obey, otherwise not. This constitution when adopted, will become a part of our state constitution; and the latter must yield to the former, only in those cases where power is given by it. It is not to yield to it in any other case whatever. For instance, there is nothing in the constitution of this state establishing the authority of a federal court. Yet the federal court when established, will be as constitutional as the superior court is now under our constitution. It appears to me merely a general clause, the amount of which is that when they pass an act, if it be in the execution of a power given by the constitution, it shall be binding on the people, otherwise not. . . .

Mr. Bloodworth. This [Supremacy] clause will be the destruction of every law which will come in competition with the laws of the United States. Those laws and regulations which have been, or shall be made in this state, must be destroyed by it, if they come in competition with the powers of congress. Is it not necessary to define the extent of its operation? . . . This clause seems to me too general, and I think its extent ought to be limited and defined. I should suppose every reasonable man would think some amendments to it was necessary.

Mr. Maclaine. Mr Chairman, that it will destroy the state sovereignty is a very popular argument. . . . Government is formed for the happiness and prosperity of the people at large. The powers given it are for their own good. We have found by several years' experience, that government taken by itself nominally, without adequate power, is not sufficient to promote their prosperity. Sufficient powers must be given to it. The powers to be given the general government, are proposed to be withdrawn from the authority of the state governments, in order to protect and secure the union at large. This proposal is made to the people. No man will deny their authority to delegate powers and recall them, in all free countries. But, says the gentleman last up, the construction of the constitution is in the power of congress, and it will destroy the sovereignty of the state governments. It may be justly said, that it diminishes the power of the state legislatures, and the diminution is necessary to the safety and prosperity of the people; but it may be fairly said, that the members of the general government, the president, senators and representatives, whom we send thither by our free suffrages to consult our common interest, will not wish to destroy the state governments, because the existence of the general government will depend on that of the state governments.

But what is the sovereignty, and who is congress? One branch—the people at large, and the other branch the states by their representatives. Do people fear the delegation of power to themselves—to their own representatives? But he [Bloodworth] objects, that the laws of the union are to be the supreme laws of the land. Is it not proper that their laws should be the law of the land, and paramount to those of any particular state? Or is it proper that the laws of any particular state should control the laws of the United States? Shall a part control the whole? To permit the local laws of any state to control the laws of the union, would be to give the general government no powers at all. If the judges are not to be bound by it, the powers of congress will be nugatory. This is self-evident and plain. Bring it home to every understanding; it is so clear it will force itself upon it. . . .

Every gentleman must see the necessity for the laws of the union to be paramount to those of the separate states; and that the powers given by this constitution must be executed. What, shall we ratify a government and then say it shall not operate?—This would be the same as not to ratify. . . .

Mr. J. Galloway. Mr. Chairman, I should make no objection to this clause were the powers granted by the constitution sufficiently defined: for I am clearly of opinion that it is absolutely necessary for every government, and especially for a general government, that its laws should be the supreme law of the land. But I hope the gentlemen of the committee will advert to the 10th section of the first article. This is a negative which the constitution of our own state does not impose upon us. I wish the committee to attend to that part of it which provides that no state shall pass any law which will impair the obligation of contracts. Our public securities are at a low ebb, and have been so for many years. We well know that this country has taken those securities as specie. This hangs over our heads as a contract. . . .

Mr. Iredell. . . . It has been asked . . . what is the meaning of that part, where it is said, that the United States shall *guarantee* to every state in the union a republican form of government, and why a *guarantee* of religious freedom was not included. The meaning of the guarantee provided was this—there being thirteen governments confederated, upon a republican principle, it was essential to the existence and harmony of the confederacy that each should be a republican government, and that no state should have a right to establish an

aristocracy or monarchy. That clause was therefore inserted to prevent any state from establishing any government but a republican one.
Every one must be convinced of the mischief that would ensue, if any
state had a right to change its government to a monarchy. . . . But consistently with this restriction the states may make what change in their
own governments they think proper. Had congress undertaken to guarantee religious freedom, or any particular species of it, they would then
have had a pretence to interfere in a subject they have nothing to do with.
Each state, so far as the clause in question does not interfere, must be
left to the operation of its own principles.

There is a degree of jealousy which it is impossible to satisfy. Jealousy
in a free government ought to be respected; but it may be carried to too
great an extent. It is impracticable to guard against all possible danger
of people's choosing their officers indiscreetly. If they have a right to
choose, they may make a bad choice. . . .

Mr. Lenoir. . . . I think it [the constitution] not proper for our adoption, as I consider that it endangers our liberties. When we consider this
system collectively, we must be surprised to think, that any set of men
who were delegated to amend the confederation, should propose to annihilate it. For that and this system are utterly different, and cannot
exist together. It has been said that the fullest confidence should be put
in those characters who formed this constitution. We will admit them in
private and public transactions to be good characters. But, sir, it appears
to me . . . that they exceeded their powers. Those gentlemen had no
sort of power to form a new constitution altogether, neither had the
citizens of this country such an idea in their view. I cannot undertake
to say what principles actuated them. I must conceive they were mistaken
in their politics, and that this system does not secure the unalienable
rights of freemen. It has some aristocratical and some monarchical features, and perhaps some of them intended the establishment of one of
these governments. Whatever might be their intent . . . it will lead to
the most dangerous aristocracy that ever was thought of—an aristocracy
established on a constitutional bottom! I conceive that this is so dangerous, that I should like as well to have no constitution at all. Their powers are almost unlimited. . . .

My constituents instructed me to oppose the adoption of this constitution. The principal reasons are as follow: The right of representation is
not fairly and explicitly preserved to the people, it being easy to evade
that privilege as provided in this system, and the terms of election being
too long. . . . The senators are chosen for six years, and two-thirds of
them with the president have most extensive powers. They may enter into
a dangerous combination. And they may be continually re-elected. The
president may be as good a man as any in existence, but he is but a man.
He may be corrupt. He has an opportunity of forming plans dangerous

to the community at large. I shall not enter into the minutiæ of this system, but I conceive that whatever may have been the intention of its framers, that it leads to a most dangerous aristocracy. It appears to me that instead of securing the sovereignty of the states, it is calculated to melt them down into one solid empire. If the citizens of this state like a consolidated government, I hope they will have virtue enough to secure their rights. I am sorry to make use of the expression, but it appears to me to be a scheme to reduce this government to an aristocracy. It guarantees a republican form of government to the states; when all these powers are in congress it will only be a form. It will be past recovery, when congress has the power of the purse and the sword. The power of the sword is in explicit terms given to it. The power of direct taxation gives the purse. They may prohibit the trial by jury, which is a most sacred and valuable right. There is nothing contained in this constitution to bar them from it. The federal courts have also appellate cognizance of law and fact: the sole cause of which is to deprive the people of that trial, which it is optional in them to grant or not. We find no provision against infringement on the rights of conscience. Ecclesiastical courts may be established, which will be destructive to our citizens. They may make any establishment they think proper. They have also an exclusive legislation in their ten miles square, to which may be added their power over the militia, who may be carried thither and kept there for life. Should any one grumble at their acts, he would be deemed a traitor, and perhaps taken up and carried to the exclusive legislation, and there tried without a jury. We are told there is no cause to fear. When we consider the great powers of congress, there is great cause of alarm. They can disarm the militia. If they were armed, they would be a resource against great oppressions. The laws of a great empire are difficult to be executed. If the laws of the union were oppressive they could not carry them into effect, if the people were possessed of proper means of defence.

It was cried out that we were in a most desperate situation, and that congress could not discharge any of their most sacred contracts. I believe it to be the case. But why give more power than is necessary? The men who went to the federal convention, went for the express purpose of amending the government, by giving it such additional powers as were necessary. If we should accede to this system, it may be thought proper by a few designing persons to destroy it in a future age, in the same manner that the old system is laid aside. The confederation was binding on all the states. It could not be destroyed but with the consent of all the states. There was an express article to that purpose. The men who were deputed to the convention, instead of amending the old, as they were solely empowered and directed to do, proposed a new system. If the best characters departed so far from their authority, what may not be apprehended from others who may be agents in the new government?

It is natural for men to aspire to power—it is the nature of mankind to be tyrannical, therefore it is necessary for us to secure our rights and liberties as far as we can; but it is asked why we should suspect men who are to be chosen by ourselves, while it is their interest to act justly, and while men have self-interest at heart? I think the reasons which I have given are sufficient to answer that question. We ought to consider the depravity of human nature, the predominant thirst of power which is in the breast of every one, the temptations our rulers may have, and the unlimited confidence placed in them by this system. These are the foundation of my fears. They would be so long in the general government that they would forget the grievances of the people of the states.

But it is said we shall be ruined if separated from the other states, which will be the case if we do not adopt. If so, I would put less confidence in those states. The states are all bound together by the confederation, and the rest cannot break from us without violating the most solemn compact. If they break that, they will this.

But it is urged that we ought to adopt, because so many other states have. In those states which have patronized and ratified it, many great men have opposed it. The motives of those states I know not. It is the goodness of the constitution we are to examine. We are to exercise our own judgments, and act independently. And as I conceive we are not out of the union, I hope this constitution will not be adopted till amendments are made. Amendments are wished for by the other states. . . .

The president has . . . great powers. He has the nomination of all officers and a qualified negative on the laws. He may delay the wheels of government. He may drive the senate to concur with his proposal. He has other extensive powers. There is no assurance of the liberty of the press. They may make it treason to write against the most arbitrary proceedings. They have power to control our elections as much as they please. It may be very oppressive on this state, and all the southern states. . . .

I wish not to be so understood as to be so averse to this system, as that I should object to all parts of it, or attempt to reflect on the reputation of those gentlemen who formed it; though it appears to me that I would not have agreed to any proposal but the amendment of the confederation. If there were any security for the liberty of the people, I would, for my own part, agree to it. But in this case, as millions yet unborn are concerned, and deeply interested in our decision, I would have the most positive and pointed security. I shall therefore hope that before this house will proceed to adopt this constitution, they will propose such amendments to it, as will make it complete; and when amendments are adopted, perhaps I will be as ready to accede to it as any man.—One thing will make it aristocratical. Its powers are very indefinite. There was a very necessary clause in the confederation, which is omitted in this system. That was a clause declaring that every power, &c. not given to congress, was reserved to the states. The omission of this clause makes the power so much greater.—Men will naturally put the fullest construction on the power given them. Therefore lay all restraint on them, and form a plan to be understood by every gentleman of this committee, and every individual of the community. . . .

JEFFERSON, MADISON, AND THE BILL OF RIGHTS

Thomas Jefferson reflects the American mind of the early years of the Republic. He was not, as he said, "of the party of federalists. But I am much farther from that of the antifederalists." Influential in converting Madison to support a Bill of Rights for the new Constitution, Jefferson favored amendments which would safeguard individual rights without sapping the energy of the national government.

1 · Madison to Jefferson · December 9, 1787

. . . As yet a large majority of the people are . . . ["much disposed to adopt the new Constitution"]. As yet also are a majority of the Assembly. What change may be produced by the united influence of exertions of Mr. Henry, Mr. Mason, and the Governor [Randolph] with some pretty able auxiliaries, is uncertain. My information leads me to suppose there must be three parties in Virginia. The first for adopting without attempting amendments. This includes Genl. [Washington] and the other deputies who signed the Constitution. . . . At the head of the 2d. party which urges amendments are the Governor and Mr. Mason. These do not object to the substance of the Government but contend for a few additional guards in favor of the Rights of the States and of the people. I am not able to enumerate the characters which fall in with their ideas, as distinguished from those of a third Class, at the head of which is Mr. Henry. This class concurs at present with the patrons of amendments, but will probably contend for such as strike at the essence of the System, and must lead to an adherence to the principle of the existing Confederation, which most thinking men are convinced is a visionary one, or to a partition of the Union into several Confederacies. . . .

2 · Jefferson to Madison · December 20, 1787

. . . I have little to fill a letter. I will therefore make up the deficiency by adding a few words on the Constitution proposed by our Convention. I like much the general idea of framing a government which should go on of itself peaceably, without needing continual recurrence to the state

Julian P. Boyd, ed., *The Papers of Thomas Jefferson* (Princeton, N.J.: Princeton University Press, 1955-1958), XII, 410.
Boyd, XII, 439-42.

legislatures. I like the organization of the government into Legislative, Judiciary and Executive. I like the power given the Legislature to levy taxes; and for that reason solely approve of the greater house being chosen by the people directly. For tho' I think a house chosen by them will be, very illy qualified to legislate for the Union, for foreign nations &c. yet this evil does not weigh against the good of preserving inviolate the fundamental principle that the people are not to be taxed but by representatives chosen immediately by themselves. I am captivated by the compromise of the opposite claims of the great and little states, of the latter to equal, and the former to proportional influence. I am much pleased too with the substitution of the method of voting by persons, instead of that of voting by states: and I like the negative given to the Executive with a third of either house, though I should have liked it better had the Judiciary been associated for that purpose, or invested with a similar and separate power. There are other good things of less moment. I will now add what I do not like. First the omission of a bill of rights providing clearly and without the aid of sophisms for freedom of religion, freedom of the press, protection against standing armies, restriction against monopolies, the eternal and unremitting force of the habeas corpus laws, and trials by jury in all matters of fact triable by the laws of the land and not by the law of Nations. To say, as Mr. Wilson does that a bill of rights was not necessary because all is reserved in the case of the general government which is not given, while in the particular ones all is given which is not reserved might do for the Audience to whom it was addressed, but is surely gratis dictum, opposed by strong inferences from the body of the instrument, as well as from the omission of the clause of our present confederation which had declared that in express terms. It was a hard conclusion to say because there has been no uniformity among the states as to the cases triable by jury, because some have been so incautious as to abandon this mode of trial, therefore the more prudent states shall be reduced to the same level of calamity. It would have been much more just and wise to have concluded the other way that as most of the states had judiciously preserved this palladium, those who had wandered should be brought back to it, and to have established general right instead of general wrong. Let me add that a bill of rights is what the people are entitled to against every government on earth, general or particular, and what no just government should refuse, or rest on inference. The second feature I dislike, and greatly dislike, is the abandonment in every instance of the necessity of rotation in office, and most particularly in the case of the President. Experience concurs with reason in concluding that the first magistrate will always be reelected if the constitution permits it. He is then an officer for life. . . . If once elected, and at a second or third election outvoted by one or two votes, he will pretend false votes, foul play, hold possession of the reins of government, be supported by the states voting for him, especially if they are the central ones lying in a compact body themselves and separating their opponents. . . . It may be said that if elections are to be attended with these disorders, the seldomer they are renewed the better. But experience shews that the only way to prevent disorder is to render them uninteresting by frequent changes. An incapacity to be elected a second time would have been the only effectual preventative. The power of removing him every fourth year by the vote of the people is a power which will not be exercised. The king of Poland is removeable every day by the Diet, yet he is never removed. . . . I do not pretend to decide what would be the best method of procuring the establishment of the manifold good things in this constitution, and of getting rid of the bad. Whether by adopting it in hopes of future amendment, or, after it has been duly weighed and canvassed by the people, after seeing the parts they generally dislike, and those they generally approve, to say to them "We see now what you wish. Send together your deputies again, let them frame a constitution for you omitting what you have condemned, and establishing the powers you approve. Even these will be a great addition to the energy of your government."—At all events I hope you will not be discouraged from other trials, if the present one should fail of it's full effect.—I have thus told you freely what I like and dislike: merely as a matter of curiosity for I know your own judgment has been formed on all these points after having heard every thing which could be urged on them. I own I am not a friend to a very energetic government. It is always oppressive. The late rebellion in Massachusetts has given more alarm than I think it should have done. Calculate that one rebellion in 13 states in the course of 11 years, is but one for each state in a century and a half. No country should be so long without one. Nor will any degree of power in the hands of government prevent insurrections. France with all it's despotism, and two or three hundred thousand men always in arms has had three insurrections in the three years I have been here in every one of which greater numbers were engaged than in Massachusetts and a great deal more blood was spilt. . . . After all, it is my principle that the will of the Majority should always prevail. If they approve the proposed Convention in all it's parts, I shall concur in it chearfully, in hopes that they will amend it whenever they shall find it work wrong. . . .

3 · Madison to Jefferson · April 22, 1788

The adversaries take very different grounds of opposition. Some are opposed to the substance of the plan; others to particular modifications only. Mr. Henry is supposed to aim at disunion. Col. Mason is growing every day more bitter, and outrageous in his efforts to carry his point; and will probably in the end be thrown by the violence of his passions into the politics of Mr. H——y. The preliminary question will

Boyd, XIII, 98-99.

be whether previous alterations shall be insisted on or not? Should this be carried in the affirmative, either a conditional ratification, or a proposal for a new Convention will ensue. In either event, I think the Constitution and the Union will be both endangered. It is not to be expected that the States which have ratified will reconsider their determinations, and submit to the alterations prescribed by Virga. and if a second Convention should be formed, it is as little to be expected that the same spirit of compromise will prevail in it as produced an amicable result to the first. It will be easy also for those who have latent views of disunion, to carry them on under the mask of contending for alterations popular in some but inadmissible in other parts of the U. States.

4 • Jefferson to Madison • July 31, 1788

I sincerely rejoice at the acceptance of our new Constitution by nine states. It is a good canvas, on which some strokes only want retouching. What these are, I think are sufficiently manifested by the general voice from North to South, which calls for a bill of rights. It seems pretty generally understood that this should go to Juries, Habeas corpus, Standing armies, Printing, Religion and Monopolies. I conceive there may be difficulty in finding general modification of these suited to the habits of all the states. But if such cannot be found then it is better to establish trials by jury, the right of Habeas corpus, freedom of the press and freedom of religion in all cases, and to abolish standing armies in time of peace, and Monopolies, in all cases, than not to do it in any. The few cases wherein these things may do evil, cannot be weighed against the multitude wherein the want of them will do evil. In disputes between a foreigner and a native, a trial by jury may be improper. But if this exception cannot be agreed to, the remedy will be to model the jury by giving the medietas linguae in civil as well as criminal cases. Why suspend the Hab. corp. in insurrections and rebellions? The parties who may be arrested may be charged instantly with a well defined crime. Of course the judge will remand them. If the publick safety requires that the government should have a man imprisoned on less probable testimony in those than in other emergencies; let him be taken and tried, retaken and retried, while the necessity continues, only giving him redress against the government for damages. Examine the history of England: see how few of the cases of the suspension of the Habeas corpus law have been worthy of that suspension. They have been either real treasons wherein the parties might as well have been charged at once, or sham-plots where it was shameful they should ever have been suspected. Yet for the few cases wherein the suspension of the hab. corp. has done real good, that operation is now become habitual, and the minds of the nation almost prepared to live under it's constant suspension. A declaration that the federal government will never restrain the presses from printing any thing they please, will not take away the liability of the printers for false facts printed. The declaration that religious faith shall be unpunished, does not give impunity to criminal acts dictated by religious error. The saying there shall be no monopolies lessens the incitements to ingenuity, which is spurred on by the hope of a monopoly for a limited time, as of 14, years; but the benefit even of limited monopolies is too doubtful to be opposed to that of their general suppression. If no check can be found to keep the number of standing troops within safe bounds, while they are tolerated as far as necessary, abandon them altogether, discipline well the militia, and guard the magazines with them. More than magazine-guards will be useless if few, and dangerous if many. No European nation can ever send against us such a regular army as we need fear, and it is hard if our militia are not equal to those of Canada or Florida. My idea then is, that tho' proper exceptions to these general rules are desireable and probably practicable, yet if the exceptions cannot be agreed on, the establishment of the rules in all cases will do ill in very few. I hope therefore a bill of rights will be formed to guard the people against the federal government, as they are already guarded against their state governments in most instances. . . .

5 · Madison to Jefferson · August 23, 1788

. . . It appears that a large majority [in North Carolina] has decided against the Constitution as it stands, and according to the information here received has made the alterations proposed by Virginia the conditions on which alone that State will unite with the others. Whether this be the precise State of the case I cannot say. It seems at least certain that she has either rejected the Constitution, or annexed conditions precedent to her ratification. It cannot be doubted that this bold step is to be ascribed in part to the influence of the minority in Virginia which lies mostly in the Southern part of the State, and to the management of its leader. It is in part ascribed also by some to assurances transmitted from leading individuals here, that New York would set the example of rejection. The event, whatever may have been its cause, with the tendency of the circular letter from the Convention of N. York, has somewhat changed the aspect of things and has given fresh hopes and exertions to those who opposed the Constitution. The object with them now will be to effect an early Convention composed of men who will essentially mutilate the system, particularly in the article of taxation, without which in my opinion the system cannot answer the purposes for which it was intended. An early Convention is in every view to be dreaded in the present temper of America. A very short period of delay would produce the double advantage of diminishing the heat and increasing the light of all parties. A trial for one year will probably suggest more real amendments than all the antecedent speculations of our most sagacious politicians.

6 · George Washington to Jefferson · August 31, 1788

The merits and defects of the proposed Constitution have been largely and ably discussed. For myself, I was ready to have embraced any tolerable compromise that was competent to save us from impending ruin; and I can say, there are scarcely any of the amendments which have been suggested to which I have *much* objection, except that which goes to the prevention of direct taxation—and that, I presume, will be more strenuously advocated and insisted upon hereafter than any other. I had indulged the expectation, that the New Government would enable those entrusted with its administration to do justice to the public creditors and retrieve the National character. But if no means are to be employed but requisitions, that expectation was vain and we may as well recur to the old Confederation. If the system can be put in operation without touching much the Pockets of the People, perhaps, it may be done; but, in my judgment, infinite circumspection and prudence are yet necessary in the experiment. It is nearly impossible for any body who has not been on the spot to conceive (from any description) what the delicacy and danger of our situation have been. Though the peril is not passed entirely; thank God! the prospect is somewhat brightening. You will probably have heard before the receipt of this letter, that the general government has been adopted by eleven States. . . .

7 · Madison to Jefferson · September 21, 1788

The Circular letter from the New York Convention has rekindled an ardor among the opponents of the federal Constitution for an *immediate* revision of it by another General Convention. You will find in one of the papers inclosed the result of the consultations in Pennsylvania on that subject. Mr. Henry and his friends in Virginia enter with great zeal into the scheme. Governour Randoph also espouses it; but with a wish to prevent if possible danger to the article which extends the power of the Government to internal as well as external taxation. It is observable that the views of the Pennsylva. meeting do not rhyme very well with those of the Southern advocates for a Convention; the objects most eagerly pursued by the latter being unnoticed in the Harrisburg proceedings. The effect of the Circular letter on other States is less well known. I conclude that it will be the same every where among those who opposed the Constitution, or contended for a conditional ratification of it. Whether an early Convention will be the result of this united effort is more than can at this moment be foretold. The measure will certainly be industriously opposed in some parts of the Union, not only by those who wish for no alterations, but by others who would prefer the other mode provided in the Constitution, as most expedient at present for introducing those supplemental safeguards to liberty against which no objections can be raised; and who would moreover approve of a Convention for amending the frame of the Government itself, as soon as time shall have somewhat corrected the feverish state of the public mind and trial have pointed its attention to the true defects of the system.

8 · Madison to Jefferson · October 17, 1788

. . . My own opinion has always been in favor of a bill of rights, provided it be so framed as not to imply powers not meant to be included in the enumeration. At the same time I have never thought the omission a material defect, nor been anxious to supply it even by *subsequent* amendment, for any other reason than that it is anxiously desired by others. I have favored it because I supposed it might be of use, and if properly executed could not be of disservice. I have not viewed it in an important light—1. because I conceive that in a certain degree, though not in the extent argued by Mr. Wilson, the rights in question are reserved by the manner in which the federal powers are granted. 2. because there is great reason to fear that a positive declaration of some of the most essential rights could not be obtained in the requisite latitude. I am sure that the rights of conscience in particular, if submitted to public definition would be narrowed much more than they are likely ever to be by an assumed power. One of the objections in New England was that the Constitution by prohibiting religious tests, opened a door for Jews Turks & infidels. 3. because the limited powers of the federal Government and the jealousy of the subordinate Governments, afford a security which has not existed in the case of the State Governments, and exists in no other. 4. because experience proves the inefficacy of a bill of rights on those occasions when its controul is most needed. Repeated violations of these parchment barriers have been committed by overbearing majorities in every State. In Virginia I have seen the bill of rights violated in every instance where it has been opposed to a popular current. Notwithstanding the explicit provision contained in that instrument for the rights of Conscience, it is well known that a religious establishment wd have taken place in that State, if the Legislative majority had found as they expected, a majority of the people in favor of the measure; and I am persuaded that if a majority of the people were now of one sect, the measure would still take place and on narrower ground than was then proposed, notwithstanding the additional obstacle which the law has since created. Wherever the real power in a Government lies, there is the danger of oppression. In our Governments the real power lies in the majority of the Community, and the invasion of private rights is *chiefly* to be apprehended, not from acts of Government contrary to the sense of its constituents, but from acts in which the Government is the mere instrument of the major number of the Constituents. This is a truth of great importance, but not yet sufficiently attended to; and is probably more strongly impressed on my mind by facts, and reflections suggested by them, than on yours which has contemplated abuses of power issuing from a very different quarter. Wherever there is an interest and power to do wrong, wrong will generally be done, and not less readily by a powerful & interested party than by a powerful and interested prince. The difference so far as it relates to the superiority of republics over monarchies, lies in the less degree of probability that interest may prompt more abuses of power in the former than in the latter; and in the security in the former agst an oppression of more than the smaller part of the Society, whereas in the former [latter] it may be extended in a manner to the whole. The difference so far as it relates to the point in question—the efficacy of a bill of rights in controuling abuses of power—lies in this: that in a monarchy the latent force of the nation is superior to that of the Sovereign, and a solemn charter of popular rights must have a great effect, as a standard for trying the validity of public acts, and a signal for rousing & uniting the superior force of the community; whereas in a popular Government, the political and physical power may be considered as vested in the same hands, that it is a majority of the people, and, consequently the tyrannical will of the Sovereign is not [to] be controuled by the dread of an appeal to any other force within the community. What use then it may be asked can a bill of rights serve in popular Governments? I answer the two following which, though less essential than in other Governments, sufficiently recommend the precaution: 1. The political truths declared in that solemn manner acquire by degrees the character of fundamental maxims of free Governments, and as they become incorporated with the national sentiment, counteract the impulses of interest and passion. 2. Altho, it be generally true as above stated that the danger of oppression lies in the interested majorities of the people rather than in usurped acts of the Government, yet there may be occasions on which the evil may spring from the latter source; and on such, a bill of rights will be a good ground for an appeal to the sense of the community. Perhaps too there may be a certain degree of danger, that a succession of artful and ambitious rulers may by gradual & well timed advances, finally erect an independent Government on the subversion of liberty. Should this danger exist at all, it is prudent to guard agst it, especially when the precaution can do no injury. At the same time I must own that I see no tendency in our Governments to danger on that side. It has been remarked that there is a tendency in all Governments to an augmentation of power at the expence of liberty. But the remark as usually understood does not appear to me well founded. Power when it has attained a certain degree of energy and independence goes on generally to further degrees. But when below that degree, the direct tendency is to further degrees of relaxation, until the abuses of liberty beget a sudden transition to an undue degree of power. With this explanation the remark may be true; and in the latter sense only is it, in my opinion applicable to the Governments in America. It is a melancholy reflection that liberty should be equally exposed to danger whether the Government have too much or too little power, and that the line which divides these extremes should be so inaccurately defined by experience.

Supposing a bill of rights to be proper the articles which ought to compose it, admit of much discussion. I am inclined to think that *absolute* restrictions in cases that are doubtful, or where emergencies may overrule them, ought to be avoided. The restrictions however strongly marked on paper will never be regarded when opposed to the decided sense of the public, and after repeated violations in extraordinary cases they will lose even their ordinary efficacy. Should a Rebellion or insurrection alarm the people as well as the Government, and a suspension of the Hab. Corp. be dictated by the alarm, no written prohibitions on earth would prevent the measure. Should an army in time of peace be gradually established in our neighborhood by Brit. or Spain, declarations on paper would have as little effect in preventing a standing force for the public safety. The best security agst these evils is to remove the pretext for them. With regard to Monopolies, they are justly classed among the greatest nuisances in Government. But is it clear that as encouragements to literary works and ingenious discoveries, they are not too valuable to be wholly renounced? Would it not suffice to reserve in all cases a right to the public to abolish the privilege at a price to be specified in the grant of it? Is there not also infinitely less danger of this abuse in our Governments than in most others? Monopolies are sacrifices of the many to the few. Where the power is in the few it is natural for them to sacrifice the many to their own partialities and corruptions. Where the power as with us is in the many not in the few the danger cannot be very great that the few will be thus favored. It is much more to be dreaded that the few will be unnecessarily sacrificed to the many. . . .

9 · Madison to Jefferson · December 8, 1788

. . . The questions which divide the public at present relate 1. to the extent of the amendments that ought to be made to the Constitution,

2. to the mode in which they ought to be made. The friends of the Constitution, some from an approbation of particular amendments, others from a spirit of conciliation, are generally agreed that the System should be revised. But they wish the revisal to be carried no farther than to supply additional guards for liberty, without abridging the sum of power transferred from the States to the general Government, or altering previous to trial, the particular structure of the latter and are fixed in opposition to the risk of another Convention, whilst the purpose can be as well answered, by the other mode provided for introducing amendments. Those who have opposed the Constitution, are on the other hand, zealous for a second Convention, and for a revisal which may either not be restrained at all, or extend at least as far as alterations have been proposed by any State. Some of this class are, no doubt, friends to an effective Government, and even to the substance of the particular Government in question. It is equally certain that there are others who urge a second Convention with the insidious hope of throwing all things into Confusion, and of subverting the fabric just established, if not the Union itself. If the first Congress embrace the policy which circumstances mark out, they will not fail to propose of themselves, every desirable safeguard for popular rights; and by thus separating the well meaning from the designing opponents fix on the latter their true character, and give to the Government its due popularity and stability. . . .

10 • Jefferson to Francis Hopkinson • March 13, 1789

. . . You say that I have been dished up to you as an antifederalist, and ask me if it be just. My opinion was never worthy enough of notice to merit citing: but since you ask it I will tell it you. I am not a Federalist, because I never submitted the whole system of my opinions to the creed of any party of men whatever in religion, in philosophy, in politics, or in any thing else where I was capable of thinking for myself. Such an addiction is the last degradation of a free and moral agent. If I could not go to heaven but with a party, I would not go there at all. Therefore I protest to you I am not of the party of federalists. But I am much farther from that of the antifederalists. I approved from the first moment, of the great mass of what is in the new constitution, the consolidation of the government, the organisation into Executive, legislative and judiciary, the subdivision of the legislative, the happy compromise of interests between the great and little states by the different manner of voting in the different houses, the voting by persons instead of states, the qualified negative on laws given to the Executive which however I should have liked better if associated with the judiciary also as in New York, and the power of taxation. I thought at first that the latter might have been limited.

A little reflection soon convinced me it ought not to be. What I disapproved from the first moment also was the want of a bill of rights to guard liberty against the legislative as well as executive branches of the government, that is to say to secure freedom in religion, freedom of the press, freedom from monopolies, freedom from unlawful imprisonment, freedom from a permanent military, and a trial by jury in all cases determinable by the laws of the land. I disapproved also the perpetual re-eligibility of the President. To these points of disapprobation I adhere. My first wish was that the 9. first conventions might accept the constitution, as the means of securing to us the great mass of good it contained, and that the 4. last might reject it, as the means of obtaining amendments. But I was corrected in this wish the moment I saw the much better plan of Massachusets [sic] and which had never occurred to me. With respect to the declaration of rights I suppose the majority of the United states are of my opinion: for I apprehend all the antifederalists, and a very respectable proportion of the federalists think that such a declaration should now be annexed. The enlightened part of Europe have given us the greatest credit for inventing this instrument of security for the rights of the people, and have been not a little surprised to see us so soon give it up. With respect to the re-eligibility of the president, I find myself differing from the majority of my countrymen, for I think there are but three states of the 11. which have desired an alteration of this. And indeed, since the thing is established, I would wish it not to be altered during the life of our great leader, whose executive talents are superior to those I beleive [sic] of any man in the world, and who alone by the authority of his name and the confidence reposed in his perfect integrity, is fully qualified to put the new government so under way as to secure it against the efforts of opposition. But having derived from our error all the good there was in it I hope we shall correct it the moment we can no longer have the same person at the helm. These, my dear friend, are my sentiments, by which you will see I was right in saying I am neither federalist nor antifederalist; that I am of neither party, nor yet a trimmer between parties. . . .

11 • Jefferson to Madison • March 15, 1789

. . . Your thoughts on the subject of the Declaration of rights in the letter of Oct. 17, I have weighed with great satisfaction. Some of them had not occurred to me before, but were acknoleged [sic] just in the moment they were presented to my mind. In the arguments in favor of a declaration of rights, you omit one which has great weight with me, the legal check which it puts into the hands of the judiciary. This is a body, which if rendered independent, and kept strictly to their own department merits great confidence for their learning and integrity. In fact what degree of confidence would be too much for a body composed of such men as Wythe, Blair, and Pendleton? On characters like these the "civium ardor prava jubentium" would make no impression. I am happy to find that on the whole you are a friend to this amendment. The Declaration of rights is like all other human blessings alloyed with some inconveniences, and not accomplishing fully it's object. But the good in this instance vastly overweighs the evil. I cannot refrain from making short answers to the objections which your letter states to have been raised. 1. That the rights in question are reserved by the manner in which the federal powers are granted. Answer. A constitutive act may certainly be so formed as to need no declaration of rights. The act itself has the force of a declaration as far as it goes: and if it goes to all material points nothing more is wanting. In the draught of a constitution which I had once a thought of proposing in Virginia, and printed afterwards, I endeavored to reach all the great objects of public liberty, and did not mean to add a declaration of rights. Probably the object was imperfectly executed: but the deficiencies would have been supplied by others in the course of discussion. But, in a constitutive act which leaves some precious articles unnoticed, and raises implications against others, a declaration of rights becomes necessary by way of supplement. This is the case of our new federal constitution. This instrument forms us into one state as to certain objects, and gives us a legislative and executive body for these objects. It should therefore guard us against their abuses of power within the feild [sic] submitted to them. 2. A positive declaration of some essential rights could not be obtained in the requisite latitude. Answer. Half a loaf is better than no bread. If we cannot secure all our rights, let us secure what we can. 3. The limited powers of the federal government and jealousy of the subordinate governments afford a security which exists in no other instance. Answer. The first member of this seems resolvable into the 1st. objection before stated. The jealousy of the subordinate governments is a precious reliance. But observe that those governments are only agents. They must have principles furnished them whereon to found their opposition. The declaration of rights will be the text whereby they will try all the acts of the federal government. In this view it is necessary to the federal government also: as by the same text they may try the opposition of the subordinate governments. 4. Experience proves the inefficacy of a bill of rights. True. But tho it is not absolutely efficacious under all circumstances, it is of great potency always, and rarely inefficacious. A brace the more will often keep up the building which would have fallen with that brace the less. There is a remarkeable difference between the characters of the inconveniences which attend a Declaration of rights, and those which attend the want of it. The inconveniences of the Declaration are that it may cramp government in it's useful exertions. But the evil of this is shortlived, moderate, and reparable. The inconveniences of the want of a Declaration are permanent, afflicting and irreparable: they are in constant progression from bad to worse. The executive in our governments is not the sole, it is scarcely the principal object of my jealousy. The tyranny of the legislatures is the most formidable dread at present, and will be for long years. That of the executive will come in it's turn, but it will be at a remote period. I know there are some among us who would now establish a monarchy. But they are inconsiderable in number and weight of character. The rising race are all republicans. We were educated in royalism: no wonder if some of us retain that idolatry still. Our young people are educated in republicanism. An apostacy from that to royalism is unprecedented and impossible. I am much pleased with the prospect that a declaration of rights will be added: and hope it will be done in that way which will not endanger the whole frame of the government, or any essential part of it. . . .

12 · Jefferson to David Humphreys · March 18, 1789

The operations which have taken place in America lately, fill me with pleasure. In the first place they realize the confidence I had that whenever our affairs get obviously wrong, the good sense of the people will interpose and set them to rights. The example of changing a constitution by assembling the wise men of the state, instead of assembling armies, will be worth as much to the world as the former examples we had given them. The constitution too which was the result of our deliberations, is unquestionably the wisest ever yet presented to men, and some of the accomodations of interest which it has adopted are greatly pleasing to me who have before had occasions of seeing how difficult those interests were to accomodate. A general concurrence of opinion seems to authorize us to say it has some defects. I am one of those who think it a defect that the important rights, not placed in security by the frame of the constitution itself, were not explicitly secured by a supplementary declaration. There are rights which it is useless to surrender to the government, and which yet, governments have always been fond to invade. These are the rights of thinking, and publishing our thoughts by speaking or writing: the right of free commerce: the right of personal freedom. There are instruments for administering the government, so peculiarly trust-worthy, that we should never leave the legislature at liberty to change them. The new constitution has secured these in the executive and legislative departments; but not in the judiciary. It should have established trials by the people themselves, that is to say by jury. There are instruments so dangerous to the rights of the nation, and which place them so totally at the mercy of their governors, that those governors, whether legislative or executive, should be restrained from keeping such instruments on

Boyd, XIV, 678.

foot but in well defined cases. Such an instrument is a standing army. We are now allowed to say such a declaration of rights, as a supplement to the constitution where that is silent, is wanting to secure us in these points. The general voice has legitimated this objection. It has not however authorized me to consider as a real defect, what I thought and still think one, the perpetual re-eligibility of the president. But three states out of 11. having declared against this, we must suppose we are wrong according to the fundamental law of every society, the lex majoris partis, to which we are bound to submit. And should the majority change their opinion, and become sensible that this trait in their constitution is wrong, I would wish it to remain uncorrected as long as we can avail ourselves of the services of our great leader, whose talents and whose weight of character I consider as peculiarly necessary to get the government so under way as that it may afterwards be carried on by subordinate characters.

13 · Jefferson to John Paul Jones · March 23, 1789

. . . Our new constitution was acceded to in the course of the last summer by all the states except N. Carolina and Rhode island. Massachusetts, Virginia and New York, tho they accepted unconditionally, yet gave it as a perpetual instruction to their future delegates never to cease urging certain amendments. N. Carolina insisted that the amendments should be made before she would accede. The most important of these amendments will be effected by adding a bill of rights; and even the friends of the Constitution are becoming sensible of the expediency of such an addition were it only to conciliate the opposition. In fact this security for liberty seems to be demanded by the general voice of America, and we may conclude it will unquestionably be added. . . . Tho' the new constitution was adopted in 11. states, yet in those of Massachusetts, Virginia, and New York it was by very small majorities; and the minorities in the last two are far from the laudable acquiescence of that of Massachusetts. Govr. Clinton in New York, and Mr. Henry in Virginia are moving heaven and earth to have a new Convention to make capital changes. But they will not succeed. There has been just opposition enough to produce probably further guards to liberty without touching the energy of the government, and this will bring over the bulk of the opposition to the side of the new government. . . .

14 · James Madison · *Speech Placing the Proposed Bill-of-Rights Amendments before the House of Representatives* · June 8, 1789

Mr. Madison rose, and reminded the House that this was the day that he had heretofore named for bringing forward amendments to the con-

Boyd, XIV, 688-89.
Annals U.S. Congress, 1st Cong. (1789-1791), Vol. 1, 440-60.

stitution, as contemplated in the fifth article of the constitution. . . . As I considered myself bound in honor and in duty to do what I have done on this subject, I shall proceed to bring the amendments before you as soon as possible, and advocate them until they shall be finally adopted or rejected by a constitutional majority of this House. With a view of drawing your attention to this important object, I shall move that this House do now resolve itself into a Committee of the whole on the state of the Union; by which an opportunity will be given, to bring forward some propositions, which I have strong hopes will meet with the unanimous approbation of this House, after the fullest discussion and most serious regard. I therefore move you, that the House now go into a committee on this business.

Mr. Smith was not inclined to interrupt the measures which the public were so anxiously expecting, by going into a Committee of the whole at this time. . . . For, said he, it must appear extremely impolitic to go into the consideration of amending the Government, before it is organized, before it has begun to operate. . . .

Mr. Jackson.—I am of opinion we ought not to be in a hurry with respect to altering the constitution. . . . What experience have we had of the good or bad qualities of this constitution? Can any gentleman affirm to me one proposition that is a certain and absolute amendment? I deny that he can. Our constitution, sir, is like a vessel just launched, and lying at the wharf; she is untried, you can hardly discover any one of her properties. It is not known how she will answer her helm, or lay her course; whether she will bear with safety the precious freight to be deposited in her hold. . . .

When the propriety of making amendments shall be obvious from experience, I trust there will be virtue enough in my country to make them. . . .

Mr. Madison.— . . . But if we continue to postpone from time to time, and refuse to let the subject come into view, it may occasion suspicions, which, though not well founded, may tend to inflame or prejudice the public mind against our decisions. They may think we are not sincere in our desire to incorporate such amendments in the constitution as will secure those rights, which they consider as not sufficiently guarded. The applications for amendments come from a very respectable number of our constituents, and it is certainly proper for Congress to consider the subject, in order to quiet that anxiety which prevails in the public mind. Indeed, I think it would have been of advantage to the Government, if it had been practicable to have made some propositions for amendments the first business we entered upon; it would have stifled the voice of complaint, and made friends of many who doubted the merits of the constitution. Our future measures would then have been more generally agreeably supported; but the justifiable anxiety to put the Government into operation prevented that; it therefore remains for us to take it up as soon as possible. . . . I only wish to introduce the great work, and, as I said before, I do not expect it will be decided immediately; but if some step is taken in the business, it will give reason to believe that we may come to a final result. This will inspire a reasonable hope in the advocates for amendments, that full justice will be done to the important subject; and I have reason to believe their expectation will not be defeated. . . .

I will state my reasons why I think it proper to propose amendments, and state the amendments themselves, so far as I think they ought to be proposed. . . . It appears to me that this House is bound by every motive of prudence, not to let the first session pass over without proposing to the State Legislatures some things to be incorporated into the constitution, that will render it as acceptable to the whole people of the United States, as it has been found acceptable to a majority of them. I wish, among other reasons why something should be done, that those who have been friendly to the adoption of this constitution may have the opportunity of proving to those who were opposed to it that they were as sincerely devoted to liberty and a Republican Government, as those who charged them with wishing the adoption of this constitution in order to lay the foundation of an aristocracy or despotism. It will be a desirable thing to extinguish from the bosom of every member of the community, any apprehensions that there are those among his countrymen who wish to deprive them of the liberty for which they valiantly fought and honorably bled. And if there are amendments desired of such a nature as will not injure the constitution, and they can be ingrafted so as to give satisfaction to the doubting part of our fellow-citizens, the friends of the Federal Government will evince that spirit of deference and concession for which they have hitherto been distinguished.

It cannot be a secret to the gentlemen in this House, that, notwithstanding the ratification of this system of Government by eleven of the thirteen United States, in some cases unanimously, in others by large majorities; yet still there is a great number of our constituents who are dissatisfied with it; among whom are many respectable for their talents and patriotism, and respectable for the jealousy they have for their liberty, which, though mistaken in its object, is laudable in its motive. There is a great body of the people falling under this description, who at present feel much inclined to join their support to the cause of Federalism, if they were satisfied on this one point. We ought not to disregard their inclination, but, on principles of amity and moderation, conform to their wishes, and expressly declare the great rights of mankind secured under this constitution. The acquiescence which our fellow-citizens show under the Government, calls upon us for a like return of moderation. But perhaps there is a stronger motive than this for our going into a consideration of the subject. It is to provide those securities for liberty which are required by a part of the community; I allude in

a particular manner to those two States [Rhode Island and North Caro-
lina] that have not thought fit to throw themselves into the bosom of
the Confederacy. It is a desirable thing, on our part as well as theirs,
that a re-union should take place as soon as possible. . . .

But I will candidly acknowledge, that, over and above all these considerations, I do conceive that the constitution may be amended; that
is to say, if all power is subject to abuse, that then it is possible the abuse
of the powers of the General Government may be guarded against in a
more secure manner than is now done, while no one advantage arising
from the exercise of that power shall be damaged or endangered by it.
We have in this way something to gain, and, if we proceed with caution,
nothing to lose. And in this case it is necessary to proceed with caution;
for while we feel all these inducements to go into a revisal of the constitution, we must feel for the constitution itself, and make that revisal a
moderate one. I should be unwilling to see a door opened for a recon-
sideration of the whole structure of the Government—for a re-considera-
tion of the principles and the substance of the powers given; because I
doubt, if such a door were opened, we should be very likely to stop at
that point which would be safe to the Government itself. But I do wish
to see a door opened to consider, so far as to incorporate those provisions
for the security of rights, against which I believe no serious objection has
been made by any class of our constituents: such as would be likely to
meet with the concurrence of two-thirds of both Houses, and the approbation of three-fourths of the State Legislatures. I will not propose
a single alteration which I do not wish to see take place, as intrinsically
proper in itself, or proper because it is wished for by a respectable number of my fellow-citizens; and therefore I shall not propose a single alteration but is likely to meet the concurrence required by the constitution. There have been objections of various kinds made against the constitution. Some were levelled against its structure because the President
was without a council; because the Senate, which is a legislative body,
had judicial powers in trials on impeachments; and because the powers
of that body were compounded in other respects, in a manner that did
not correspond with a particular theory; because it grants more power
than is supposed to be necessary for every good purpose, and controls
the ordinary powers of the State Governments. I know some respectable
characters who opposed this Government on these grounds; but I believe that the great mass of the people who opposed it, disliked it because
it did not contain effectual provisions against encroachments on particular rights, and those safeguards which they have been long accustomed
to have interposed between them and the magistrate who exercises the
sovereign power; nor ought we to consider them safe, while a great number of our fellow-citizens think these securities necessary.

It is a fortunate thing that the objection to the Government has been
made on the ground I stated; because it will be practicable, on that

ground, to obviate the objection, so far as to satisfy the public mind that their liberties will be perpetual, and this without endangering any part of the constitution, which is considered as essential to the existence of the Government by those who promoted its adoption.

[Madison then proceeded to list the amendments.]

The first of these amendments relates to what may be called a bill of rights. I will own that I never considered this provision so essential to the federal constitution, as to make it improper to ratify it, until such an amendment was added; at the same time, I always conceived, that in a certain form, and to a certain extent, such a provision was neither improper nor altogether useless. . . .

It has been said, that it is unnecessary to load the constitution with this provision, because it was not found effectual in the constitution of the particular States. It is true, there are a few particular States in which some of the most valuable articles have not, at one time or other, been violated; but it does not follow but they may have, to a certain degree, a salutary effect against the abuse of power. If they are incorporated into the constitution, independent tribunals of justice will consider themselves in a peculiar manner the guardians of those rights; they will be an impenetrable bulwark against every assumption of power in the legislative or executive; they will be naturally led to resist every encroachment upon rights expressly stipulated for in the constitution by the declaration of rights. Besides this security, there is a great probability that such a declaration in the federal system would be enforced; because the State Legislatures will jealously and closely watch the operations of this Government, and be able to resist with more effect every assumption of power, than any other power on earth can do; and the greatest opponents to a Federal Government admit the State Legislatures to be sure guardians of the people's liberty. I conclude, from this view of the subject, that it will be proper in itself, and highly politic, for the tranquillity of the public mind, and the stability of the Government, that we should offer something, in the form I have proposed, to be incorporated in the system of Government, as a declaration of the rights of the people. . . .

I wish also, in revising the constitution, we may throw into that section, which interdicts the abuse of certain powers in the State Legislatures, some other provisions of equal, if not greater importance than those already made. The words, "No State shall pass any bill of attainder, *ex post facto* law," &c. were wise and proper restrictions in the constitution. I think there is more danger of those powers being abused by the State Governments than by the Government of the United States. The same may be said of other powers which they possess, if not controlled by the general principle, that laws are unconstitutional which infringe the rights of the community. I should therefore wish to extend this interdiction, and add, as I have stated in the 5th resolution, that no State shall violate the equal right of conscience, freedom of the press, or trial by jury in criminal cases; because it is proper that every Government should be disarmed of powers which trench upon those particular rights. I know, in some of the State constitutions, the power of the Government is controlled by such a declaration; but others are not. I cannot see any reason against obtaining even a double security on those points; and nothing can give a more sincere proof of the attachment of those who opposed this constitution to these great and important rights, than to see them join in obtaining the security I have now proposed; because it must be admitted, on all hands, that the State Governments are as liable to attack these invaluable privileges as the General Government is, and therefore ought to be as cautiously guarded against. . . .

I find, from looking into the amendments proposed by the State conventions, that several are particularly anxious that it should be declared in the constitution, that the powers not therein delegated should be reserved to the several States. Perhaps words which may define this more precisely than the whole of the instrument now does, may be considered as superfluous. I admit they may be deemed unnecessary; but there can be no harm in making such a declaration, if gentlemen will allow that the fact is as stated. I am sure I understand it so, and do therefore propose it.

There are the points on which I wish to see a revision of the constitution take place. How far they will accord with the sense of this body, I cannot take upon me absolutely to determine; but I believe every gentleman will readily admit that nothing is in contemplation, so far as I have mentioned, that can endanger the beauty of the Government in any one important feature, even in the eyes of its most sanguine admirers. I have proposed nothing that does not appear to me as proper in itself, or eligible as patronized by a respectable number of our fellow-citizens; and if we can make the constitution better in the opinion of those who are opposed to it, without weakening its frame, or abridging its usefulness, in the judgment of those who are attached to it, we act the part of wise and liberal men to make such alterations as shall produce that effect.

IV · MUST WE CONTINUE
THE STATES RIGHTS DEBATE?

Essay 🎋

Laying the foundations of government in a constitutional text is one thing; supplying the motive power of governing, something else. A constitution is a lifeless thing, a paper contrivance, merely the license to begin governing. "Governments, like clocks," William Penn once observed, "go from the motion men give them. . . ." [1] So it was with the government established in 1789. The new political system might have been launched by men who wished to cling to old ways and customary institutions. It was, in fact, set in motion by men determined to break away from the biases and prejudices of the past and embark on a bold new course.

The Constitution contained no guarantee that it would "endure for all ages to come," and be adaptable to the various crises certain to arise. Framed in general language, it was susceptible to widely divergent and not wholly unreasonable interpretations. Madison's statesmanship represents an extraordinary embodiment of the alternatives. At the Philadelphia convention he was a staunch Federalist; later on he helped to lay the foundation of "dual federalism." [2] In the debate of 1791 on establishment of a national bank, he had argued that *interference with the power of the States was no constitutional criterion of the powers of Congress. If the power was not given, Congress could not exercise it; if given, they might exercise it, although it should interfere with the laws, or even the Constitution of the States.*" [3] In 1819, Madison deplored the Supreme Court's tendency "to convert a limited into an unlimited Gov't." "There is certainly," he went on, "a reasonable medium between expounding the Constitution with the strictness of a penal law, or other ordinary statute, and expounding it with a laxity which may vary its essential character, and encroach on the local sovereignties with which it was meant to be reconcilable. *The very existence of these local sovereignties is a controul on the pleas for a constructive amplification of the powers of the General Gov't.*" [4] The Father of the Constitution deplored the statesmanship of Chief Justice Marshall who, during the formative years, entrenched nationalist policy through constitutional interpretation so firmly as to be almost impregnable.

The Constitution, Marshall argued, was not a compact of sovereign states; it was "ordained and established in the name of the people." Deriving its authority from the people, the Constitution altered the former position of the states as free and independent units of government. It has been said, Marshall observed, that "the states were sovereign, were completely independent, and were connected with each other only by a league." Prior to 1789, the Chief Justice conceded the truth of this proposition. "But, when these allied sovereigns converted their league into a government, when they converted their congress of ambassadors . . . into a legislature, empowered to enact laws on the most interesting subjects, the whole character in which the states appear underwent a change." [5] Striking at the jugular vein of the states rights argument, Marshall continued: "It has been contended that, if a law passed by a State, in the exercise of its acknowledged sovereignty, comes into conflict with a law passed by congress in pursuance of the constitution, they affect the subject, and each other, like equal opposing powers. But the framers of our constitution foresaw this state of things, and provided for it by declaring the supremacy not only of itself, but of the laws made in pursuance of it." [6]

The necessary-and-proper clause gives Congress a discretionary choice of means for carrying its enumerated powers into execution. The tenth amendment does not limit this freedom of selection. Thus, Marshall established not only the proposition that national powers must be liberally construed, but also the equally decisive principle that the tenth amendment does not create in the states an independent limitation on such authority. Summarizing Chief Justice Marshall's position, Professor Corwin writes:

> When the Supremacy Clause is given its due operation no subject-matter whatever is withdrawn from the control of the delegated powers of the United States by the fact alone that the same subject-matter also lies within the jurisdiction of the reserved powers of the state; for when national and State power, correctly defined in other respects, comes into conflict in consequence of attempting to govern simultaneously the same subject-matter, the former has always the right of way. [7]

Marshall's robust nationalism did not go unchallenged. His critics objected that his rulings created a unified system of government. Enumeration of powers had proved to be "a vain attempt to confine what is necessarily illimitable." "The government has been fundamentally altered by the progress of opinion," Hugh Swinton Legaré wrote in 1828. "Instead of being any longer one of enumerated powers and a circumscribed sphere, as it was beyond all doubt intended to be, it knows absolutely no bounds but the will of a majority of Congress.

. . ." "That argument," Legaré concluded, "cannot be sound which necessarily converts a government of enumerated into one of indefinite powers, and a confederacy of republics into a gigantic and consolidated empire." [8]

After Marshall's death in 1835, the course of American federalism was significantly altered. As if in answer to fears of consolidation, President Jackson appointed Roger Brooke Taney as Chief Justice Marshall's successor. During the next generation (1835-1864), the Court, under Taney's leadership, redefined federalism in terms more favorable to state power. An important incidental result was a greatly enhanced role for the judiciary.

Under the concept of federalism entertained by Marshall's critics, the Constitution was a compact of sovereign states, not an ordinance of the people. "Dual federalism," as this notion has come to be known, means two mutually exclusive, reciprocally limited fields of power—that of the national government and that of the states. The two authorities confront each other as equals across a precise constitutional line, defining their respective jurisdictions.

"Dual federalism" was spelled out in a series of opinions delivered in the *License Cases,* decided in 1847. Said Chief Justice Taney:

> The constitution of the United States declares that that constitution and the laws of the United States which shall be made in pursuance thereof, and all treaties made, or which shall be made, under the authority of the United States, shall be the supreme law of the land. It follows that a law of congress, regulating commerce with foreign nations, or among the several States, is the supreme law; and if the law of a state is in conflict with it, the law of congress must prevail, and the state law cease to operate so far as it is repugnant to the law of the United States.
>
> It is equally clear that the power of congress over this subject does not extend further than regulation of commerce with foreign nations and among the several States; and that beyond these limits the States have never surrendered their power over trade and commerce, and may still exercise it free from any controlling power on the part of the general government. Every State, therefore, may regulate its own internal traffic, according to its own judgment, and upon its own views of the interest and well-being of its citizens. . . .
>
> It is unquestionably no easy task to mark, by a certain and definite line, the division between foreign and domestic commerce, and to fix the precise point, in relation to every imported article, where the paramount power of congress terminates, and that of the State begins. The constitution itself does not attempt to define these limits. They cannot be determined by the laws of congress or the States, as neither can, by its own legislation, enlarge its own powers, or restrict those of the other. And as the constitution itself does not draw the line, the question is necessarily one for judicial decision, and depending altogether upon the words of the constitution.[9]

The Taney Court enforced nation-state equality. Within the powers allegedly reserved by the tenth amendment, the states were sovereign. Final authority to determine the scope of state powers rested with the national judiciary, an impartial body presumably standing aloof from the sovereign pretensions of both the national government and the states, not, as Marshall had insisted, merely an instrument of the national government. In cases involving a clash of sovereignties, Marshall asked one question: does the Congress have the power? Taney asked two questions: does Congress have the power and do the states have any rights precluding congressional action?

The Taney concept of federal-state relations meant a greatly enlarged role for the Supreme Court. "As the constitution itself does not draw the line," Chief Justice Taney observed, "the question is necessarily one for judicial decision, and depending altogether on the words of the constitution." [10] But the Constitution's words draw no line either. Supreme Court Justices assumed the responsibility for doing what the framers and the first Congress had deliberately left undone. With this assertion of the sovereign prerogative of choice, there was but a short step from *national* supremacy to *judicial* supremacy.

In practice, judicial supremacy has precipitated two major crises— three if we count the belated stir aroused by the proposed "disunion amendments" of 1963. Distrustful of any further drive toward unity, Chief Justice Taney ruled in the *Dred Scott* case,[11] that Congress could not abolish slavery even in the territories. Slavery was a subject matter reserved unqualifiedly and exclusively to the states. Taney's failure to recognize slavery as a problem national in scope, demanding national authority to deal with it, helped to bring on the Civil War.

Large business corporations operating across state boundaries created America's second crisis in federal-state relations. By switching from the doctrine of national supremacy to that of dual federalism, the Supreme Court defeated both state and national attempts to regulate business enterprise. At both levels "Uncle Sam" was finally "tied," as Justice Stone said, "in a hard knot." [12] State regulations were vetoed by applying the doctrine of national supremacy, holding that since the problem was national, corrective action must come from Congress. When Congress responded to this invitation, state power was interposed. National action was regarded as an invasion of the domain reserved to the states. The tenth amendment was applied as if it read, all powers not *expressly* delegated are reserved, instead of all powers not delegated are reserved. Outlawing congressional authority to regulate child labor under the commerce power, Justice Day observed:

> In interpreting the Constitution it must never be forgotten that the Nation is made up of States to which are entrusted the powers of local government. And to them and to the people powers not *expressly* [sic] delegated to the Na-

tional Government are reserved. . . . The power of the States to regulate their purely internal affairs by such laws as seem wise to the local authority is inherent and has never been surrendered to the general government. . . .[13]

The Court divided five to four. Five Supreme Court Justices amended the tenth amendment by interpolating in it the word "expressly." The very word the Congress of 1789 had deliberately refused to insert, became, for all practical purposes, the law of the land. By judicial fiat, certain subject matters—manufacturing, agriculture and employer-employee relations—were put beyond the reach of national authority.

"Dual federalism," as an instrument of judicial government, reached its climax in a series of decisions upsetting New Deal legislation. The redundancy of the tenth amendment—"powers not delegated are reserved"—then became a notorious judicial device for defeating the power to govern. In a notable dissent of 1936,[14] Justice Stone discredited this judicial perversion in language of unmatched vehemence. Several weeks later, still pondering the subject, he wrote Charles A. Beard: "Have you ever found in your researches any indication that the framers of the [tenth] Amendment intended the reserve powers of the states to constitute a limitation on the powers of Congress?" As it turned out, Beard's search served only to confirm Stone's belief that no such limitation had been intended. "I have always held," the Justice reflected, "that the framers of the Constitution intended to create a strong government, adequate to deal with every situation. I think they would have been surprised, even after the Tenth Amendment, to learn that the Constitution reserved a legislative field to the states. It granted power to the National Government and, in the vernacular of the farmer, 'the tail goes with the hide.' "[15] In 1936, six Supreme Court justices, bent on slaying the New Deal, had again inserted "expressly" before the word "delegated."

It remained for Justice Stone, writing in 1941 for a unanimous Court, to set the tenth amendment in the context of history:

> Our conclusion is unaffected by the Tenth Amendment. . . . The amendment states but a truism that all is retained which has not been surrendered. There is nothing in the history of its adoption to suggest that it was more than declaratory of the relationship between the national and state governments as it had been established by the Constitution before the amendment or that its purpose was other than to allay fears that the new national government might seek to exercise powers not granted, and that the states might not be able to exercise fully their reserved powers. . . . From the beginning and for many years the Amendment has been construed as not depriving the National government of authority to resort to all means for the exercise of granted power which are appropriate and plainly adopted to the permitted end.[16]

Though it was a landmark case—at issue was the constitutionality of the Fair Labor Standards Act of 1938—Chief Justice Hughes, uncertain as to its validity, had concurred in the decision, but assigned the opinion to Justice Stone. Hughes' position was consistent. In the Jones-Laughlin case of 1937, the high-water mark of his liberal interpretation of the commerce clause, he cited the "explicit reservation of the Tenth Amendment" as an independent limitation on national power. "The authority of the Federal Government," he went on

> may not be pushed to such an extreme as to destroy the distinction, which the commerce clause itself establishes, between commerce "among the several States" and the internal concerns of a State. That distinction between what is national and what is local in the activities of commerce is vital to the maintenance of our Federal system. . . . Undoubtedly the scope of this [commerce] power must be considered in the light of our dual system of government and may not be extended so as to embrace effects upon the interstate commerce so indirect and remote that to embrace them, in view of our complex society, would effectually obliterate the distinction between what is national and what is local and create a completely centralized government. . . .[16a]

Within the Court itself the states rights debate continued. Justice Stone's words in *U.S.* v. *Darby* underscore the most dramatic judicial reversal in American history. The Federalist and Antifederalist agreement on the nationalistic nature of the Constitution, as of 1788-1789, had at long last been confirmed. Antifederalists, opposing ratification, had charged that the Constitution established a consolidated system. Federalists, favoring a strengthened national government, insisted that the powers granted to it be left "indefinite." As adopted, the Constitution thus embodied potentialities favored by the Federalists and feared by Antifederalists.

Confronted by President Roosevelt's audacious threat of February 5, 1937 to "pack" the Supreme Court with justices of his own political persuasion, the Court had retreated—"switched in time," a wag put it, "to save nine." Back of this remarkable shift in constitutional doctrine and decisions lay a fundamental change in political and constitutional theory. From about 1890 on, priority of national power was used to inhibit the exercise of state power, and vice versa, by those who found all government regulation distasteful. Before 1932, the laissez-faire dogma accorded each individual nearly complete freedom over wages, prices, and profits. Liberty meant the union of social power and private right. After 1937, the orientation of American political thought became basically collectivistic. It was recognized that no individual, no group, can profit or suffer without affecting the interests of all. Liberty could be infringed by forces other than government, and those other forces, chiefly economic, may require the affirmative action of government to counteract them. Promotion of the general welfare became recognized as inherent in government at all levels.[17]

After almost two centuries of constitutional debate, the issue of federalism is still not settled. In 1954 the Supreme Court outlawed racial segregation in public schools. The familiar cry—invasion of states rights—was again heard. Proposals for federal aid to education, usually a state rather than a national function in the United States, raise the specter of federal dictation of educational policy and content. In 1962, the Court stepped into another area heretofore reserved to the states, implying that election districts must have some reasonable relation to population distribution. All of these problems had become national in scope, but judicial attempts to deal with them on that level stirred passionate feelings against the unity federal action portended.

The relentless drive toward national unity has been the result of necessity rather than doctrinaire preference. Speaking in 1958, and again in September 1963, Chief Justice Warren conceded that the national government had at times become too deeply enmeshed in matters properly within the prerogatives of the states. But, as he explained, the fault lies more often than not with the states themselves:

> When the state governments fail to satisfy the needs of the people, the people appeal to the Federal Government. Whether the question is one of the advancement of human knowledge through research, of law and order, or the right of all persons to equal protection of the law, the Federal Government need become involved only when the states fail to act.[18]

The Chief Justice's point was vividly illustrated in the historic case of *Baker* v. *Carr*.[19] For half a century Tennessee, along with other states, had failed to protect the basic democratic right of franchise by refusing properly to apportion its electoral districts. The Supreme Court, reversing a stand previously taken, asserted its responsibility for correcting this miscarriage of democratic justice. States rights reaction borders on the outrageous. If ratified, the "Dis-Union" Amendments now pending would take us back to the monstrous political predicament the Constitution was designed to remedy.

Several states had already endorsed one or more of these "amendments," when, in May 1963, Chief Justice Warren called for a "great national debate." Professor John P. Roche of Brandeis University demurred, reminding the Chief Justice that states rights had been thoroughly explored from 1787 to 1789. "Must we seriously consider . . . a return to the Articles of Confederation?" Professor Roche asked.[20] The short answer is "yes." An issue persistently discussed, not merely over a period of two years but for nearly two centuries—on the public platform, in the press, in legislative halls, and in Supreme Court opinions—clearly was not resolved in 1789. Nor is it settled today. In the long discussions before the Civil War, reason had failed to resolve the issue. And even after an "indestructible union of indestructible states" was confirmed by resort to force, the discussion still goes on. A debate capable of generating heat for so long cannot be reasonably considered lacking in the essential fuel of controversy on either side.

The explanation of this never-ending wrangle may lie in the Constitution itself, and in the nature of the government it establishes. Chief Justice Marshall was accustomed to reiterate the telling reminder: "we must never forget, that it is a *Constitution* we are expounding." [21] Like an oracle, it speaks ambiguously. Neither friends nor enemies of the proposed constitution could be certain as to the nature of the government it ordained. Antifederalists, trying to defeat ratification, argued with conviction that it would lead to consolidation. Hamilton, an ardent consolidationist, signed reluctantly on the common-sense ground that it is impossible to hesitate between anarchy and the mere possibility of a truly national government.

What was said on both sides in the ratifying debates is even more ambiguous than the document itself. One commentator has dubbed *The Federalist*—still uncritically accepted as the Constitution's authoritative gloss—a "split personality." [22] Nor was James Madison, as sometimes portrayed, the sole equivocator. In a series of essays designed to sway a widely divergent constituency, it was not unnatural that both contributors should becloud hotly controverted issues.[23] When John Taylor set out to prove that Chief Justice Marshall had, through spurious interpretation, converted a compact of sovereign states into a consolidated empire, he drew indiscriminately from Hamilton's and Madison's numbers of *The Federalist*.[24] Marshall enlisted the support of America's political classic—that "great authority," he called it—to demonstrate that federal judicial power must extend to Supreme Court review of state court decisions arising under the federal Constitution or laws of the United States. Yet Spencer Roane resorted to this same resourceful arsenal for the ammunition he used to blast Marshall's alleged usurpations.[25] Perhaps to placate the rising storm of protest, Marshall himself, on occasion, made concessions to the claims of state sovereignty, thus supplying grist for the judicial mills of his successors.[26]

Antifederalists today would turn the clock back; they would scuttle the Constitution and return us to the monstrous *imperium in imperio,* so convincingly discredited in the years both before and after 1776. Their proposals seem absurd, yet debate—one of the normal "wastes of democracy," as Louis D. Brandeis called it—must be tolerated. Distrust of power at all levels, of whatever orientation, is still the American watchword. Eternal vigilance is still the price of liberty. Power concentrated in Washington and in the President is not an unmitigated blessing. Jefferson declared that "the jealousy of the subordinate governments is a precious reliance." [27] A century and a half later, Brandeis thanked "God for the limitations inherent in our federal system." [28] Nor have the methods of the welfare state reached such a peak of perfection as to make them immune to discussion and criticism. We still need to bear in mind old John Randolph's trenchant caveat: "You can cover whole skins of parchment with limitations, but power alone can limit power." [29] Conflict between federal and state authority means "vibrations of power," and this, Hamilton said, is "the genius of our government." [30]

The states rights debate must continue. Federalists should be the last to suggest a moratorium. Informed exploration of the record—and the compelling verdict of history—redound overwhelmingly to their advantage. Nevertheless, Jefferson's admonition of 1821 is applicable as much to the national government and the states as to Congress, the Executive, and the Court. The "healing balm" of our Constitution, he said, is that "each party should prudently shrink from all approach to the line of demarcation, instead of rashly overleaping it, or throwing grapples ahead to haul to hereafter." [31] That the Constitution drew no "line of demarcation" limiting national power *vis-à-vis* the states does not detract from the wisdom of Jefferson's advice. The tenth amendment may be a "truism," but history demonstrates its continuing force as a compelling reminder of America's search for union without unity.

Notes 𝒥𝕥🙰

1. Thorpe, ed., *The Federal and State Constitutions of the United States of America* (1909), V, 3054.
2. See Corwin, "James Madison, Layman, Publicist, and Exegete," *New York University Literary Review*, 27 (1952), 277. Corwin, "National Power and State Interposition 1787-1861," *Michigan Literary Review*, 10 (1912), 535.
3. Hunt, ed., *The Writings of James Madison*, 6 (1906), p. 28, *supra*, note 21; emphasis added.
4. *The Writings of James Madison*, 8, *id.*, Hunt, 451-52; emphasis added.
5. *Gibbons* v. *Ogden*, 6 U.S. (9 Wheat.) 1, 3 (1824).
6. *Id.*, 16-17.
7. Corwin, *The Commerce Power versus States Rights*, pp. 12-13 (1936).
8. Legaré, *Writings*, 2 (1843); a review of Kent's *Commentaries*, pp. 123, 130, 131. Continuing, Legaré wrote: "If any one wishes to be convinced how little, even the wisest men, are able to foresee the results of their own political contrivances, let him read the constitution, with the contemporaneous exposition of it contained (even) in *The Federalist*; and then turn to this part of Kent's work. . . . He will find that this extraordinary revolution has been brought about, in good degree by the Supreme Court of the United States, which has applied to the Constitution—very innocently, no doubt, and with commanding ability in argument—and thus given authority and currency to such canons of interpretation, as necessarily lead to these extravagant results. Above all, he will be perfectly satisfied that that high tribunal affords . . . no barrier whatever against the usurpations of Congress—and that the rights of the weaker part of this confederacy may, to an extent, be wantonly and tyrannically violated, under color of law, [the most grievous shape of oppression] by men neither interested in its destiny nor subject to its control, without any means of redress being left to it, except such as are inconsistent with all idea of order and government. Perhaps . . . he will conclude that the American people have not been sufficiently careful, at the beginning of their unprecedented

experiment in politics, what principles they suffered to be established—perhaps he may look forward to the future, with anxiety and alarm, as holding forth a prospect of a rapid accumulation of power in the hands of those who have already abused it, or, on the contrary, with a strong hope that experience will teach wisdom and diversified interests and conflicting pretensions, lead to moderation in conduct—perhaps . . . he might wish to see proper means adopted to bring back the government to its first principle, and put an end to the unhappy jealousies and heart-burnings which are beginning to embitter one part of our people against another. . . ." Pp. 123-124. For an echo of Legaré's sentiment, see the statement of Mr. Lloyd Lowrey presenting the "Dis-Union" Amendments of 1962, below.

9. *License Cases*, 16 U.S. (5 How.) 513, 515-16 (1846). See also the equally pointed language of Justices McLean (*id.*, 530) and Daniel (*id.*, 558).

10. *Id.*, 516.

11. *Scott* v. *Sandford*, 19 U.S. (19 How.) 393 (1856).

12. Quoted in Mason, *Harlan Fiske Stone: Pillar of the Law* (1956), p. 426.

13. *Hammer* v. *Dagenhart*, 247 U.S. 251, 275-76 (1918); emphasis added.

14. *United States* v. *Butler*, 297 U.S. 1, 78 (1936).

15. Quoted in Mason, *op. cit., supra*, note 39, 411.

16. *United States* v. *Darby*, 312 U.S. 100, 123-24 (1941).

16a. *N.L.R.B.* v. *Jones-Laughlin*, 301 U.S. 1, 30, 37 (1937).

17. The shift of judicial approach comes out clearly in *West Coast Hotel Co.* v. *Parrish*, 300 U.S. 379 (1937). Sustaining the Washington State minimum wage law for women, Chief Justice Hughes said:

> The Constitution does not speak of freedom of contract. It speaks of liberty and prohibits the deprivation of liberty without due process of law. In prohibiting that deprivation the Constitution does not recognize an absolute and uncontrollable liberty. Liberty in each of its phases has its history and connotation. But the liberty safeguarded is liberty in a *social organization which requires the protection of law against the evils which menace the health, safety, morals and welfare* of the people. Liberty under the Constitution is thus necessarily subject to the restraints of due process, and regulation which is reasonable in relation to its subject and is adapted in the interests of the community is due process.

Id., 391; emphasis added. See, in this connection, Miller, "An Affirmative Thrust to Due Process of Law," *George Washington Literary Review*, 30 (1962), 399.

18. Quoted in Mason & Beaney, *The Supreme Court in a Free Society* (1959), p. 310. See also Chief Justice Warren's address of Sept. 25, in *The New York Times*, Sept. 26, 1963, p. 29, col. 5.

19. *Supra*, note 2.

20. *The New York Times*, June 2, 1963, sec. 4, p. 10B, col. 8.

21. *McCulloch* v. *Maryland, supra*, note 27, 422.

22. Adair, "The Authorship of the Disputed Federalist Papers," *William & Mary Quarterly*, 1 (3rd ser., 1944), 97. See Mason, "The Federalist: A Split Personality," *American Historical Review*, 57 (1962), 625.

23. See Mason, "The Nature of Our Federal Union Reconsidered," *Political Science Quarterly*, 65 (1950), 502.

24. Madison was not, as sometimes pictured, the sole states rights culprit. His most significant concession occurred in *The Federalist*, Nos. 39 and 45. In the latter essay, he wrote, "the States will retain, under the proposed Constitution, a very extensive portion of active sovereignty. . . . The powers delegated by the proposed Constitution to the federal government are few and defined. Those which are to remain to the State governments are numerous and indefinite." *The Federalist*, No. 45, pp. 326, 328.

In *The Federalist*, No. 9, p. 128, Hamilton declared that "the proposed constitution, so far from implying an abolition of the State governments, makes them constituent parts of the national sovereignty, by allowing them a direct representation in the Senate, and leaves in their possession certain *exclusive* and very important portions of sovereign power." (Emphasis added.) Yet Taylor was wary. "The ambiguity of this sentence arises from the interpolation of the words national sovereignty. . . ." Taylor, *New Views of the Constitution of the United States* (1823), p. 65. Thus, while "Mr. Hamilton seems to *intimate*, that the constitution has created two sovereignties . . . each invested with exclusive powers, [he has made one sovereign over the other] by the representation [of the inferior sovereignty] in the Senate." *Id.*, 66-67. (Emphasis added.)

Taylor suggests that Hamilton planted the seeds of nullification, by saying in *The Federalist*, No. 28, pp. 225, 226:

Power being almost always the rival of power, the general government will at all times stand ready to check the usurpations of the state governments, and these will have the same disposition towards the general government. . . .

[The people] are in a situation, through the medium of their State governments, to take measures for their own defence, with all the celerity, regularity, and system, of independent nations.

In *The Federalist*, No. 31, p. 239, Hamilton declared flatly that, "The State governments, by their original constitutions, are invested with complete sovereignty." In *The Federalist*, No. 32, pp. 241, 243, Hamilton was:

willing here to allow, in its full extent, the justness of the reasoning which requires that the individual States should possess an independent and uncontrollable authority to raise their own revenues. . . . I affirm that (with the sole exception of duties on imports and exports) they would, under the plan of the convention, retain that authority in the most absolute and unqualified sense; and that an attempt on the part of the national government to abridge them in the exercise of it, would be a violent assumption of power, unwarranted by any article or clause of its constitution. . . .

The necessity of a concurrent jurisdiction in certain cases results from the division of sovereign power. . . .

In *The Federalist*, No. 33, pp. 245-46, Hamilton undercut the basis of Marshall's jurisprudence, saying: "The declaration itself [necessary-and-proper clause], though it may be chargeable with tautology or redundancy, is at least perfectly harmless."

Small wonder Taylor could write that "The principles I am advocating are forcibly sustained in" *The Federalist*. Taylor, *op. cit., supra*, p. 75.

25. *Cohens* v. *Virginia*, 5 U.S. (6 Wheat.) 82, 108-9 (1821); and Roane, "On the Lottery Decision," *Richmond Inquirer*, June 8, 1821; reprinted in *The John P. Branch Historical Papers*, 2 (June 1906), p. 170.

26. See *Cohens* v. *Virginia, supra*, note 46, p. 106: "These States are constituent parts of the United States. They are members of one great empire—for some purposes sovereign, for some purposes subordinate." In *Gibbons* v. *Ogden, supra*, note 32, p. 12, Marshall, conceding the states' power to impose inspection laws, referred to the inspection laws as "a portion of that immense mass of legislation . . . not surrendered to the general government; all which can be most advantageously exercised by the States themselves." See also *Willson* v. *the Blackbird Creek Marsh Co.*, 8 U.S. (2 Peters) 105 (1829). Even in *Charles River Bridge* v. *Warren Bridge*, 12 U.S. (11 Peters) 496 (1837), Chief Justice Taney was not wholly lacking in support drawn from John Marshall. Taney was able to cite four precedents drawn from the Marshall era: *Providence Bank* v. *Billings*, 9 U.S. (4 Peters) 171 (1830); *Beatty* v. *Knowles*, 9 U.S. (4 Peters) 36 (1830); *United States* v. *Arrendondo*, 10 U.S. (6 Peters) 315 (1832); *Jackson* v. *Lampshire*, 8 U.S. (3 Peters) 419 (1830). The *Providence Bank*

case, *supra*, supplied quotable words from Marshall's opinion. For this footnote I am indebted to an unpublished paper, "The Constitutional Revolution of 1837 and the Myth of Marshall's Monolith," by my friend, Dr. Gerald Garvey.

27. Jefferson to Madison, March 15, 1789, in *The Papers of Thomas Jefferson*, 14, ed. Boyd (1950), p. 660.
28. Quoted in Mason, *Brandeis: A Free Man's Life* (1946), p. 621.
29. Bruce, *John Randolph of Roanoke*, II (1922), p. 211.
30. Hamilton to Rufus King, June 3, 1802, in *The Works of Alexander Hamilton*, 10, ed. Lodge (1904), p. 439.
31. Jefferson to Spencer Roane, June 27, 1821, in *The Writings of Thomas Jefferson*, 10, ed. Ford (1899), p. 189, Note 1. Compare Jefferson's opinion of May 3, 1790 on federal-state relations in the Georgia Land Grants Controversy:

> The right of the general government is, in my opinion, to be maintained. The case is sound; and the means of doing it as practicable as can ever occur. But respect and friendship should, I think, mark the conduct of the general towards the particular governments, and explanations should be asked, and time and colour given them to tread back their steps, before coercion is held up to their view. . . . I should think it better then that the first measures, while firm, be yet so temperate as to secure their alliance and aid to the general government. Might not the eclat of a proclamation revolt their pride and passion, and throw them hastily into the opposite scale?

The Papers of Thomas Jefferson, 16, *op. cit.*, *supra*, note 54, pp. 407-8 (Boyd ed., 1961). Compare Hamilton's language in *The Federalist*, No. 36, p. 262: "As neither [the federal nor State governments] can *control* the other [in the objects of taxation], each will have an obvious and sensible interest in this reciprocal forbearance." In 1944, Mr. Justice Frankfurter wrote:

> The interpenetrations of modern society have not wiped out state lines. It is not for us to make inroads upon our federal system either by indifference to its maintenance or excessive regard for the unifying sources of modern technology. Scholastic reasoning may prove that no activity is isolated within the boundaries of a single State, but that cannot justify absorption of legislative power by the United States of every activity.

Polish Nat'l Alliance v. *NLRB*, 322 U.S. 643, 650 (1944).

Documents ॐ

Nearly two centuries ago an infant nation boldly asserted the original right of a free people to organize a government and assign different departments their respective powers. Immediately following this "very great exertion," symbolized by a written constitution "designed to be permanent," the first Congress proposed, and the States ratified, the amendments, known as the Bill of Rights. The rights identified and guaranteed against government invasion are enforceable by courts.

The cosmic gap between the enduring implications of this initial achievement and the destructive potentialities of the proposed "Dis-Union" Amendments of December 1962, emerges with singular clarity on the following pages.

1 · *The Bill of Rights* · 1789

ART. I. Congress shall make no law respecting an establishment of religion, or prohibiting the free exercise thereof; or abridging the freedom of speech, or of the press, or the right of the people peaceably to assemble and to petition the government for a redress of grievances.

ART. II. A well regulated militia being necessary to the security of a free state, the right of the people to keep and bear arms shall not be infringed.

ART. III. No soldier shall, in time of peace, be quartered in any house, without the consent of the owner; nor in time of war, but in a manner to be prescribed by law.

ART. IV. The right of the people to be secure in their persons, houses, papers and effects, against unreasonable searches and seizures, shall not be violated, and no warrants shall issue, but upon probable cause, supported by oath or affirmation, and particularly describing the place to be searched and the persons or things to be seized.

ART. V. No person shall be held to answer for a capital, or otherwise infamous crime, unless on a presentment or indictment of a grand jury, except in cases arising in the land or naval forces, or in the militia, when in actual service in time of war or public danger; nor shall any person be subject for the same offence to be twice put in jeopardy of life or limb; nor shall be compelled in any criminal case to be a witness against himself, nor be deprived of life, liberty or property, without due process of law; nor shall private property be taken for public use, without just compensation.

ART. VI. In all criminal prosecutions, the accused shall enjoy the right to a speedy and public trial, by an impartial jury of the state and district wherein the crime shall have been committed, which district shall have been previously ascertained by law, and to be informed of the nature and cause of the accusation; to be confronted with the witnesses against him; to have compulsory process for obtaining witnesses in his favor, and to have the assistance of counsel for his defence.

ART. VII. In suits at common law, where the value in controversy shall exceed twenty dollars, the right of trial by jury shall be preserved, and no fact tried by a jury shall be otherwise re-examined in any court of the United States, than according to the rules of the common law.

ART. VIII. Excessive bail shall not be required, nor excessive fines imposed, nor cruel and unusual punishments inflicted.

ART. IX. The enumeration in the constitution, of certain rights, shall not be construed to deny or disparage others retained by the people.

ART. X. The powers not delegated to the United States by the constitution, nor prohibited by it to the states, are reserved to the states respectively, or to the people.

2 · Proposed "Dis-Union" Amendments · 1962

In presenting the amendments Mr. Lloyd W. Lowrey of California, Chairman of the National Legislative Conference Committee, read to the General Assembly a Statement of Principles, as follows:

The characteristic of our constitutional government, which has contributed most to the development of democratic processes and the preservation of human rights, is the division of the powers of government between the nation and the states on the one hand and between the executive, legislative and judicial departments of both state and federal governments on the other.

Over the years we have escaped the evils of despotism and totalitarianism. It is only when each division of the whole governmental structure insists upon the right to exercise its powers, unrestrained by any other division, that the proper balance can be maintained and constitutional government, as we understand it, preserved.

It is the responsibility of the central government to protect the people from invasion by the states of those rights which are guaranteed to them by the Federal Constitution. It is equally the obligation of the states to initiate and to prosecute to fruition the necessary procedures to protect the states and the people from unwarranted assumption of power by any department of the federal government.

The most sacred of all public officials, whether state or federal, and the highest patriotic responsibility of all citizens is to preserve, protect and defend the Constitution, including that portion of the Constitution intended to guarantee a government of dual sovereignty. When it becomes apparent that purposely or inadvertently, any department or agency of government has embarked upon a course calculated to destroy the balance of power essential to our system, it behooves all other departments and agencies acting within their respective spheres of jurisdiction to take all steps within their power necessary to avert the impending evil. We believe that grave imbalance now exists.

Some federal judicial decisions involving powers of the federal and state governments carry a strong bias on the federal side, and consequently are bringing about a strong shift toward the extension of federal powers and the restraining of state powers. This shift tends to accelerate as each decision forms the basis and starting point for another extension of federal domination.

A greater degree of restraint on the part of the United States Supreme

State Government, The Journal of State Affairs, Vol. XXXVI (Winter 1963), pp. 10-15, *passim.*

Court can do much, but experience shows that it is not likely to be sufficient. The basic difficulty is that the Supreme Court's decisions concerning the balance between federal and state power are final and can be
changed in practice only if the states can muster sufficient interest in
Congress, backed by a three-fourths majority of the states themselves to
amend the Constitution. While the founding fathers fully expected and
wished the words of the Constitution to have this degree of finality, it is
impossible to believe that they envisaged such potency for the pronounce-
ments of nine judges appointed by the President and confirmed by the
Senate. The Supreme Court is, after all, an organ of the federal government. It is one of the three branches of the national government, and in
conflicts over federal and state power, the Court is necessarily an agency
of one of the parties in interest. As such, its decisions should not be
assigned the same finality as the words of the Constitution itself. There is
need for an easier method of setting such decisions straight when they are
unsound.

To amend the Federal Constitution to correct specific decisions of the
federal courts on specific points is desirable, but it will not necessarily
stop the continuing drift toward more complete federal domination. The
present situation has taken a long time to develop and may take a long
time to remedy. Accordingly, some more fundamental and far-reaching
change in the Federal Constitution is necessary to preserve and protect
the states.

We appeal most earnestly to all branches of the federal government,
and particularly to the highest federal court, to take diligent and impartial reflection upon the dangers to the nation inherent in the trends
herein described. We urge them to evaluate the possibilities of an all-
powerful central government with unlimited control over the lives of
the people, the very opposite of self-government under a federal system.

It is the ultimate of political ingenuity to achieve a vigorous federal
system in which dynamic states combine with a responsible central government for the good of the people. Your committee is dedicated to this
objective.

RESOLUTION NO. 1

The first proposal was then read to the General Assembly. Like each of
the other recommendations by the committee, it was in the form of a
resolution offered for the consideration of each of the state legislatures,
for action in January. The first resolution reads:

Section 1. Article V of the Constitution of the United States is hereby
amended to read as follows: The Congress, whenever two-thirds of both
Houses shall deem it necessary, or, on the application of the Legislatures of
two-thirds of the several states, shall propose amendments to this Constitution,

which shall be valid to all intents and purposes, as part of this Constitution, when ratified by the Legislatures of three-fourths of the several states. Whenever applications from the Legislatures of two-thirds of the total number of states of the United States shall contain identical texts of an amendment to be proposed, the President of the Senate and the Speaker of the House of Representatives shall so certify, and the amendment as contained in the application shall be deemed to have been proposed, without further action by Congress. No State, without its consent, shall be deprived of its equal suffrage in the Senate." *

RESOLUTION NO. 2

Section 1. No provision of this Constitution, or any amendment thereto, shall restrict or limit any state in the apportionment of representation in its legislature.

Section 2. The judicial power of the United States shall not extend to any suit in law or equity, or to any controversy, relating to apportionment of representation in a state legislature.

RESOLUTION NO. 3

Section 1. Upon demand of the legislatures of five states, no two of which shall share any common boundary, made within two years after the rendition of any judgment of the Supreme Court relating to the rights reserved to the states or to the people by this Constitution, such judgment shall be reviewed by a Court composed of the chief justices of the highest courts of the several states to be known as the Court of the Union. The sole issue before the Court of the Union shall be whether the power or jurisdiction sought to be exercised on the part of the United States is a power granted to it under this Constitution.

Section 2. Three-fourths of the justices of the Court of the Union shall constitute a quorum, but it shall require concurrence of a majority of the entire Court to reverse a decision of the Supreme Court. In event of incapacity of the chief justice of the highest court of any state to sit upon the Court of the Union, his place shall be filled by another justice of such state court selected by affirmative vote of a majority of its membership.

Section 3. On the first Monday of the third calendar month following the ratification of this amendment, the chief justices of the highest courts of the several states shall convene at the national capital, at which time the Court of the Union shall be organized and shall adopt rules governing its procedure.

Section 4. Decisions of the Court of the Union upon matters within its Jurisdiction shall be final and shall not thereafter be overruled by any court and may be changed only by an amendment of this Constitution.

* This Resolution was anticipated in Resolution 13 of the Randolph Plan. See Introduction, *supra,* note 3.

Section 5. The Congress shall make provision for the housing of the Court of the Union and the expenses of its operation.*

* Meeting in Chicago, August 1963, the American Bar Association turned thumbs down on these proposals. Without dissent, it rejected Resolution No. 1 that would cut Congress out of its historic role of introducing, debating, and submitting constitutional amendments to the states for ratification. Also without dissent, it rejected Resolution No. 3 that would set up a Court of the Union, empowered to overrule, under certain conditions, the Supreme Court. By a vote of 136 to 74, the lawyers also turned down Resolution No. 2, denying the federal courts jurisdiction over apportionment of seats in the State legislatures. See Irving Dilliard, "A.B.A. Took Right Stand," *Sunday American* (Chicago), editorial page, August 25, 1963.

The A.B.A.'s overwhelming opposition represents a serious setback, but the drive to push the amendments through to ratification will doubtless continue.

Selected Bibliography 🌿

PRIMARY SOURCES

DOCUMENTS

Documentary History of the Constitution of the United States (Washington: Department of State, 1905). Vols. IV and V.

The Debates in the Several State Conventions on the Adoption of the Federal Constitution, Jonathan Elliot, ed. (Philadelphia: J. P. Lippincott, 1861). Vols. III and V.

The Records of the Federal Convention of 1787, Max Farrand, ed. (New Haven: Yale University Press, 1911). 4 vols.

Essays on the Constitution of the United States, 1787-1788, Paul Leicester Ford, ed. (Brooklyn, N.Y.: Historical Printing Club, 1892).

Pamphlets on the Constitution, Paul Leicester Ford, ed. (Brooklyn, N.Y., 1888).

The Delegate from New York, or, *Proceedings of the Federal Convention of 1787, from the notes of John Lansing, Jr.,* Joseph R. Strayer, ed. (Princeton: Princeton University Press, 1939).

LETTERS

The Papers of Thomas Jefferson, Julian P. Boyd, ed. (Princeton: Princeton University Press, 1951-   ). Vols. XII-XVI.

The Letters of Richard Henry Lee, James Ballagh, ed. (New York: The Macmillan Company, 1914). Vol. II.

The Writings of James Madison, Gaillard P. Hunt, ed. (New York: G. P. Putnam's Sons, 1904). Vol. V.

The Writings of George Washington, Jared Sparks, ed. (Boston: 1837). Vol. IX.

SECONDARY WORKS

Bancroft, George, *History of the Formation of the Constitution of the United States of America* (New York: D. Appleton & Co., 1889). Vol. II.

Beard, Charles A., *An Economic Interpretation of the Constitution* (New York: The Macmillan Company, 1913).

Beveridge, Albert J., *The Life of John Marshall* (New York: Houghton-Mifflin Co., 1916). Vol. I.

Brant, Irving, *James Madison: Father of the Constitution, 1787-1800* (New York: Bobbs-Merrill Co., 1950).

Brown, Robert E., *Charles Beard and the Constitution* (Princeton: Princeton University Press, 1956).

Elkins, Stanley and McKitrick, Eric, "Founding Fathers," *Political Science Quarterly,* 76:181-216 (1961).

Henry, William Wirt, *Patrick Henry: Life, Correspondence and Speeches* (New York: Charles Scribner's Sons, 1891). Vol. III.

Jensen, Merrill, *The New Nation: a History of the United States during the Confederation, 1781-1789* (New York: Alfred A. Knopf, Inc., 1950).

Lee, R. H., *Memoir of the Life of Richard Henry Lee* (Philadelphia: Carey and Lea, 1825).

Kenyon, Cecelia M., "Men of Little Faith: the Anti-Federalists on the Nature of Representative Government," *William and Mary Quarterly,* 12:3-143 (1955).

Main, Jackson Turner, *The Antifederalists: Critics of the Constitution* (Chapel Hill: University of North Carolina Press, 1961).

Mason, Alpheus Thomas, "Our Federal Union Reconsidered," *Political Science Quarterly,* 55:502-521 (1950).

———, *The Supreme Court: Palladium of Freedom* (Ann Arbor: University of Michigan Press, 1962). Chs. 1 and 2.

McDonald, Forrest, *We the People: the Economic Origins of the Constitution* (Chicago: University of Chicago Press, 1958).

McLaughlin, Andrew C., *The Confederation and the Constitution, 1783-1789* (New York: Harper and Brothers, 1905).

Ranny, John C., "The Bases of American Federalism," *William and Mary Quarterly,* 1:139-156 (1956).

Rowland, Kate Mason, *The Life of George Mason* (New York: G. P. Putnam's Sons, 1892). Vol. II.

Rutland, Robert, *The Birth of the Bill of Rights* (Chapel Hill: University of North Carolina Press, 1955).

Swindler, W. F., "The Current Challenge to Federalism: the Confederating Proposals." 52 *Georgetown Law Journal,* 52:1-41 (Fall 1963).

Wright, Benjamin F., *Consensus and Continuity, 1776-1787* (Boston, 1958).

In December 1963, Burton C. Bernard, Esq., of Granite City, Illinois, prepared a valuable bibliography, exclusive of newspaper articles, covering the three proposed States Rights Amendments.

THE STATES

CONNECTICUT

Steiner, Bernard Christian, *Connecticut's Ratification of the Federal Constitution* (American Antiquarian Society. Proceedings, Worcester, Mass., 1915) n.s. 5, v. 25, pp. 70-127.

DELAWARE

Munroe, John A., *Federalist Delaware, 1775-1815* (New Brunswick, N.J.: Rutgers University Press, 1954).

GEORGIA

Abbott, W. W., "The Structure of Politics in Georgia, 1782-1789," *William and Mary Quarterly*, 3rd series, 14:47-65 (1957).

Coleman, Kenneth. *The American Revolution in Georgia, 1763-1789* (Athens, Ga., 1958).

MARYLAND

Crowl, Philip A., *Maryland During and After the Revolution* (Baltimore: Johns Hopkins Press, 1943).

————, "Antifederalism in Maryland, 1787-1788," *William and Mary Quarterly*, 3rd series, 4:446-469 (1947).

MASSACHUSETTS

East, R. A., "The Massachusetts Conservatives in the Critical Period," in Richard B. Morris, ed., *The Era of the American Revolution* (1939).

Harding, Samuel B., *The Federal Constitution in Massachusetts* (New York: Longmans, Green & Co., 1896).

NEW HAMPSHIRE

Walker, Joseph B., *The New Hampshire Federal Convention, 1788* (Boston: Cupples & Hurd, 1880).

NEW JERSEY

McCormick, Richard P., *Experiment in Independence: New Jersey in the Critical Period, 1783-1787* (New Brunswick, N.J.: Rutgers University Press, 1950).

NEW YORK

Miner, C. E., "The Ratification of the Constitution in New York," *Columbia University Publications in History, Political Science and Public Law*, vol. 94.

Cochran, Thomas C., *New York in the Confederation: An Economic Study* (Philadelphia: University of Pennsylvania Press, 1932).

Spaulding, E. Wilder, *New York in the Critical Period, 1783-1789* (New York: Columbia University Press, 1932).

NORTH CAROLINA

Newsome, A. R., "North Carolina's Ratification of the Federal Constitution," *North Carolina Historical Review*, 17:287-301 (1940).

Pool, William C., "An Economic Interpretation of the Federal Constitution in North Carolina," *North Carolina Historical Review*, 27:119-141, 289-313, 437-461 (1950).

Trenholme, Louise, *The Ratification of the Federal Constitution in North Carolina* (New York, 1932).

PENNSYLVANIA

Brunhouse, Robert L., *The Counter Revolution in Pennsylvania, 1776-1790* (Harrisburg: Pennsylvania Historical Commission, 1942).

McMaster, J. B., and Stone, F. D., *Pennsylvania and the Federal Constitution, 1788* (Philadelphia: Inquirer Printing and Publishing Co., 1942).

SOUTH CAROLINA

Brunhouse, Robert L., ed., "David Ramsey—On Ratification in South Carolina," *Journal of Southern History*, 9:549-55 (1943).

Freeman, H. Hart, *The Valley of Virginia in the American Revolution* (Chapel Hill: University of North Carolina Press, 1942).

Thomas, Robert E., "The Virginia Convention of 1788," *Journal of Southern History*, 19:63-72 (1954).

Some Other ⟨⟨⟨ Spectrum Books